Communication f

Communication for Teachers

Joseph L. Chesebro

The State University of New York at Brockport

James C. McCroskey

West Virginia University

Allyn and Bacon

Boston ■ London ■ Toronto ■ Sydney ■ Tokyo ■ Singapore

Series Editor: *Karon Bowers*
Editorial Assistant: *Jennifer Trebby*
Editorial Production Administrator: *Bryan Woodhouse*
Composition and Prepress Buyer: *Linda Cox*
Editorial Production Service: *Chestnut Hill Enterprises*
Electronic Composition: *Peggy Cabot, Cabot Computer Services*
Manufacturing Buyer: *Julie McNeill*
Cover Administrator: *Kristina Mose-Libon*

Library of Congress Cataloging-in-Publication Data

Communication for teachers / edited by Joseph L. Chesebro, James C. McCroskey.
    p. cm.
    Includes bibliographical references and index.
    ISBN 0-205-31887-8
       1. Communication in education.   2. Interaction analysis in eduation.
   3. Teacher–student relationships. I. Chesebro, Joseph L. II. McCroskey, James C.
LB1033.5 .C62 2002
371.102'2—dc21   2001046133

CONTENTS

PREFACE

We created this book with one goal in mind: to take much of the research on teacher communication, synthesize it, and translate it into practical suggestions that can help new teachers communicate more effectively with their students. Specifically, *Communication for Teachers* is aimed at graduate teaching assistants and new faculty members, in both communication and other fields. These two groups may find themselves in short orientation courses or workshops or semester-long practicum courses in which they are taught "the basics" of teaching. We consider this book ideal for use in such courses.

Each chapter is well-grounded in research in the relevant areas of instructional communication and educational psychology. More important, each chapter has been written with newer teachers in mind. Though each chapter addresses relevant theories, the focus is on applying the theories to practical classroom situations and teacher–student interactions. Most source citations have been omitted in order to make the content more immediate and accessible to readers. Readers wishing to learn more about a particular chapter can refer to the references listed at the end of each chapter. We prefer this conversational approach because it enables us to almost "talk" to new teachers and tell them what we wish we had known when we began our teaching careers.

We believe that this book fills an important need in the area of graduate assistant and new teacher training. We recognize that there are other quality books available related to teacher communication. However, these are not aimed specifically at graduate teaching assistants and new college teaching faculty. This distinction is important. Even when this book was little more than an idea, we realized through discussions with colleagues who are responsible for training graduate teaching assistants (many of whom were happy to contribute to this work!) that there was not really a book available to meet their needs. We also recognized that, although a great deal of instructional communication research has been generated in the past twenty-five years, there has been no book that synthesizes all of that information or discusses the ways in which it can be used to help teachers improve their teaching. So, we attempted to fill these voids.

We have organized *Communication for Teachers* into three sections. Because we believe that effective teaching is student-centered, we begin by focusing on students. This section examines objectives and goals we have for our students, the ways in which students listen, reasons our students may not be willing to communicate in our classrooms and students' motives for communicating with teachers, and ways in which our teaching behavior is influenced by our students. We can learn a great deal from our students, and once we better understand them, we will be in a better position to teach them more effectively. Therefore, the second section builds on the first by discussing a variety of teacher-related factors in student–teacher communication, such as immediacy, the relevance of content to students' needs and interests, clear teaching, teacher communication styles, teacher use of humor in the classroom, teacher misbehaviors, and factors related to student motivation to learn. The third section takes what has been learned in the first two sections and applies it to important contexts that new teachers face or may face, such as distance education and communicating with students from other cultures or of various ages. The last chapter synthesizes everything from previous chapters into some principles that can help new teachers "put everything together." Finally, there is an Appendix, which has been included to help teaching assistant trainers train their new assistants more effectively. We anticipate that this book will enable newer teachers to improve their teaching in a variety of meaningful ways and that, as a result, teaching will be both more effective and more fun for teachers and their students. So to new teachers, we say congratulations for choosing a meaningful profession. We hope this book helps you become a better professional.

Joe Chesebro and *James McCroskey*

Acknowledgments

I would like to thank several people for helping to make this book possible. I have received considerable guidance and encouragement over the years and on this project from my coeditor James McCroskey. I also am indebted to all of the contributors for their enthusiasm for this project and for their excellent chapters. I have been fortunate to work with three great people at Allyn and Bacon: editor Karon Bowers and her two editorial assistants, Jennifer Becker and Sarah Kelly. Their expertise and support have helped make this a great experience. I am thankful to have worked with the excellent faculty in the communication programs at the State University of New York at Brockport, at Ball State University, and at West Virginia University, and in the Educational Psychology program at West Virginia University. They have taught me a great deal about communicating, writing, teaching, and learning. I am also grateful for the helpful comments provided by the following reviewers: Joe Ayres, Washington State University; Katherine Hendrix, University of Memphis; John and Virginia Jones, University of Illinois at Chicago; and Katherine Thweatt, West Virginia University. Finally, I would like to thank my first three great teachers—my grandmothers Isabelle and Lucille, and my mother Linda—as well as my most patient teacher, my wife Jen. They helped make this book possible.

Joe Chesebro

SECTION ONE

Our Students

Quality teaching is student centered. This section examines a number of student characteristics and behaviors which will enable newer teachers to tailor their teaching so that it meets the needs, interests, and abilities of their students.

CHAPTER

1 Learning Goals and Objectives

JAMES C. MCCROSKEY
West Virginia University

The field of educational psychology has long been sensitive to the desirability of establishing learning objectives for instruction (Bloom, 1956; Krathwohl, Bloom, & Masia, 1964). Consequently, most undergraduate education majors study the nature and use of objectives. Unfortunately, most graduate teaching assistants and beginning college teachers, not to mention even most highly experienced college teachers, have never had a course in education. This situation is not unlike a person who has studied biology for eight years, but who has never studied medicine, becoming a physician. Would you want this person to take care of you if you were sick?

Although this deplorable situation is one of higher education's darker secrets, it is not likely to be changed in the near future. If you are one of these new college teachers, do not feel alone. Most of your colleagues either are or have been in a similar position. How on earth are you supposed to become a professional educator when all you know about the teaching process has come at the receiving end? Good question, but one that can't be answered fully in just this chapter. We can, however, begin by helping you understand just what college teaching (or teaching at any other level) really is all about. And that probably is not what you think it is at this moment.

Teaching is about content, getting students to learn information. Right? If only it were as simple as that. This is the most common misconception noneducators have about teaching. This misconception is what led people to believe that the invention of the printing press would make it possible to do away with teachers—because now all the prospective student needed was to read the book. Didn't happen, did it? Later, this same misconception led people to believe that, when radios and radio stations became widely available, radios would replace teachers. Students could stay home and just listen to the radio to get their lessons. Again, didn't happen, did it? But, of course, once TV came onto the scene (particularly color television) it was clear to the people who believed that content was all teaching was about that TV would put traditional teaching out of business. Didn't happen, did it? Currently the people who hold the misconception about content being what teaching is about happily point to the Internet and profoundly predict that education, particularly higher education, will soon be the province of the Internet.coms instead of colleges and universities. Will it happen? Put your money on the lottery; the odds are much better.

Domains of Learning

It is generally accepted that there are three broad domains of learning: cognitive, psychomotor, and affective. To understand what teaching is all about, we need to be familiar with all three.

Cognitive Learning

The cognitive domain of learning is concerned with the process of acquiring knowledge—the content aspect of education. At the lowest level, knowledge refers to a specific unit of information, such as the date of an historical event, how to define a given word, or what a driver is expected to do when he or she sees a stop sign. At the middle level, knowledge relates to methods of inquiry, such as hypothesis testing, mastering generalizations or principles, and comprehending larger theories. At the highest level of cognitive learning, knowledge is concerned with the ability to interpret, analyze, and synthesize the knowledge acquired at the lower levels with new information that the learner will confront in later life.

Cognitive learning objectives center on the lower level of the domain in early childhood education, and in beginning courses in high school and college, and move to the higher levels as the student progresses to more advanced instruction in a subject area. Thus, even in many college courses, since students typically have not been introduced to many subject matter areas before entering college, learning objectives may center on the lowest level of the cognitive domain. A primary function of such courses is to establish schema (organizational systems) for processing information in that particular subject matter. If the student does not take more advanced courses in the given subject matter area, he or she will still know this basic material, but he or she will be highly unlikely to be able to deal with larger theories in the area, much less develop the cognitive skills necessary to interpret, analyze, and synthesize information in that content field. Mediated forms of communication, such as books, television, and more recently the Internet, have been found to be helpful to teachers in educating students at the lower levels of cognitive learning. However, these forms have been found much less helpful at the higher levels.

Psychomotor Learning

While cognitive learning is concerned with "knowing," psychomotor learning is concerned with "doing." At the lowest level, this domain relates to basic control of physical behaviors, such as a baby learning to hold a rattle handed to her or him by a parent or focusing her or his eyes on a toy hanging over the bed. At a moderate level, psychomotor learning is concerned with such behaviors as writing, walking, running, jumping, throwing, hammering, and sawing. At the higher levels, concern centers on more complex behaviors such as typing or keyboarding, speaking a foreign language or an already known language with a different accent, playing a piano or other musical instrument, driving a vehicle or replacing the engine in that vehicle, or shooting a basketball while five other people are trying to prevent that behavior.

Psychomotor learning objectives tend to be valued in the lower grades, but seem to lose some of their importance in educational systems at each higher level. Consider the relative importance ascribed to English and mathematics, for example, compared to driver education, physical education, and typing (or keyboarding). This discrepancy exists in spite of the fact that driver education and physical education are likely to aid one to live a longer and healthier life and typing is the psychomotor skill required to permit one to work with the most sophisticated computers. In addition, psychomotor skills that lead to vocations such as carpentry, auto mechanics, and chiropractic are typically relegated to "trade" schools or junior colleges because they are deemed unworthy of inclusion by institutions that center on "intellectual" pursuits.

Affective Learning

Affective learning is concerned with the student's attitudes, beliefs, and values that relate to the knowledge and psychomotor skills the student acquires. The affective domain is most centrally associated with a student's behavioral choices. A student may know what to do and have the psychomotor skills to do it, but if the student does not have a positive attitude toward doing it, it most likely will not be done. Affective learning is the domain of learning that receives the least attention from many college teachers. If fact, many college professors openly decry any interest at all in the affective domain. On college campuses, particularly in the more traditional disciplines, it is not at all unusual to hear a professor say something like: "I am hired to teach students math. It is not my job to make them like it!" This kind of comment certainly is not restricted to math professors. But, whatever the discipline referenced, such a comment is a blatant expression of the professor's ignorance about what a professional educator's job really entails. With this type of attitude, a book or TV set might be a worthy replacement for this professor. At least they would be less likely to harm students' growth.

At higher levels, the emphasis on psychomotor learning declines in most disciplines. However, both the cognitive and the affective domains remain critical in all disciplines at all levels. What is it worth for a student to learn about great literature, if he or she also learns to hate reading that literature? What is it worth for a student to learn elementary statistics, if he or she also learns to disrespect statistical probability? What is it worth for a person to learn to be a physician, if he or she also learns to devalue human life? Unfortunately, all of these types of outcomes are common in classrooms where professors forget that they are teaching people, not content. If the affect of the learner is ignored, a competent job of teaching is not being done.

Long-Term Goals

Almost all of our long-term goals for education are based on appropriate affective learning. Long-term goals are those that are concerned with what will become of the student later on, well after he or she no longer is in our class. Such goals may deal with such global concerns as the student becoming a good citizen and a contributing member of society. They may be concerned with such things as developing an appreciation for art, music, film, or literature; adopting a healthy lifestyle; or becoming a lifelong learner. However, goals also may be concerned with somewhat more immediate matters, such as the student choosing to enroll in another course in the subject matter you teach, being able to perform satisfactorily in an advanced course that follows yours, or choosing a career that draws on the subject you teach.

Employing an old analogy, the long-term goals are the forest whereas our daily instructional objectives are the trees. Often professors lose sight of the long-term goals, which are much more central to what higher education is all about, and focus virtually all of their attention and communication on the immediate, lower-level cognitive learning goals. If professors focus only on short-term goals, it is natural for students to learn to do likewise. Thus students develop an orientation that all learning is temporary, and that forgetting what was learned last semester is not only acceptable, but normal—and possibly even necessary.

For a professor to focus on short-term cognitive learning objectives may be, at least in part, a function of the professor's being sensitive to her or his limitations. As teachers we often see ourselves as having a very limited "span of control." That is, we feel we can directly impact only those students who are in our classes right now. It certainly is easier to see the impact we have on those students, but that does not mean our impact stops when the student completes our class. In fact, most of our important impact (positive or negative) will come later. If we turn a student on to what we teach (be it math, English, engineering, or whatever), that student will be more likely to succeed in later courses in that subject matter. However, if we turn that student off, the student may not even take another course in the area, much less succeed in the course. In a very real sense, we may terminate the student's career in our field. In fact, a professor's "I don't have to make them like it" approach is most likely to have precisely that result.

The Role of Communication

It is probably evident at this point that we believe the role of affective learning is critical to the success of a professor or teaching assistant in higher education. This communication-based view (Hurt, Scott, & McCroskey, 1978; McCroskey, 1998) is not the view commonly expressed in colleges of arts and sciences, fine arts, or engineering. Nor even is it always the view expressed in colleges of education. In public discussions of how to improve public schools or colleges, it is a position rarely heard. Nor is this lack of attention to the affective domain of learning one of recent origin. Throughout history, attention has focused primarily on cognitive learning, and to a lesser extent on psychomotor learning. Attention to affective learning frequently has been missing entirely. The quality of instruction has suffered consistently as the result.

It is important that we do not give the impression that cognitive and psychomotor learning are unimportant. Far from that, they are vitally important. But they do not provide the critical learning element necessary to meet the long-term objectives of higher education. That element is positive affect for the subject being taught. If cognitive and psychomotor objectives receive all of the attention, and affective learning is ignored, higher education cannot meet its most important goals.

"Communication" as an academic field is still very young. Hence, it probably should not be surprising that most of the attention it paid to instruction in its early years was focused on the medium of instruction—print, radio, TV, satellite, Internet. Only in the last 25 years or so have a significant number of people in the field of human communication (as opposed to mediated communication) directed their research focus on improving live teacher–student interactions and the outcomes of those interactions. For the most part, the remaining chapters in this book focus on the live teacher–student context and attempt to integrate research and experience to provide advice for the beginning college teacher.

College professors and graduate teaching assistants function as professional communicators. As a consequence, what research has discovered about how human communication functions and how it can be improved can be applied in the context of instruction as well as other contexts in which professional communicators function. As has been noted previously (Hurt, Scott, & McCroskey, 1978), the difference between knowing and teaching is communication in the classroom.

REFERENCES AND SUGGESTED READING

Bloom, B. S. (1956). *Taxonomy of educational objectives (Handbook I: Cognitive domain)*. New York: McKay.

Hurt, H. T., Scott, M. D., & McCroskey, J. C. (1978). *Communication in the classroom*. Reading, MA: Addison-Wesley.

Krathwohl, D. R., Bloom, B. S., & Masia, B. B. (1964). *Taxonomy of educational objectives (Handbook II: Affective domain)*. New York: McKay.

McCroskey, J. C. (1998) *An introduction to communication in the classroom* (2nd ed.). Acton, MA: Tapestry Press.

CHAPTER

2

Student Listening Behavior

JOSEPH L. CHESEBRO
State University of New York at Brockport

Starting a book on teacher communication by first talking about students might seem strange. To better understand this focus, it is important to note that communication is defined as the process by which one or more persons stimulates meaning in the mind of another using verbal and nonverbal messages (McCroskey, 1992). A close look at this definition reveals that attempts at communication are useless unless the appropriate meaning is stimulated in the receiver's (the listener's) mind. In a sense, the whole process is centered around what our messages end up meaning to our receivers. In the classroom, this means that the "bottom line" for teachers consists of whatever messages are received by students. Thus, it makes much sense to examine students' listening behavior. Without understanding the way in which students listen and process teachers' messages, teachers should not expect to be very successful at stimulating the desired meaning in their students' minds.

For teachers (especially new ones), concerns other than student listening usually come to mind first, such as "How will I fill the whole hour with this material?" "How can I explain this?" or "What if they look bored or are talking instead of paying attention?" Teachers often fail to see that the answers to all of these questions can be found to some extent by understanding their students' listening behavior. The teacher who understands the components of listening behavior and the factors that influence the way people listen will understand how to structure a class period to maximize students' attention to the material and will present that material in a way that is clear and maintains student interest.

But there is an even more fundamental reason to learn about student listening behavior. If the point of teaching is for students to learn, and students usually cannot learn if they do not listen effectively in class, then teachers owe it to their students to learn about how students listen. In other words, teachers should teach in a way that is most conducive to effective student listening and learning. This point sounds obvious, but it often eludes teachers. Lecturing is a prime example. Of all the public speakers we encounter, consider the number we enjoy seeing speak for at least an hour at a time. Outside of stand-up comedians and motivational speakers, there probably are few. Even assuming we enjoy seeing those speakers speak for so long, how much do we remember from the hour-long presentations? When put like that, the idea of listening to an hour-long lecture sounds silly. Still, it is pretty typical of teaching. Of course, note taking and question and answer periods help aid memory, but most teachers would benefit from a greater understanding of how their students are listening to them and interpreting their messages. With this in mind, this chapter presents the major parts of the listening process and provides suggestions for teaching in a way that is conducive to effective student listening and learning.

The Listening Process

As with many communication concepts, several definitions and models of listening exist. This is not the forum in which to review or debate all of these. Regardless of the specific models of listening behavior that exist, most agree that listening involves sensing, attending to, interpreting, remembering, and responding to stimuli (the sights and sounds we listen to). This chapter will discuss each of these aspects of the listening process as they relate to classroom learning.

Sensing and Attending

Sensing refers to our five senses and all of the information listeners can gain from them. The senses of hearing and sight are most relevant to the present discussion of listening. Before students fully listen to anything, they first sense it by hearing it, seeing it, or both. In the classroom, there are a number of things students can sense: the lawnmower outside, the two students talking and laughing in the back, the attractive student in the next seat over, the student with the loud cough, and maybe even the teacher. Add to all of this sensory information any psychological distractions: another class in which a student may be struggling, problems with financial aid, anxiety about an upcoming speech, what's going on during the weekend, problems with a boyfriend or girlfriend, problems at work, problems with a roommate or with family at home, and so forth.

Given this abundance of available sensory stimuli, it is clear that teachers are not guaranteed their students' attention. Students may be able to sense everything, but they cannot keep their focus on everything and therefore they must be selective in their attention. Something must be sacrificed, and unless teachers are responsive to their students' listening behavior it may be the teacher's message that is ignored.

Teachers should be aware that attention to classroom messages takes effort and that attention spans are short when compared to the typical length of a lecture. Studies in vigilance, or sustained attention (attempts to pay attention to one thing for a long period of time), reveal that after students attend to the same stimulus for a while, the quality of their attention diminishes (Perry and Laurie,

1992). As time passes, students are more likely to daydream or become distracted by other classroom stimuli. Teachers should keep this in mind when lecturing. The longer they lecture, the greater the chance that their students' attention to the class material will fade. As a result, it is a good rule of thumb to lecture for no more than 20 minutes at a time. At regular intervals, teachers should pause to ask questions, provide demonstrations, or conduct activities. This variety will enable students to attend to each of the different attentional tasks (lecturing, questions, activity) without having to attend to any one task long enough to challenge the stamina of their attention.

So far, it is clear that students' attention is an important part of the teaching process. It is quite selective, and even when it is focused it can be fleeting. Providing a variety of classroom messages is one thing a teacher can do to maximize students' attention to classroom messages. Other things teachers may do will be discussed in later chapters on teacher immediacy and content relevance. Of course, attention is only one part of the listening process. Once teachers have students' attention, they must make sure that the messages received by the students are the same ones intended to be sent by the teacher. In other words, teachers must make sure that their messages are interpreted accurately.

Interpreting

It is important for teachers to remember that each student in the classroom is approaching classroom messages from his or her own unique perspective. Collectively, students have grown up in different areas or states, been brought up by different kinds of families, experienced a variety of life events, and taken a unique combination of classes before taking yours. Therefore, a classroom of 20 people essentially is a classroom of 20 different points of view that may interpret your classroom messages in 20 different ways. The good news for teachers is that students also have shared a number of similar experiences and that teachers can capitalize on those similarities to increase the likelihood that classroom messages are perceived consistently.

As people learn from their experiences in life (both in and out of school), the information they learn is organized mentally, almost as if each new piece of information one learns is "filed" away into a complex "filing" system. The name given to this structure or system has varied, but the three main terms used to describe the way information is organized in our minds are schema, scripts, and frames. Rather than exploring the differences between each of the three terms, the term *schema* will be used throughout the remainder of the chapter to refer to the way in which information is organized mentally.

Schemas are mental representations of knowledge. It is useful to think of a schema as being like a mental "filing cabinet," "blueprint," or "concept map" of how groups of similar information are organized in our mind. Not entirely unlike an outline in a student's notes, each schema is organized around a central topic and contains more specific material related to the central topic. Schemas have a number of properties (Baddeley, 1990). People can have a schema for any area of knowledge they possess. For example, a psychology major may have a well-developed schema in which information about major theories, methods of research, and approaches to psychology are organized, while the non–psychology major may have no such mental structure. Another property of schemas is that they may be imbedded within each other. For example, the psychology student who has to take the common psychology statistics course is using her math schema within the context of her psychology schema. Schemas also may vary in abstraction. In other words, people have schemas for concrete ideas such as directions to friends' houses but also for such abstract concepts as love and justice. Schemas also have some fixed parts and some variable parts. For example, once students have been at school at least a semester, they have a consistent schema for what happens during classes: Students arrive on time, the teacher takes attendance, class proceeds, and during the last 10 minutes of class students fidget and pack their materials in their bags to communicate their readiness to leave the class as soon as possible. However, there is much room for variety within that general schema, as each class will have its own unique features.

Another important aspect of schemas is that they differ in the extent to which they are developed. Each individual will have some well-developed schemas and some weaker ones. Teachers may have a well-developed schema for their own subject but have little or no schema for another subject. The idea of schema complexity is important when considering the way in which a person will interpret a message. For example, imagine two friends—Friend A, who knows much about football (developed schema), and Friend B, who knows very little (no schema). Imagine a third friend starting a conversation about football by saying something like "the Bills will do all right this year, but they need to get a new free safety, change their defense to a 4-3, and move to a 1 back system." Consider whether Friend A or Friend B is more likely to (1) understand the message and interpret it correctly, and (2) remember the message for a longer amount of time. According to schema theory, person A will understand the message because a schema is in place that will allow the message to be interpreted correctly (Edwards and McDonald, 1993). Person B has no such schema in place, and therefore will have a harder time understanding and remembering the message. Schemas help people interpret incoming information, and if no schema exists, we are less likely to accurately remember or recall the information at a later date (Brownell, 1996). Instead, information is likely to be distorted to fit existing schema (Brewer, 1977) or forgotten.

It is important for teachers to understand the importance of schema so they can teach in a way that enables students to correctly interpret classroom messages. Teachers first should consider the extent to which their students' schemas for the subject are likely to be developed. In order to enable students to develop their own schema for the course material and remember what may at first be very new information, teachers should make every effort to tie new information into schemas that students already have. For example, teachers should start by using terminology that is familiar to students before using more complex terminology. In other words, language should be on the students' level before moving onto more complex levels. For example, a colleague of mine once introduced the "peripheral route of processing of persuasive messages" by calling it the "Homer Simpson way of processing persuasive messages." Even though neither of these terms is completely clear, one is much more likely than to the other to "tap into" students' schemas. Once students are able to tie new information into existing schemas and understand the gist of the material, they will be more prepared to develop their own schema for the material. Again, the value of having a student-centered approach to teaching is clear: Teachers who consider their students' points of view and schemas are more likely to teach so that students will attend to and understand classroom messages. However, understanding is not enough, as students also have to remember that which is being taught.

Remembering

This section will discuss the ways in which remembering is an important stage of the listening process, especially student listening. In doing so, several aspects of memory, learning, and educational psychology are discussed.

Timing and Memory.   The way in which teachers and students use their time is important in terms of memory. The existence of primacy and recency effects means that students are most likely to remember the information that is presented earliest and latest in a class. This explains why teachers should preview and review their most important content at the beginning and end of their classes. The way students use time to learn and remember also influences memory. It is much better to study or learn in small chunks of time rather than larger ones (reviewed by Baddeley, 1990). When taking 5 hours to study or learn, it would be better to learn in one-hour blocks for 5 days rather than trying to learn everything in one 5-hour block of time. This is another reason teachers should take breaks from presenting material to allow for activities. By taking breaks, information is grouped into smaller units, and if each small unit is previewed and reviewed at the beginning and end, primacy and recency effects also should lead to improved memory. In addition to understanding the importance of timing, teachers and students should understand the importance of the way in which information is processed. This is detailed in the next section on types of memory and information processing.

Models of Memory.   Several models of memory have been offered to explain how the process works. An early approach held that there were memory stores or systems: sensory, short-term, or working memory, and long-term memory (Atkinson & Shiffrin, 1968). Anything that can be sensed is temporarily stored in the sensory register for only 3 to 4 seconds. Information in the sensory register that we attend to by focusing on it is in our short-term memory store, and it may last there for seconds up to about one minute (as when we are introduced to someone; we attend to his or her name but may forget it in a matter of seconds). The process by which information is retained long enough to be stored in long-term memory is called *rehearsal*. Information is rehearsed when someone processes it mentally in order to remember it. Atkinson and Shiffrin held that the more information was rehearsed while in short-term memory, the greater the chance that it would survive to be stored as a long-term memory. This explains the logic behind repeating someone's name to ourselves upon being introduced in order to remember it.

Although simple rehearsal can help memories last longer, some memory researchers began to realize that the way in which information is rehearsed is also an important factor influencing memory. Shifting the focus from different types of memory (short-, long-term) to the quality of rehearsal, Craik and Lockhart (1972) presented a model of memory that focused on levels of processing. In doing so, they identified two types of rehearsal: maintenance and elaborative. Maintenance rehearsal is a more simple kind, in which information might be repeated (as with names or phone numbers). Although this type of approach can enable someone to prevent forgetting information, it is not thought to ensure the long-term learning that is achieved through elaborative rehearsal. Elaborative rehearsal involves greater effort than maintenance rehearsal and may involve the use of mnemonic devices (e.g., ROYGBIV for the colors of the spectrum), and linking to existing memories (e.g., when hearing someone's name thinking of someone we already know by that name so that we remember the new person), and thinking of examples of new information (thinking about amusement park rides to remember such physics concepts as centrifugal force), along with other means of effortful processing. The difference between these types of rehearsal is that elaborative processing takes more effort than maintenance rehearsal and is more likely to lead to long-term learning (notice how it often involves attaching new information to existing schemas).

Regardless of the different theoretical approaches to memory, theorists tend to agree that some type of effortful processing is needed to assure long-term learning. The effort that elaborative rehearsal requires helps students develop new schemas for material or attach material to existing schemas. Teachers can encourage this type of processing by teaching students about it, asking questions that require students to elaborate on the material, creating activities that require students to elaborate on the material, and if possible, by using essay test questions that require integration rather than multiple-choice questions (which tend to rely on maintenance rehearsal—memorization).

Metacognition.   Recognizing the importance of elaboration, educational researchers have focused much attention on a process known as *metacognition*, which involves an awareness of one's own thinking and information processing and a monitoring of this processing while learning (Flavell, 1981). A student who is metacognitively aware is participating in elaborative rehearsal by being aware of learning strategies and employing them in the classroom. Furthermore, studies comparing high-achieving and lower-achieving students indicate that higher achievers are more likely to use more metacognitive strategies (Romainville, 1994). At first, it might seem odd to encourage students to spend so much time thinking about thinking, as they already are busy taking notes and trying to "get" everything the teacher is saying. However, listeners actually can process information much faster than people speak, meaning that a thought-speech differential exists (Wolvin & Coakley, 1996). As a result, students actually do have "room" to think about thinking and employ learning strategies while in the classroom.

Lundsteen (1993) offers a number of metacognitive strategies that students might find useful (and that teachers might wish to encourage). Students may consciously direct their attention to important parts of the message by reminding themselves to identify the central idea or try to identify the most important point of the lecture. Students doing this would be less likely to daydream and suffer from attention lapses because they actually have a goal for the class session that they want to achieve. Students can also employ a self-questioning strategy while listening to the teacher, in which they develop questions that they then attempt to answer themselves. For example, a teacher reading this chapter would ask the self-question "This stuff about student learning is interesting, but how should my teaching change to improve my students' listening behavior?" In doing so, this "student" would be focusing his attention, elaborating, and attaching new material to existing schemas. Students also may use the strategy of asking teachers to clarify or try paraphrasing the teacher's message ("So what you mean by this is . . .") back to the teacher to assure that their interpretation is correct. Strategies already mentioned, such as forming examples or linking information to past experiences, also are metacognitive strategies. Colin Rose and Malcolm Nicholl (1997), whose Accelerated Learning program recognizes the importance of metacognition, also offer some strategies. One strategy is to try to get an overview of the subject at the beginning of the semester, whether that means flipping through the book or previewing the teacher's syllabus. Notice how this strategy would help provide the framework for a new schema for the material. As mentioned earlier, Rose and Nicholl also suggest the strategy of identifying the core idea of a subject in order to add to the foundation gained by skimming the material. A third strategy is for each student to identify that which she or he already knows about the subject. This strategy has a few benefits. First, it activates all the schemas that are relevant to the topic. Second, it is a positive starting point, in that it gives the student a chance to recognize all she already has learned about the subject. Third, it enables the student to see the areas in which she needs to learn more and more fully develop her knowledge.

Regardless of the strategies being used, notice the benefits of metacognition. It involves focused attention and diverse methods of elaborative processing, both of which are conducive to long-term learning. Also notice that, as with other aspects of the listening process, elaborative processing takes much effort to effectively remember information. The activity level required for effective learning is clear. Unfortunately, students (and teachers) often fall into a passive pattern of talk → take notes → move on to the next point in the outline. However, teachers can do a number of things to foster more active processing and metacognition in their students: Take breaks and have students write questions about the material, have students pair up and review by "teaching" the material to each other (they will have to understand the material well to be able to teach it), encourage students to ask questions, devote class periods in the beginning and middle of the semester to have students discuss what they have learned about the subject, have students come up with new examples of concepts, have students discuss concepts in their own words when reviewing, and of course, teach students about metacognition and strategies they can use to improve their own learning. Though the discussion of memory and metacognition may at first seem very student-focused and "out of the teacher's hand," it is clear that teachers can do a great deal in the classroom to facilitate their students' learning. Furthermore, notice that none of the strategies involved lecturing, and that they instead involve a variety of approaches, making them very conducive to holding students' attention.

Multiple Intelligences.   There is one final area of educational psychology that is relevant to student listening, because it suggests that students listen in different ways. In his 1983 book *Frames of Mind*, Howard Gardner articulates a new way of viewing intelligence by arguing that the traditional view of intelligence (IQ) is unsatisfactory and that people can be intelligent in different ways. Specifically, he identified seven intelligences that everyone possesses to some extent, indicating that each person has a mix of intelligences, some of which are stronger than others. The eight intelligences (he later added one) along with their characteristics are listed in Box 2.1.

Gardner's approach to intelligence is useful to teachers because it suggests that students learn in different ways (and teachers teach in different ways). Notice that the typical approach to teaching favors the linguistic or logical-mathematical intelligences. Because classrooms are likely to be comprised of students with different intelligence profiles (some highly intelligent interpersonally, others kinesthetically, etc.), teaching should be informed by knowledge of multiple intelligences, and teachers should attempt to teach in a way that will enable the students to learn the information effectively.

This is not a suggestion that teachers teach every piece of information in eight different ways. Instead, it is a suggestion that teachers use a variety of methods in teaching in order to involve all students. Rather than consistently teaching by lecturing, teachers can enhance their students' learning experience by challenging them to learn and think in different ways. In the process of doing this, teachers are likely to "tap into" each student's learning style. This may sound difficult, but teachers have a number of approaches at their disposal. For example, when teaching outlining in a public speaking course, teachers can have each student represent a part of a speech and then have the students physically move about the room and arrange themselves in the most appropriate outline form (relying on kinesthetic, spatial intelligences) and have them explain their choices (relying on interpersonal intelligences). When teaching audience analysis in the same class, the teacher could have the students role-play to act like different types of audiences while the teacher is speaking and then explain the appropriate ways to adjust to each type of audience (interpersonal intelligence). Also, the teacher could assign short introductory speeches but could require students to bring in a tape or CD of theme music (to be played before, during, or after the speech) that

BOX **2.1**   **The Eight Intelligences**

Intelligence	Characteristics
1. Linguistic	Proficiency with language (reading, writing) and word use
2. Logical-mathematical	Ability to reason and think logically and systematically
3. Body-kinesthetic	Effectiveness at using the body to solve problems; enjoyment of activity; adeptness with hands
4. Interpersonal	Ability to communicate well with others and understand others
5. Intrapersonal	Ability to understand oneself and to reflect and monitor one's own abilities and feelings
6. Spatial	Ability to visualize and have a sense of space and direction
7. Naturalist	Ability to understand nature and have comfort with natural surroundings
8. Musical	Ability to understand music and its components (pitch, rhythm, harmony, etc.)

best represents their personality (intrapersonal and musical intelligences, and possibly interpersonal intelligence—if the choice of music stimulates conversation). Although these ideas may look like little more than "fun and games," they are instructionally sound ideas. Again, they are a departure from lecturing, and the variety is likely to stimulate and hold students' attention. They are likely to be fun for students. They "tap into" a variety of intelligences. Finally, they are all very much task-related and can be used to illustrate class concepts and help students strengthen their schema for the material.

Notice that memory requires much work by students and their teachers. Consistent with the other stages of listening, this stage takes effort. However, students who attempt to learn actively and teachers who encourage active learning and teach with variety are likely to achieve success in the classroom.

Responding

Some models of listening include responding as one of the final stages (Brownell, 1996; Wolvin & Coakley, 1996). This will not be discussed in detail here as it is covered to some extent in the Mottet and Richmond chapter on students' nonverbal communication in the classroom. For new teachers, students' responses can be intimidating, as students who look bored or students who are talking to others may be distracting. However, new teachers should remember that looks of boredom, confusion, enjoyment, and enthusiasm all can help the teacher by serving as feedback on what he or she is saying and doing. Teachers should monitor student responses and remember that they can be useful in helping teachers continually improve their teaching.

By starting the teaching process with a focus on student listening, the ultimate goal of student learning—and the means by which teachers can help students achieve this goal—is made clear. Given the ground covered by this chapter, the importance and challenge of listening is apparent. Each stage of the listening process requires effort on the part of the listener. The listener must focus attention, work to correctly interpret information, elaborate on information to remember it, and think carefully to offer an appropriate response. If listening is this challenging for students, then teachers are faced with an even greater task.

The careful (and metacognitive) reader will note that this chapter has not assumed that students will even *want* to listen to teachers. It would be nice to think so, and it is often the case with some students, but to really be sure students are listening, teachers have to take great care in their teaching. After all, they have to gain their students' attention, teach so that students can correctly understand the material, enable students to remember the material, and take advantage of the feedback they get from their students' responses. To do all of this successfully, teachers must divide their time wisely (to maintain students' attention and enable them to remember information more effectively), teach clearly (much more on this in Chapter 8), create situations that require students to employ metacognition and elaborative processing, present material in different ways to appeal to students with different types of intelligences, and in general, use variety and do much more than just lecture and assume that students are listening. If new teachers do these things, then those earlier questions about filling time and students who appear bored will probably not be an issue anymore.

REFERENCES AND SUGGESTED READINGS

Atkinson, R. C., & Shiffrin, R. M. (1968). Human memory: A proposed system and its control processes. In K. W. Spence (Ed.), *The psychology of learning and motivation: advances in research and theory Vol. 2* (pp. 89–195). New York: Academic Press.

Baddeley, A. (1990). *Human memory: Theory and practice.* Boston: Allyn & Bacon.

Bartlett, F. C. (1932). *Remembering.* Cambridge, MA: Cambridge University Press.

Brewer, W. F. (1977). Memory for the pragmatic implications of sentences. *Memory and cognition, 5,* 673–678.

Borkowski, J. G., Cart, M., & Pressley, M., (1987). "Spontaneous" strategy use: Perspectives from metacognitive theory. *Intelligence, 11,* 61–67.

Broadbent, D. E. (1958). *Perception and communication.* London: Pergamon Press.

Brownell, J. (1996). *Listening: Attitudes, principles,*

and skills. Boston: Allyn & Bacon.

Coakley, C., & Wolvin, A. (1996). Listening in the educational environment. In M. Purdy & D. Borisoff (Eds.), *Listening in Everyday Life: A personal and professional approach* (pp. 179–212). Lanham, MD: University Press of America.

Craik, F. I. M., & Lockhart, R. S. (1972). Levels of processing: A framework for memory research. *Journal of verbal learning and verbal behavior, 11,* 671–684.

Edwards, R., & McDonald, J. (1993). Schema theory and listening. In A. Wolvin & C. G. Coakley (Eds.), *Perspectives on listening* (pp. 60–77). New York: Ablex Publishing.

Flavell, J. H. (1976). Metacognitive aspects of problem solving. In L. B. Resnick (Ed.), *The nature of intelligence.* Hillsdale, NJ: Lawrence Erlbaum.

Flavell, J. H. (1981). Cognitive monitoring. In W. P. Dickson (Ed.), *Children's oral communication skills* (pp. 35–38). New York: Academic Press.

Gardner, H. (1983). *Frames of mind: The theory of multiple intelligences.* New York: Basic Books.

Kahneman, D. (1973). *Attention and effort.* Englewood Cliffs, NJ: Prentice-Hall.

Lawson, M. J. (1984) Being executive about metacognition. In J. R. Kirby (Ed.), *Cognitive strategies and educational performance.* Orlando, FL: Academic Press.

Lundsteen, S. W. (1993). Metacognitive listening. In A. Wolvin & C. G. Coakley (Eds.), *Perspectives on listening* (pp. 106–123). New York: Ablex Publishing.

McCroskey, J. C. (1992). *An introduction to communication in the classroom.* Edina, MN: Burgess.

Minsky, M. L. (1975). A framework for representing knowledge. In P. H. Winston (Ed.), *The psychology of computer vision* (pp. 211–227). New York: McGraw-Hill.

Perry, A. R., & Laurie, C. A. (1992). Sustained attention and the Type A behavior pattern: The effect of daydreaming on performance. *Journal of General Psychology, 119,* 217–229.

Purdy, M., & Borisoff, D. (1996). *Listening in everyday life: A personal and professional approach.* Lanham, MD: University Press of America.

Romainville, M. (1994). Awareness of cognitive strategies: The relationship between university students' metacognition and their performance. *Studies in Higher Education, 19,* 359–367.

Rose, C., & Nicholl, M. J. (1997). *Accelerated learning for the 21st century.* New York: Dell Publishing.

Rumelhart, D. E. (1975). Notes on a schema for stories. In D. G. Bobrow & A. Collins (Eds.), *Representation and understanding* (pp. 211–236). New York: Academic Press.

Schank, R. C. (1975). *Conceptual information processing.* Amsterdam: North-Holland.

Stroh, C. M. (1971). *Vigilance: The problem of sustained attention.* Oxford, NY: Pergamon Press.

Wolvin, A., & Coakley, C. G. (1993). *Perspectives on listening.* New York: Ablex Publishing.

Wolvin, A., & Coakley, C. G. (1996). *Listening* (5th ed.). Boston: McGraw-Hill.

Yerkovich, F. R., & Thorndyke, P. W. (1981). An evaluation of alternative functional models of narrative schemata. *Journal of Verbal Learning and Verbal Behavior, 20,* 454–469.

3 Willingness to Communicate and Communication Apprehension in the Classroom

LINDA L. MCCROSKEY

California State University, Long Beach

JAMES C. MCCROSKEY

West Virginia University

Unlike those in most educational systems in other cultures, students in the U.S. system are expected to be verbal participants in their education. For many of these students, this expectation will not be met. From first grade with "show and tell," to second grade with reading out loud, to fourth grade with oral book reports, to sixth grade with oral current events, to eighth grade with oral presentations for science projects, to tenth grade with public speaking classes, to twelfth grade with oral lab reports—for these students, school is hell. Then on to college with group projects, class presentations, more public speaking classes, and seemingly every class syllabus indicating the percentage of the final grade that will be based on "class participation." Whatever the percentage, 20 percent or 50 percent, these students know they will not fare well. One person in five who reads this book is among them.

Whether you are an experienced teacher or a beginning teaching assistant, it is important that you understand what these students face. To get some sense of it, develop a mental image of what frightens you most. Maybe it is flying, heights, roller coasters, snakes, mice, water, the dark, spiders, taking standardized tests, earthquakes, tornados, or hurricanes. Whatever it is, now visualize having to confront it *every time you enter a classroom and for the whole time you are in the classroom.* The number-one fear of adult North Americans is having to give a public speech (death is third). But many teachers never hesitate to make such an event part of their required history, geology, sociology, or English class.

Most teachers do this not because they enjoy torturing their students. They just don't know any better. Others, ignorant of what scientific research has discovered, even think such assignments will be "good for them," help them "come out of their shell," or prepare them for "the real world." None of these things are true. In fact, the truth is almost the opposite of these myths.

Notice that we referred to these teachers as "ignorant," not stupid. They are just unaware of the facts relating to quiet people. Even professors of communication believed these myths until about 30 years ago, when research in this area started to open their eyes to a world they didn't even know existed. The purpose of this chapter is to raise the veil of ignorance that may exist for you in this regard. On the other hand, if you are already familiar with the research on quiet people, we hope this chapter will help you understand its implications for classroom instruction.

Willingness to Communicate

People differ greatly in the degree to which they communicate. At the extremes, some students hardly ever speak, while others seem to talk continuously. Teachers also vary widely in terms of how much they talk. Some seem to be talking to their classes all day long, while others seldom talk.

This variability in talking behavior has been the object of study for decades. In fact, research in this area represents one of the longest, continuous streams of research in the social sciences. In recent years four branches of this research have formed. One of these is directed toward the problem acknowledged at the beginning of this chapter—"communication apprehension" (CA): (Beatty, McCroskey, & Heisel, 1998; McCroskey, 1970, 1984). CA is an individual's level of fear or anxiety associated with either real or anticipated communication with another person or persons. About 20 percent of the population in North America are considered "communication apprehensives" (CAs). That is, these people are generally apprehensive about virtually all forms of oral communication—whether it involves talking with one other person, a small group, a large meeting, or public speaking.

CA is one of the two main reasons that people engage in reduced oral communication. The other is "self-perceived communication competence" (SPCC) (McCroskey & McCroskey, 1988). SPCC refers to the degree to which a person believes he or she is competent to perform various communication tasks. This should not be confused with actual communication competence. It represents the way someone thinks about his or her competence, not what the level of competence really is. If people think they are communicatively competent, they are much more likely to initiate communication. In contrast, if they do not feel competent, they are much less likely to initiate communication. SPCC clearly is related to self-esteem. People with high self-esteem also tend to have higher SPCC. People with low self-esteem tend to have both low SPCC and high CA.

The other two branches investigate "shyness" and "willingness to communicate." Shyness (McCroskey & Richmond, 1982) refers to the actual frequency of a person's talking. A person who refrains from talking much of the time, whatever the reason, can be referred to as a "shy" person. Shyness, then, represents a behavioral pattern and not necessarily a person's preferences toward communication or a person's anxiety about communication. If you don't talk much, you are shy. Research has indicated that approximately 40 percent of the people in the North American culture report that they are currently shy—and an additional 40 percent recall being shy at sometime in their life.

"Willingness to communicate" (WTC) (McCroskey, 1992; McCroskey & Richmond, 1987) refers to an individual's preference to initiate or avoid communication. A person who prefers to initiate communication in many circumstances is referred to as highly willing to communicate. In contrast, people who prefer to avoid communication in most circumstances are seen as not willing to communicate.

WTC, then, refers to a person's *preferences* with regard to initiating or avoiding communication, while "shyness" refers to the person's actual *behavior* with regard to initiating or avoiding communication. While it would be expected that in most situations a person would behave in the way he or she prefers to behave, it should be recognized that many other factors may influence people's choices in addition to their behavior preferences. Most of us would prefer not to take a test, but we have taken many anyway. Of course, being forced to make this choice contrary to our preferences may cause us considerable anxiety, raise our stress level, or even make us angry.

The WTC Trait

Consistent behavioral tendencies with regard to the frequency and amount of talk by an individual have been noted in the social science literature for decades. Such regularity in communication behavior across communication contexts suggests the presence of a traitlike personality variable. This willingness-to-communicate trait drives the individual's behavior across contexts and explains why people with different levels of this trait can be observed engaging in differing behavioral patterns (McCroskey, 1992).

Research by Cattell (1973) and by Buss and Plomin (1975) initially suggested that genetics plays a major role in WTC. Recent research has provided substantial support for this theory. With the advancement of the communibiological approach to the study of communication (Beatty & McCroskey, 2001; Beatty, McCroskey, & Heisel, 1998) it has become clear that most communication traits are likely to be heavily influenced by genetic factors. It is also recognized that a trait may have varying strength as a function of the general context in which communication takes place. For example, most people are far more likely to initiate communication in a dyadic (two-person) context than to volunteer to give a public speech in front of several hundred people. However, some people seem to be programmed in an opposite way—they are quick to volunteer for public performances but much less likely to initiate communication in a social context. It is important, therefore, that we look at general contexts to understand how people vary in willingness to communicate.

Types of Contexts

Although there are many types of communication contexts, we will focus on seven of the most general types here. Four types are distinguished by the number of people involved. These four are particularly relevant to communication in the classroom. They are: dyadic, small group, large group, and public (sometimes referred to as "person-to-group"). The other three are distinguished by the relationships among the participants in the communication. They are strangers, acquaintances, and friends.

Dyadic communication involves two people. It includes what we normally call "conversation." When two students talk together, or when a teacher and student talk together, we have dyadic communication. The overwhelming majority of the communication in which most people engage is dyadic. It is the least threatening type of communication for most (but definitely not all) people, so it is the type of context in which most people are most willing to communicate. Many students who will never ask a question or give an answer in front of a class will be quite willing to talk to the teacher outside of the class when no other students are present.

Small group communication involves more people than dyadic, but the upper limit of people to be considered a small group is a matter of judgment. In classrooms, most small groups range in membership from 4 to 7. Breaking into such groups provides more opportunities for students to talk about a given topic than would exist in a general class discussion. People vary greatly in their response to communication opportunities in small groups, some being highly talkative, but others choosing to say virtually nothing unless pushed into doing so by other group members.

Large group communication represents the normal class in school. It also characterizes the Parent-Teacher Association meeting. This is an environment that is often arranged so that one or a few people are at the front and there are many seats for others facing the front. This type of communication includes people talking from the front and others asking or answering questions or making statements from the audience. This is the typical small lecture class in schools—the teacher is the primary speaker, but students ask and answer questions or participate in other ways. Within this type of context, fewer audience members/students participate than would do so in the small group setting. In fact, research in classrooms indicates that 20 percent of the students account for over 80 percent of the participation in this communication setting.

Person-to-group communication (public speaking) places the burden of initiating communication on one person, while the others function primarily as listeners. In many cases it is assumed that one person will do all the talking and, when he or she is done, the group will break up or else another speaker will take over. This communication environment typifies the large lecture class in higher education. There may be from about 40 to over 1,000 students, and one lecturer. Usually students are not expected to participate in these classes, and may even be restricted from doing so—either by instruction or as a function of the media employed (TV, Internet, etc.). Many students resent this type of instruction because they can't participate orally. Others prefer this type of instruction because they can't be forced to participate orally.

On the first day of class it is not unusual for all of the students to be strangers, particularly in higher education. Of course, every day we talk to strangers in our normal pattern of life—the checkout clerk at the store, the service person at the restaurant, the sales clerk at the department store, and so forth. Whenever we travel, most of our interactions will be with strangers. Many people find talking with strangers very difficult. Others are actually more comfortable initiating interactions with strangers than they are with anyone else. In any event, communicating with strangers can be very strained: People have a difficult time deciding just how to interact and what to expect from others whom they do not know well.

With the possible exception of very large universities, most classrooms, after the first few days, become places where acquaintances interact. While students may not know one another beyond the context of the classroom, they at least have a perception of each other within this context. Most instructors will never know their students any better than this. Relationships within this context are limited, and high self-disclosure usually is not looked upon favorably. Communication is very purposeful and socializing is kept to a comparatively low level. Manifestations of WTC may be the highest in this context. That is, people's behavior may be most characteristic of their general WTC trait. People with high WTC will talk a lot, people with low WTC may not talk at all.

The final context type, friends, occurs mostly in upper-division and graduate classes. The students get to know each other well, and often the teacher and students know each other in social contexts outside the classroom. Of course, this does not necessarily mean that everyone in the context is friends with everyone else (some people may actually dislike one another very much). The critical element is that people know one another well and know how to communicate with each other. Generally, this is the context in which the most communication will occur. More people are likely to communicate more. Strong conflict may also be expressed in this kind of setting, whereas in the stranger and acquaintance contexts it is more likely to be considered inappropriate and thus stifled.

Special Constraints

People have a willingness-to-communicate trait which, in general, can predict how much they want to communicate across various contexts and with various people. Although trait WTC is very strong, people will vary to some extent in the degree to which they actually communicate—even in highly similar contexts and/or with highly similar types of receivers. Because situations are different, behavior may change even though the person's level of trait WTC stays the same.

Both situational constraints and personal constraints can impact a student's WTC in the classroom—and the same holds true for the teacher.

There are numerous situational factors that may have an impact on students' WTC in the classroom. Something as simple as the temperature in the room can have a very noticeable impact. When a classroom is too warm (over 72 degrees), the teacher may notice a significant drop in total participation in classroom interaction. Warmth tends to slow down intellectual processes and make students drowsy. When that happens, WTC will decrease.

Teachers often reduce students' WTC by not appearing open to student communication or by being highly evaluative of what students say. If students think talk is not acceptable or desirable, or if they feel they are likely to be criticized for what they say, most of them are bright enough to stay silent. It is not that they are less willing to communicate in all classrooms, it is just that they are not willing to communicate in this particular one.

In some situations students put high pressure on one another not to communicate in the classroom. While this may be a general orientation, it is more likely to be related to something specific, such as when it is shortly before the time for the class to end. The student may still want to participate, but recognizes the other students will punish her or him for doing so.

Students' WTC may also be reduced as a function of affective concerns. If the student does not like the subject matter, or does not like the teacher, the student's WTC is very likely to be sharply reduced.

These are just a few of the situational constraints that may exist. Others include such things as an upcoming holiday, a student activity later in the day, a visitor in the room, and so on. The instructor may have no way of knowing why the normally verbal student is quiet on a given day; even the student may not know why. The best advice for the teacher in any event is to simply recognize that the student does not want to talk and to leave the student alone. Even if the student knows why he or she does not want to talk, it may be something he or she does not want to share with the teacher. Often it is a personal rather than a situational constraint.

There are an unlimited number of personal constraints that may influence a student's WTC in the classroom. The one that teachers usually suspect first is sometimes actually the correct one—the student has not prepared well enough for class. This, however, is not as common as most teachers think. Sometimes, for example, the student is fully prepared but just doesn't have anything to say.

A student's health may have a big impact on her or his WTC. If one is not feeling well, it is reasonable to want to refrain from communicating. Sometimes the student is just feeling tired and having a hard time following what is going on.

More serious student concerns can also be present. Sometimes instructors are asking questions of the class that the student thinks call for self-disclosure, which he or she is unwilling to do. Sometimes the student is having personal or family problems and just does not want to share those with the rest of the students. Just because a person is an instructor does not mean that person is entitled to violate a student's desire for privacy.

As we indicated with situational constraints previously, the instructor who recognizes that the student wants to remain silent should leave the student alone. Students are people, and people have the right to be quiet if they want to. While quietness has a price for the student, it is not the right of the instructor to force the student to communicate, and coercing the student to communicate against her or his will can only damage the relationship between that teacher and student.

Correlates of WTC

As we noted previously, two of the major reasons people prefer to engage in reduced communication are a low level of SPCC and a high level of CA. Scores on measures of both of these are substantially correlated with the measure of WTC. As SPCC scores go up and/or CA scores go down, WTC goes up. Alternatively, as SPCC scores go down and/or CA scores go up, WTC goes down.

While theoretically this suggests that SPCC and CA are causes of WTC, we need to remember that all three of these are genetically based, hence at least to some extent, the measures of each of these are redundant measures of the same thing(s). We believe the factors producing the temperament variables extroversion and neuroticism are manifestations of a person's genetically determined brain structures. Extroversion is positively correlated with WTC and SPCC but negatively correlated with CA. Neuroticism is positively correlated with CA but negatively correlated with extroversion and WTC. Thus, people with high SPCC and WTC are non-neurotic extroverts, while people with high CA are neurotic introverts. Thus, thinking of SPCC and CA as causes of WTC probably is not a productive approach. Probably it is better to think of them as triggers for WTC. When a person becomes aware that he or she is apprehensive or unsure of himself or herself, it is likely that this triggers a reduction in WTC. In contrast when a person is relaxed or highly confident of his or her abilities, it is likely that this triggers an increase in WTC. Thus, it is best to think of the interaction of these variables as functions of an integrated system.

We believe the last step in this system is shyness, which is triggered (again, not caused) by reduced WTC or enhanced by increased WTC. Thus any behavioral outcomes are a function of all of these variables, but are manifested for others to observe through communication behaviors associated with either high or low shyness.

Effects of WTC, SPCC, CA, and Shyness

Each of the variables in this system produces outcomes or effects. Some are quite obvious, others are less so. For WTC and SPCC, the effects are most obvious.

The primary effect of low WTC is to increase the probability of shy behavior, while the primary effect of high WTC is to decrease the probability of shy behavior. Similarly, the effect of high SPCC is to increase the probability of having a higher WTC, while the primary effect of low SPCC is to increase the probability of having a lower WTC. Neither of these is directly associated with behavioral outcomes.

There are four distinct, although not unrelated, effects that can be produced by high CA: internal discomfort, communication avoidance, communication withdrawal, and overcommunication. Each of these effects can be observed in most classrooms, although few students manifest all four effects.

Internal Discomfort.   The only effect of CA that is universal, across both individuals and types of CA, is an internally experienced feeling of discomfort. High physiological arousal is common in many communication situations. People who are low in CA interpret this arousal as excitement. These people channel their arousal into the act of communicating and regularly report it to be helpful to them. In contrast, people with high CA interpret this arousal as fear. This perception tends to increase the arousal even more, and this fear/arousal/fear cycle sometimes escalates to the point at which the person is terrified.

The cognitive response to real or anticipated communication, then, can range from mild concern to abject terror, with a variety of physiological changes being produced as well. The blood pressure can increase, the heart rate go up, more perspiration may occur, the hands may tremble, the voice may quake, and/or the mouth may go dry. In extreme cases fainting is likely to occur, and even heart attacks are possible (though rare).

Excessive arousal, then, can have a very debilitating impact on a communicator, just as it can on an athlete. Both athletes and public speakers have been known to regurgitate just before they perform, or worse, while they are performing. More commonly, communicators forget what they want to talk about, experience hands that shake so much they cannot read their notes, or have their mouths go so dry that they can barely speak. Highly apprehensive students who know or believe they are going to have to communicate in class have great difficulty learning the material in class, much less retaining it for exams or application later. These students concentrate so hard on trying to figure out how to cope with the communication demands that they may learn little of what the instructor is trying to teach.

Such experiences are both unpleasant and unrewarding, but usually not terminal. However, some cases have been observed in which people have had heart attacks and died while giving a public speech. While such an extreme experience is uncommon, it is not unheard of. More commonly, particularly in the classroom context, students find ways to avoid having to speak if public speaking is a severe problem for them. They simply refuse to experience the extreme internal discomfort because anticipating it is so unpleasant it forces them to choose between the options of "fight or flight." Overwhelmingly, their choice is to flee through one of the next two possible effects of CA—avoidance or withdrawal. If these avenues are cut off by a well-meaning but ignorant instructor, the extreme reactions noted above are highly likely to occur. If the reactions are severe enough, and a student is injured in any way, of course, this opens the instructor to possible negative legal consequences.

Communication Avoidance. Most people who have high CA have the extreme type of experience noted above no more than once, if they have it at all. The experience is so traumatic, or they foresee it as being so traumatic, they take the steps necessary to be sure it does not happen again. They avoid situations in which the feared communication might be required. Often, without even being fully conscious they are doing so, people with high CA make choices in their lives that minimize their chances of being forced into communication.

Research has uncovered many methods that people use to avoid being forced to communicate. It has been found that people with high CA choose housing that is in more remote areas or in remote areas within dormitories and apartment buildings. They go into occupations that they believe have low communication demands. They refuse (typical of females) or do not ask for (typical of males) a date. They do not show up for job interviews.

In school, the people with high CA do not sign up for classes known to require communication, unless the course itself is required. They drop classes when they learn part of the grade is based on "class participation." They simply stay home "sick" on days when they are expected to perform for show and tell, current events, book reports, science projects, or any other public speaking events. They choose majors that do not have classes requiring such communication performances. They prefer large lecture classes over small, interactive classes, and enroll for them when possible.

Communication Withdrawal. Sometimes it is not possible for a person to avoid communication altogether. Communication demands sometimes arise unexpectedly. People with high CA are then forced to resort to the other "flight" response—to withdraw as quickly and fully as possible. Sometimes this can be done physically—actual physical departure. In other cases it is accomplished psychologically, by tuning out what is going on, or by minimizing one's participation.

Research has indicated a variety of options that are employed to accomplish withdrawal. Students choose seats on the side or in the back of the room where they are least likely to be called upon. In small groups they try to sit in an inconspicuous place where attention is less likely to be directed toward them. Some will simply say "I don't know" when asked a question, even if they do know. Another effective dodge is to respond with irrelevant comments when called upon. After a few of these responses virtually no one will bother the student again. Of course, these students do not raise their hands to participate even when they do know the answer.

Overcommunication. A small minority of students with high CA choose the final option. They decide to fight rather than flee. These people go out of their way to place themselves into communication situations in the hope that, with enough experience, they can beat the CA problem. Often the behaviors these people engage in seem so unlike those of a person who is afraid of communication that others may think they actually are low in CA.

Students who choose this "fight" option may voluntarily register for a public speaking course, or even join the debate team or drama club. They may run for a student government office. They may volunteer to serve as chair of committees. They may raise their hands to answer a question in class, even if they have no clue what the answer is. They tend to force themselves into the conversations of others. Not surprisingly, these are the very people who sometimes are thought to "talk too much." However, it is not the quantity of their talk that is so problematic, it is the negative quality of it.

While it is rare that a person can take on his or her CA and come out the victor, some people claim they have been victorious in such battles. In most instances, however, these people never were high in the CA trait. They were moderate in terms of trait CA but were bothered by one or more context-based or receiver-based concerns. Through practice and/or study they became better in their problem area(s) and simply overestimate the amount they have changed.

Changing traits of any kind is most difficult and normally requires the assistance of a trained professional. However, because these traits have a strong genetic base, even trained professionals may not be able to produce substantial change—they cannot change genes, at least they cannot at the present time. It may be possible some day.

While instructors cannot change their students' traits, there are things they can do that will make them part of the solution rather than part of the problem. That is, they can do things in their classrooms that will help highly apprehensive students have an easier time coping with their CA while maximizing their opportunity to learn. We will consider these at the end of this chapter.

The effects of shyness are much more direct and visible than those of CA. To summarize in advance, shy people get the worst end of just about everything. In order to avoid confusion, let us summarize some of what has been said before. Some people are much more willing to communicate than others, and some people are much less willing to communicate than others. Many, but not all, of the less willing are high communication apprehensives. People, apprehensive or not, who are less willing to communicate are very likely to engage in shy behavior—they will avoid communication and talk less when put in a position in which communication is expected. The outcomes of shyness, then, are a function of reduced communication.

The North American culture places a very high value on communication. This is not true of all cultures, hence what we say here probably will not apply generally. Put simply, in this culture, people who communicate more are perceived by others more positively. People who are shy are evaluated more negatively. While shyness in children often is seen as cute, shyness in adults is seen as a sign of many personality and/or intellectual deficits. They are discriminated against in the workplace, shunned in the social arena, and disabled in the classroom. Since this research has been thoroughly summarized elsewhere (Daly, Caughlin, & Stafford, 1997, McCroskey, 1977a, 1977b; Richmond & McCroskey, 1998), we will only address some of the instructional problems here.

People who are quiet are perceived to be less competent and less intelligent than more talkative people. These perceptions have a direct impact in the school environment. Although there is at least some positive impact (e.g., quiet students are less likely to get into trouble with the teacher), most of the impact is very negative.

Instructors' expectations are a major problem. Most faculty expect that quiet students will do less well and, as a result, treat these students as if they are less intelligent. The quiet student is less likely to be called on in class (which, of course, is just what the quiet student wants) and thus this student has fewer opportunities to correct learning mistakes. Quiet students receive less attention from the instructor, and thus receive less reinforcement when they do something well. As a function of their desire to avoid communication with instructors, quiet students also ask for assistance less frequently and volunteer to participate less, thus having fewer opportunities to learn and be positively reinforced.

Because many classes are graded in part on the basis of class participation, quiet students often receive lower grades than their more talkative peers, even though their achievement might actually be equal or even superior to that of their peers. In a very real sense, then, quiet students are discriminated against from grade school through graduate school. The impact of this discrimination is cumulative over the many years of the individual's schooling. By the time young people complete high school, their learning, as measured by standardized achievement tests, is affected. Even though there is no meaningful difference in intelligence, quiet students on average score lower on precollege achievement tests than do their talkative peers. At the college level quiet students have substantially lower grade point averages than more talkative students by the end of their freshman year. By the end of the typical four-year program, this gap has widened to approximately half a grade point. While that may seem like not very much, it is a gap that will make the difference between getting into or not getting into graduate school for many students. Because of their willingness to engage in communication with their instructors and their peers, more verbal students have more opportunities for learning and reinforcement than quiet students. The ultimate effect of talkativeness in college classrooms is increased learning and self-confidence.

In the college setting, in addition to a learning environment there is a social environment. As you might expect, quiet students do not fare well in this environment either. To establish social relationships it is necessary to talk to people. Quiet students do not want to do that, hence they have fewer relationships. In fact, when asked to list the first names of their friends, many quiet students at the college level cannot record a single name. Not surprisingly, quiet students report having far fewer dates than more verbal students. However, quiet students report a higher percentage of exclusive dating behaviors. It seems that if they find someone willing to date them, they become very committed to that relationship. Over half of quiet college students marry within one year of graduation, whereas only 10 percent of the more verbal students do so.

Differential attitudes and behaviors related to communication do not affect only students. Instructors are also affected. Research indicates that quiet teachers are not liked as much as more talkative instructors. This impacts not only instructors' student evaluations (which are often used to determine whether the instructor will continue to be employed) but also their teaching effectiveness. Students are less inclined to follow the recommendations of quiet instructors than those of more talkative teachers, they develop negative attitudes toward those teachers, and they record lower evaluations of those teachers. This is a potential problem for instructors in all disciplines.

Quiet people almost universally recognize their quietness, particularly by the time they finish undergraduate school. Most seek employment opportunities in which communication demands are low. However, graduate students focused on preparing themselves for a research career with low communication demands often find themselves working as graduate teaching assistants or teachers of regular undergraduate classes or labs. Still others complete their degrees and then find that almost all research positions are at major universities where they will also be expected to teach, possibly even to teach mass lecture classes enrolling 200 or more students. Such circumstances are extremely difficult for both the new instructors and their students.

Preventing and Reducing
Student Problems in the Classroom

Approximately 40 percent of college students consider themselves to be shy. These are the quiet students in the classroom. These are the students who will not do as well as their peers with the typical insensitive instructor. If you would like to make your classroom more sensitive and enabling for your students, it is best to treat all quiet students as if they were high communication apprehensives. If you do this you will make the environment much more tolerable for all quiet students—and for many more verbal students as well. There are five general methods for accomplishing this objective: (1) reduce oral communication demands, (2) make communication a rewarding experience, (3) be consistent about communication, (4) reduce ambiguity, novelty, and evaluation, and (5) increase student control over success. We will consider each of these in turn.

Reduce Oral Communication Demands

With the exceptions of classes on public speaking and oral foreign language, talk need not be a focal activity in the classroom for all students. Communication demands can be reduced without sacrificing learning by doing the following.

1. *Avoid testing through talk.* There are many ways for students to demonstrate that they have learned (written tests, performing given tasks, etc.). Be certain that what you are testing is what is supposed to be learned in your class, not how little a high CA who is forced to talk can remember under pressure.

2. *Avoid grading on participation.* In spite of what instructors continue to say (and probably believe), research indicates that what is graded is *quantity* of participation in most cases, not *quality*. Grading on talking directly handicaps quiet students. Not only will the student be unlikely to talk anyway, unless forced to do so, he or she will be so worried about communication it will interfere with her or his learning. If you consider requiring participation because you assume it will enhance learning, you should remember that students learn primarily through their eyes and their ears, not through their mouths.

3. *Avoid alphabetical seating.* This type of seating has little advantage to it, other than providing a minor convenience for taking roll. It has the high potential for placing quiet students right in the areas with the highest communication demands. Research indicates that this will *not* increase their communication, but it will reduce their learning. To the extent that you can, given the class you are teaching, let the students select their own seats so they do not get in high interaction areas if they do not want to. You can always have the students put their names on a seating chart so you can take roll, even if it is not alphabetical.

4. *Avoid randomly calling on students to respond.* Such a procedure drives students who are afraid to communicate up the wall, and more importantly, reduces their learning by causing them to worry about being forced to communicate rather than to pay attention to the lesson.

None of these suggestions requires any major change in the instructional system, yet each can contribute to making the classroom a more comfortable place for learning by reducing communication demands. It must be stressed here that it is the demands for oral communication that are being reduced, not the oral communication. None of these suggestions in any way interferes with students who want to communicate.

Make Communication a Rewarding Experience

Although you are not likely to change a student's level of trait CA by doing so, you can help the student see your classroom as a context in which he or she may feel comfortable communicating. This can be done, and has been done, by many teachers who have taken the effort to do so. These are some suggestions about how to proceed.

1. *Praise students when they participate, particularly the quiet ones.* It seems so obvious that if we want students to communicate we should praise communication. But observation indicates that many instructors really do not do that. Even if the student with high CA says nothing for weeks, simply observing that everyone else is praised for talking increases the likelihood that the student will eventually do so, too.

2. *Try to avoid indicating that any answer is completely "wrong."* Sometimes students give wrong answers to questions posed in class. Try to reward the

effort anyway. Sometimes this is difficult, but it is worth trying. Find something positive about the answer, even if it is something like: "That answer is not completely correct, but it is one of the answers most commonly given. Let's look at how we can improve on it." This approach reduces the "risk factor" for being wrong.

3. *Try not to punish any student for talking.* If students are disruptive, make it very clear to everyone that it is the disruption that is being punished. Continue to encourage the student who was punished to participate. This will help make clear that communication is valued in your classroom, but disruptions are not.

These methods will lead quiet students to perceive communication in a more positive light, and communicating in your classroom as less threatening. Even though they may continue to avoid communication in another classroom, you may convince them that it is OK to talk in your class, even if only occasionally. After all, a little is better than none at all.

Be Consistent about Communication

Students often learn to be "helpless" in the classroom. They can't figure out what they need to do to be rewarded and/or avoid punishment, so they choose to do nothing, or as little as possible. Learned helplessness is generated by inconsistent rewards, absence of rewards, and punishments. You can reduce the potential for learned helplessness in your classroom by the following:

1. *Try to be consistent in how you handle student talk.* Try to make it so the students can be reasonably certain of your response before they speak, so they do not get unexpected responses to their talk, particularly negative ones.

2. *Be very clear about any rules you must have regarding talking.* Don't depend entirely on your own judgment. Check with students to determine their perceptions. Their judgments are the ones that count. Give everyone at least one chance to break a talk rule before being punished. Give the quiet ones even more chances; they don't need to be further conditioned to believe that talk and punishment go together.

Reduce Ambiguity, Novelty, and Evaluation

Uncertainty makes people uncomfortable, and that discomfort is even worse for students with high communication apprehension. They, and many other quiet students, are not likely to ask questions to clear things up. Some specific things you should consider are:

1. *Make all assignments as clear and unambiguous as you can.* Give all students the opportunity to ask questions about them. If possible, give the students an

e-mail address to which than can address questions. Many quiet people simply will not ask questions in class, but many are likely to do so in the relative comfort of the e-mail system.

2. *Be very clear about your grading system.* Make certain that all students understand how they will be evaluated. Remember not to place much emphasis on the evaluation of any kind of talk.

3. *Avoid surprises.* It is fine to do things that are different, but do not put the student on the spot for not understanding the "new" system. Remember, quiet students often will accept failure rather than communicate to succeed.

Increase Student Control over Success

A student who feels in control of how well he or she will do in a class has confidence. Confident students are more likely to communicate than those who lack confidence. To accomplish this you may be able to do the following:

1. *Give the student options.* The more options the student has, the more he or she can select options that fit her or his own style of learning. The quiet student can avoid those options that require a lot of communication.

2. *Be certain that the student can avoid communication and still do well in the course.* If the term project in the course requires an oral presentation and counts a third of the final grade, the quiet student may feel helpless. If possible, then, that project should be able to be presented in writing, or some other type of project altogether should be permissible.

You probably have recognized by now that none of the suggestions noted in the above sections requires any major amount of extra effort on the part of the instructor. These are steps that can be taken with little effort, but their impact on quiet students can be very important to those students' success.

The term "sensitivity" probably has been overused in recent years, but it is appropriate here. If you are sensitive to how your teaching behaviors might be perceived by your quiet students, you probably will have little trouble becoming part of the solution to their problem. If you are insensitive to those students, you will be part of the problem.

REFERENCES AND SUGGESTED READINGS

Beatty, M. J., & McCroskey, J. C. (2001). *The biology of communication: A communibiological perspective.* Cresskill, NJ: Hampton Press.

Beatty, M. J., McCroskey, J. C., & Heisel, A. D. (1998). Communication apprehension as temperamental expression: A communibiological paradigm. *Communication Monographs, 65,* 197–219.

Buss, A. H., & Plomin, R. (1975). *A temperament theory of personality.* New York: Wiley.

Cattell, R. B. (1973). *Personality and mood by questionnaire.* San Francisco: Jossey-Bass.

Daly, J. A., Caughlin, J. P., & Stafford, L. (1997). Correlates and consequences of social-communicative anxiety. In J. A. Daly, J. C. McCroskey, J. Ayres, T. Hopf, and D. M.

Ayres (Eds.), *Avoiding communication: Shyness reticence, and communication apprehension* (2nd ed., pp. 21–71), Cresskill, NJ: Hampton Press.

McCroskey, J. C. (1970). Measures of communication-bound anxiety. *Speech Monographs, 37,* 269–277.

McCroskey, J. C. (1977a). Classroom consequences of communication apprehension. *Communication Education, 26,* 27–33.

McCroskey, J. C. (1977b). Oral communication apprehension: A summary of recent theory and research. *Human Communication Research, 4,* 78–96.

McCroskey, J. C. (1984). The communication apprehension perspective. In J. A. Daly and J. C. McCroskey (Eds.), *Avoiding communication* (pp. 13–38), Beverly Hills, CA: Sage.

McCroskey, J. C. (1992). Reliability and validity of the willingness to communicate scale. *Communication Quarterly, 40,* 16–25.

McCroskey, J. C., & McCroskey, L. L. (1988). Self-report as an approach to measuring communication competence. *Communication Research Reports, 5,* 108–113.

McCroskey, J. C., & Richmond, V. P. (1982). Communication apprehension and shyness: Conceptual and operational distinctions. *Central States Speech Journal, 33,* 458–468.

McCroskey, J. C., & Richmond, V. P. (1987). Willingness to communicate. In J. C. McCroskey & J. A. Daly (Eds.), *Personality and interpersonal communication* (pp. 129–156), Beverly Hills, CA: Sage.

Richmond, V. P., & McCroskey, J. C. (1998). *Communication: Apprehension, avoidance, and effectiveness* (5th ed.). Boston: Allyn & Bacon.

4 Students' Motives for Communicating with Their Instructors

MATTHEW M. MARTIN
West Virginia University

SCOTT A. MYERS
West Virginia University

TIMOTHY P. MOTTET
Southwest Texas State University

As college instructors, we are well aware of the role communication plays in the classroom. In some cases, we may be too aware. Researchers have studied the effects of instructor communication across a wide variety of classroom contexts and have generally concluded that instructor communication significantly and positively affects students' perceived motivation, learning, and satisfaction, among other outcomes. As a result of these studies, college instructors have the ability to modify their instructional behaviors and skills that can promote learning, ensure a safe learning environment, and create a supportive classroom climate.

However, what has remained understudied is student communication in the classroom. As any instructor can attest, college students *do* and *can* engage in communication in the classroom for a variety of reasons. For some students, a willingness to communicate with their classmates or their instructors may be based on their personalities, their desire to forge new relationships, or their need to attain information. Yet, little is known about the reasons, or motives, why students communicate with their instructors.

Back in the 1960s, Schutz identified three main reasons for why people communicate with others: affection, inclusion, and control. *Affection* is the need to communicate with others to express caring and love. *Inclusion* is the need to communicate with others to participate in and maintain relationships. *Control* is the need to communicate with others in order to maintain power and influence others. Schutz argued that people communicate with others in order to satisfy these needs.

Building on the work of Schutz, in 1988, Rubin, Perse, and Barbato were interested in why people talk, with whom people talk, and what people talk about. In doing so, they identified three other motives (in addition to affection, inclusion, and control) for why people communicate with others. These three were pleasure, relaxation, and escape. *Pleasure* involves the need to be excited or entertained. *Relaxation* deals with a need to rest or to feel less tense. *Escape* focuses on a need to avoid other activities and worries. Rubin argued that these six motives influence how and why people communicate. However, she also made it clear that in different contexts, people have different motives, or reasons, for communicating with others.

This chapter explores why and how students communicate with their instructors. For the last several years, we have studied the motives students have for communicating with their instructors. In doing so, we have identified five of them: relational, functional, excuse-making, participation, and sycophancy.

When students communicate for *relational* purposes, they are trying to develop personal relationships with their instructors. Communication for *functional* reasons includes learning more about the material and the assignments in the course. Students also communicate to offer *excuses,* attempting to explain why work is late or missing or to challenge grading criteria. A fourth reason students have for communicating is for *participation.* Students want to demonstrate to their instructors that they are interested in the class and that they understand the material. A fifth reason is *sycophancy,* getting on the instructor's good side. Students may communicate in order to make a favorable impression or to get the instructor's approval. The following section looks at each of these reasons more closely.

Students' Motives

One reason students communicate with teachers is for *relational* purposes. Students might perceive their instructors as someone they could be friends with, someone with whom they could discuss daily events. Talking about the local football team, the new blockbuster movie, or the local restaurant scene are all examples of topics that teachers and students may talk about. Research in the area of interpersonal communication consistently shows that people are attracted to others who are similar to themselves. Often during interactions, people search for commonalities. If the teacher has not seen the recent movie, the student may talk about a musical group that both of them like. If the teacher and student do not share any common interests, they might possibly talk about weekend activities or current events in the news. The focus of relational communication is more on the individuals involved than on any issues involving the course content.

Why would students spend time talking to instructors about things that do not concern the course? One explanation could be that students genuinely believe that the instructors are potential friends, people who are actually interested in having a relationship outside of the classroom. Students may possibly see this type of communication as a way of learning more about their teachers, their likes and dislikes. Or as was mentioned earlier, students may realize the benefit of having a cordial relationship with their instructors. This is not to say that students intend to manipulate their instructors or take advantage of their relationships. Instead, students recognize the potential benefit of having instructors who know them and enjoy talking to them about their interests.

This type of communication would seemingly occur before or after a class session. In fact, if this type of communication took place during the course lecture on a regular basis and the teacher allowed it, it would probably be considered a teacher misbehavior. Students might enjoy playing the game of "Let's have the teacher talk about anything besides the course material." If the teacher allows the game to be played, or even initiates the game, this would be a misbehavior. Understandably, students do not react positively to instructor misbehavior. Thus, for most students, this type of communication would occur before or after a class session, in order to maximize the relational impact.

A second reason students communicate with their instructors is for *functional* purposes. Students need information about the course. The best source of information about the course is often the instructor. Students ask their instructors questions in order to learn what the expectations of the course are, to better understand the material, and to clarify the requirements for assignments and exams. Even if this information is provided in a syllabus or a textbook, students may feel more comfortable or reassured hearing the same information from instructors themselves.

Functional communication is considered to be instrumental. People communicate for this reason with a specific goal in mind. They want information; thus they ask questions. The information that is gained is used to succeed in the course. Unless students need some information about the course (i.e., directions, assignments), they are not heard from. "Is this going to be on the test" is an example of a communication message that is asked purely for functional purposes. A benefit of students talking for functional purposes is that instructors' responses often clarify to all students what is expected and desired from them.

A third reason students communicate with their instructors is for *excuse-making*. When work is late, when work is incomplete, when students are late for class or fail to attend altogether, students often inform their instructors of the reasons why. While almost all students will find it necessary to explain an absence or late work to an instructor at one time or another, other students habitually seem to have excuses for every day of the week.

Instructors by midterm are often able to identify those students who communicate primarily for excuse-making. These students are often seldom heard from, except when they have a problem that prevents them from succeeding in the course. One recent student of ours had a horrible semester: she had several grandparents die, her parents spent time in the hospital, she had several car accidents on her way to class (along with a flat tire or two), she had a bad case of mono (but was too sick to go see a doctor), her ex-boyfriend was stalking her, her dog was sick after eating her paper, her computer contracted numerous viruses that erased her hard drive, and the electric company would regularly turn off her power the night before exams. The only time this student would talk to the instructor was to give an excuse. She seldom asked about what she missed or what she would need to do to make up any assignments. Students who make excuses are usually not those who communicate for functional purposes. Those who communicate for functional purposes usually know the requirements for the class assignments and the deadlines or are seeking out this information.

Another reason students have for communicating with their instructors is to *participate*. Some classes tend to encourage interaction, while others actually discourage student involvement. In some classes, student participation is actually required. While the type of class and the instructor influence the quality and quantity of student interaction, another factor to consider is a student's motive to participate. When students believe that their classmates and instructors value their contributions, talking in class is a way of demonstrating that they are paying attention and are interested. Additionally, a way of showing understanding of the material is to be actively involved.

On the continuum of participation, there are the extremes. At one extreme, you have students who do not participate no matter what. These students could be rewarded for participating (i.e., given extra points or candy) or punished for not participating (i.e., receive a lower grade), and yet they do not participate. This is not to say that they are not interested or that learning is not taking place. In fact, these students may be communication apprehensive, a communication problem that was covered in Chapter 3. Others may have been socialized not to participate. These students learned early to merely listen and take notes. At the other extreme, there are the students who participate too much. Every class session, they have something to share with the class. Almost everyone has witnessed a student like this. Every time an instructor asks a question, the same people raise their hands (and maybe even make some noises and gestures in order to get called on). Class just is not class unless these students share their opinions with everyone else. Luckily, most students are not at the extremes. Many times students increase or decrease their participation depending on the instructor, the course, the content, and/or the format of the class.

The final motive that students have for communicating with their instructors is the motive of *sycophancy*. Sycophancy is a more polite way of saying "brown-nosing" or "sucking up." At times, students communicate with their instructors not because they like them or because they need any information about the course, but because they want to make a good impression. They want to appear as students who value and appreciate the instructor. This is not to say that students cannot compliment their instructors or acknowledge a job well done by their instructors. But when students make these statements just so they appear in a more positive light in the eyes of their instructors, these students are communicating for the motive of sycophancy.

Some students work harder at making a good impression than spending time working on their assignments or studying for their exams. One student of ours once tried to explain his poor performance on an exam by stating that as he was preparing to study for the exam, he stumbled across a couple of research articles written by the instructor. Since the articles were so stimulating and significant, the student was unable to tear himself away from the articles, and thus was not able to study sufficiently for the exam (here we have a combination of excuse-making and sycophancy). While the instructor's head may have grown slightly bigger, the instructor was not impressed enough to allow any type of extra credit work to increase the student's grade. There is nothing wrong with students sharing positive feedback with their instructors, but if the praise is expected to be a substitute for competency and/or the sincerity of the praise remains questionable, then students are communicating for sycophantic rather than relational reasons.

It should be noted that the communication motives discussed here are not mutually exclusive. In other words, students may be motivated to communicate with their instructors for multiple reasons. While students may be predominantly motivated by one motive, such as functional, these students also communicate for the other motives as well. These communication motives are also not exhaustive. While students report that these are frequent reasons why they communicate with their instructors, students may also communicate with their instructors to obtain information about the instructor's area of study, to inquire whether a particular class serves as a prerequisite for others, to ask about college and/or university policy, or to inquire about other faculty in the instructor's department. The following section reviews some of the research findings yielded from a program of research examining students' motives for communicating with their instructors.

Research on Students' Motives

In 1999, we introduced our instrument for measuring motives students have for communicating with their instructors (see Box 4.1). Since then, we and our colleagues have conducted a series of studies to explore the relationship between students' motives and other variables. The following paragraphs review this research.

Our first study involved asking students why they communicate with their instructors (Martin, Myers, & Mottet, 1999). Students generated a list of various reasons for why they communicate. This list of reasons was then given in questionnaire format to other students. For each of the reasons, students were asked to rate on a Likert-type scale, from *exactly like me* (5) to *not at all like me* (1) how each of the statements reflected their own reasons for talking to their instructors. Factor analysis resulted in identifying five motives that students report having:

relational, functional, participation, excuse-making, and sycophancy. For the five motives, students reported communicating most frequently for the functional motive, while communicating the least frequently for the relational motive.

In this study, we also examined the relationship between students' motives for communicating with their instructors with their interpersonal motives for communicating with others in general. Students who reported talking to others because it is fun, relaxing, and to show others that they care also reported that they talk to their instructors for the relational motive. Students who reported communicating with others out of a need for control stated that they talk more frequently to their instructors to satisfy excuse-making and sycophancy needs.

In our second study, we examined the relationship between students' motives for communicating with their instructors with affective and cognitive learning (Martin, Mottet, & Myers, 2000). We expected that the reason students talk to their teachers should be related to how well they like the course and the instructor. Our results did show that there was a relationship between affect and communication. Affect for the course was positively related to the relational, functional, and participation motives, while affect for the instructor was positively related to the relational and functional motives. Additionally, students' report of their cognitive learning was positively related to the motives of relational, functional, and participation motives. Seemingly, students are more communicatively active when they like the course and the instructor. Students also feel they are learning more when they are participating (i.e., communicating) more in class.

Our third study focused on how students' sociocommunicative orientations and instructors' sociocommunicate styles (see Chapter 9) influence the motives students have for communicating (Martin, Mottet, & Myers, 1999). Sociocommunicative orientations and styles are based on individuals' levels of assertiveness and responsiveness. When people report being both highly assertive and responsive, they are considered to be competent communicators. People who are assertive but not responsive are rated as aggressive; responsive but not assertive are regarded as being communicatively submissive. When people are neither assertive nor responsive, they are considered noncompetent.

In regard to sociocommunicative style, when students perceive their instructors as being competent or submissive, students report communicating for the functional motive. In other words, when students perceive their instructors as catering to the needs of others, they ask more questions about the material and assignments. Concerning their own sociocommunicative orientations, when students perceive themselves as being competent communicators, they report communicating more for the motives of relational, functional, participation, and excuse-making more so than students who perceive themselves as one of the other sociocommunicative orientations. Students high in responsiveness reported communicating more for sycophancy than students low in responsiveness. In this study, we also looked at whether men and women differed in their motives for communicating. Men reported communicating more for relational and sycophancy reasons while women reported communicating more for functional reasons. The results from this study indicate that while both student and instructor communication characteristics influence why students communicate, student communication characteristics may play a greater role in influencing why students do or do not communicate with their instructors.

To better understand the role instructor behavior plays in influencing students' motives, the relationship between students' motives and instructors' use of behavior alteration techniques (BATs) was then investigated (Martin, Heisel, & Valencic, 2000). BATs are communication strategies that instructors use to influence students. Results from this study showed that nearly none of the BATs were related to the functional motive while nearly all of the BATs were related to the participation motive. Whether students communicated to find out information about the class did not seem to be related to the instructor's use of these techniques. On the other hand, whenever instructors used strategies to get students more involved in the classroom, students reported a greater motive to communicate to participate. Additionally, the relational motive was related to the instructors use of positive BATs while the excuse-making and sycophancy motives were related to the instructors use of negative BATs. When instructors used liking, rewarding, and confirming strategies, students reported communicating more for the relational motive. However, when instructors used strategies such as punishment, guilt, and legitimate authority, students reported communicating more for the excuse-making and sycophancy motives.

Further investigating the influence of instructor communication, we asked students to rate their instructors' communicator style and to report on their motives for communicating with their instructors (Myers, Mottet, & Martin, 2000). In this study, we found that when students perceived their instructors as impression-leaving, friendly, and contentious (i.e., argumentative), they communicated more for the relational motive. Similar to the results obtained in our third study, when students perceived their instructors as being friendly, they communicated more for functional motives. The animated, contentious, and friendly attributes predicted students' participation while the attentive and contentious attributes predicted students' use of excuse-making. Students also reported communicating more for sycophancy when the instructor was perceived as friendly and contentious.

In our most recent study, the relationship between students' trait communication apprehension and their motives for communicating was investigated (Martin, Valencic, & Heisel, 2000). We also included class motivation as a study variable. As one would expect, communication-apprehensive students talk less to their instructors, especially for the relational, functional, and participation motives. As far as motivation, when students are communicating for relational and participation motives, students report greater motivation about the class overall. Additionally, the motive of excuse-making is negatively related to motivation. When students have low motivation, they appear to also have a low need to explain their lack of attendance or failure in handing in work.

While these studies have explored students' motives, further work needs to be conducted to arrive at a better understanding of the role motives play in the classroom with the hope of improving the student-instructor relationship and thus student learning. One area that we are paying more attention to now is why students do not talk to their instructors. The next section reviews several of the reasons students give for not talking to their instructors.

Why Students Do Not Talk to Their Instructors

Just as students have reasons for why they talk to instructors, students also have reasons for why they avoid or do not approach their instructors. If there is value in students communicating with their instructors as some of our research has indicated, we must also recognize why students do not communicate with their instructors. Based on this need, we asked a group of students to list five reasons why they personally do not talk to their instructors. We classified their responses into three categories: student characteristics, teacher characteristics, and environmental characteristics.

Student Characteristics

A primary reason students do not interact with instructors is based on their own communication apprehension. Not only are students afraid to communicate in general, but they are also afraid to communicate with someone of higher status who has power over them (i.e., grades). For some students, talking to a teacher is not even an idea that they would consider, let alone a behavior that they would do. Students also state that they are afraid of appearing ignorant. "What if I am asking the teacher about something she already said" and "What if I show how stupid I am by asking a dumb question" are examples that students gave for not interacting with their instructors.

Other reasons that students give for not communicating involve lack of affect and/or motivation. When students do not like the course or the instructor, they are less inclined to have a need to talk with the instructor. This reason for not communicating is consistent with the results we reported on earlier where students with greater affect for the course and instructor communicate more for the motives of relational, functional, and participation. Students also point to their own lack of motivation. When students do not care about the class, do not care about succeeding, and fail to attend class regularly, they also do not feel any need to communicate with their instructors.

One final reason students give for not communicating is the avoidance of being considered a teacher's pet. Students do not want to appear to be "kissing up" to the instructor. While some students clearly communicate with their instructors to make a favorable impression, (remember, students report communicating more frequently for sycophancy than for relational motives), some students would not consider being viewed as a person who is trying to make points or get special considerations via flattery or insincere comments.

Teacher Characteristics

Of the teacher characteristics that students listed as reasons for not communicating, a common theme among the responses was the instructor's lack of sensitivity and caring. When teachers do not appear interested in students, when teachers have a pattern of not showing respect towards students, and when teachers are verbally abusive towards students, students reply that they do not want to talk to their instructors. This makes sense. Why talk to someone who obviously does not care about you and who might respond to your attempt of communication by attacking you? We approach that which gives us pleasure, and we avoid that which gives us pain.

Another reason students give for not communicating with their instructors is the lack of feedback provided by the instructors. When students feel that previous attempts at communication have been unsuccessful, they are less likely to attempt to communicate with their instructors in the future. When attempts for help and clarification have failed in the past, students tend to look elsewhere (or possibly nowhere) for help, instead of talking to their instructors. In these instances, students have made an attempt to communicate with their instructors, but feel that the instructors are not overly interested or helpful. While not stated explicitly by students, there is the feeling that some students might generalize one bad experience with an instructor to all of their instructors. In other words, because one instructor was not helpful, students do not attempt to communicate with their other instructors in the future. Future research needs to explore the validity of this notion.

Environmental Characteristics

Students also mentioned several environmental characteristics that influence why they do not communicate with their instructors. One issue is time. Students state that they do not have enough time to communicate with their instructors. Because the class is not designed for student participation or because students have to go to a class immediately afterwards, there is no time to talk to their instructors. Students also report that lack of convenient office hours prevents them from communicating more frequently with their instructors. A final reason was that communicating with instructors was unnecessary. In explaining this last statement, students stated the class was easy enough and/or that the instructor's help or assistance was unnecessary. "I can succeed in this class without communicating with the instructor, so why bother?" was one common statement.

To better understand why students communicate with their instructors, we need to examine further the reasons why students do not communicate with their instructors. This is especially true if we are going to argue for the value of getting students to communicate with their instructors (i.e., for the motives of relational, functional, and participation). By examining the communication factors that repel students from teachers, we can enhance the factors that attract students to us, therefore improving the student-teacher relationship.

BOX 4.1

Motives	Scale Items
Relational	to learn about him/her personally so we can develop a friendship to build a personal relationship to learn more about the teacher personally because I find him/her interesting because we share common interests
Functional	to clarify the material to get assistance on the assignments/exams to learn how I can improve in the class to ask questions about the material to get academic advice to get more information on the requirements of the course
Participation	to appear involved in class because my input is vital for class discussion to demonstrate that I understand the material to demonstrate my intelligence because my classmates value my contribution to class discussions because my instructor values class participation
Excuse-Making	to explain why work is late to explain absences to explain why I do not have my work done to challenge a grade I received to explain why my work does not meet the instructor's expectations to explain the quality of my work
Sycophancy	to pretend I'm interested in the course to give the instructor the impression that I like him/her to give the impression that I think the instructor is an effective teacher to give the impression that I'm learning a lot from the instructor to give the impression that I'm interested in the course content to get special permission/privileges not granted to all students

Note: Students rate on a Likert-type scale, from *exactly like me* (5) to *not at all like me* (1) how each of the statements reflects their reasons for talking to their instructors.

Conclusion

No matter what class or subject matter one teaches, effective teaching and learning remain dependent on a teacher–student relationship grounded in communication. In this chapter, we discussed five motives that students have for communicating with their instructors. Whether a student communicates for one of these motives depends on student characteristics, instructor characteristics, and environmental characteristics. Of the five motives, three motives appear to be more advantageous in the classroom: relational, functional, and participation. These student motives are related to students' reports of their own learning and motivation. Seemingly then, students should be encouraged to communicate for these reasons. At the same time, instructors should appear responsive to the needs and concerns of their students, should refrain from being verbally aggressive, and should make themselves available for consultation.

The motives of excuse-making and sycophancy do not appear to be related to instructional outcomes. In other words, there is no relationship between these two motives and students' learning and motivation. While certain instructor behaviors may encourage students to communicate for excuse making and sycophancy reasons (e.g., when instructors use negative BATs), students are only responding to the demands of the instructor. If instructors dominate the classroom with legitimate authority and multiple rules, students will have to spend more time explaining why they broke the rules.

Many of the college instructors we know teach because they enjoy working with and nurturing students. This requires communication outside of merely providing a clear, insightful lecture. The instructional communication literature argues over and over again about the importance of establishing a positive relationship between the students in a class and the instructor. Beyond recognizing that students may communicate for different reasons in a given situation, instructors should also do their best to get their students to be actively involved and to provide a good, positive classroom experience.

REFERENCES AND SUGGESTED READINGS

Martin, M. M., Heisel, A. D., & Valencic, K. M. (2000, April). *Students' motives for communicating with their instructors IV: Considering instructors' use of BATs.* Paper presented at the Eastern Communication Association Convention, Pittsburgh, PA.

Martin, M. M., Myers, S. A., & Mottet, T. P. (1999). Students' motives for communicating with their instructors. *Communication Education, 48*, 155–164.

Martin, M. M., Mottet, T. P., & Myers, S. A. (1999, November). *Students' motives for communicating with their instructors III: Considering socio-communicative style and sex differences.* Paper

presented at the National Communication Association Convention, Chicago.

Martin, M. M., Mottet, T. P., & Myers, S. A. (2000). The relationship between students' motives for communicating with their instructors with affective learning, cognitive learning, and satisfaction. *Psychological Reports, 87*, 830–834.

Martin, M. M., Valencic, K. M., & Heisel, A. D. (2000, November). *The relationship between students' motives for communicating with their instructors with communication apprehension.* Paper presented at the National Communication Association Convention, Seattle.

Myers, S. A., Mottet, T. P., & Martin, M. M. (2000). The relationship between student communication motives and perceived instructor style. *Communication Research Reports, 17,* 161–170.

Rubin, R. B., & Martin, M. M. (1998). Interpersonal communication motives. In J. C. McCroskey, J. A. Daly, M. M. Martin, & M. J. Beatty (Eds.), *Communication and personality: Trait perspectives* (pp. 287–308). Cresskill, NJ: Hampton Press.

Rubin, R. B., Perse, E. M., & Barbato, C. A. (1988). Conceptualization and measurement of interpersonal communication motives. *Human Communication Research, 14,* 602–628.

Schutz, W. C. (1966). *The interpersonal underworld.* Palo Alto, CA: Science and Behavior Books.

5

Student Nonverbal Communication and Its Influence on Teachers and Teaching

TIMOTHY P. MOTTET
Southwest Texas State University

VIRGINIA P. RICHMOND
West Virginia University

For several years now we have worked with public school teachers who are pursuing their graduate degrees and with graduate teaching assistants who teach multiple sections of a basic course. Consistently we hear anecdotal evidence that indicates that instructors who teach the same course year after year, or who teach multiple sections of the same course, walk away from their classes having had entirely different classroom experiences. Many of these instructors have a difficult and frustrating time articulating why their classroom experiences remain so divergent. They question themselves and their self-efficacy as they attempt to find plausible explanations for such inconsistencies. Since many of these instructors teach the *same* course content in the *same* classroom during the *same* school term, the only variable that appears to change is the student.

Although we would like to think that we're immune from our students' behavior, we're not (Brophy & Good, 1974). Students react to our teaching in a variety of ways. Some remain active and interactive. They laugh at our jokes and even seem to enjoy them. Some remain passive and apathetic. They remain "too cool to care" and laugh at us rather than our jokes. Still others remain entirely lost. They would laugh at our jokes if they understood them.

The focus of this chapter is on students and how they have been shown to influence teachers and their teaching. Specifically, this chapter will examine student nonverbal behaviors and how these behaviors influence how we perceive and ultimately teach students. This chapter is divided into five sections. The first section explains why we consider this chapter to be important, especially for new teachers and their professional development. The second section explains our focus, which is student nonverbal communication. The third and fourth sections examine the research literature from the education and communication disciplines. The fifth and final section examines implications for the classroom and provides teachers with suggestions for how they might use this information.

Students Influence Teachers?

Yes! Many teachers leave their education programs or their in-service teacher training workshops getting only half of the story. We learn how our behavior influences students and their learning. Much of the education and communication research examines teaching and learning as a linear, one-directional relationship. Research studies often ignore the transactional and relational aspects of how students and their behaviors influence teachers and their teaching. In fact, Brophy and Good (1974) suggest that teachers' actions toward students are actually reactions to students' behavior.

Another reason for focusing on students results from what we know about teacher expectations and how these expectations influence our teaching. Since the publication of *Pygmalion in the Classroom* (Rosenthal & Jacobson, 1968), there has been much interest and attention paid to the effects of teachers' expectations of students on the achievement of those students. Rosenthal and Jacobson reported on a study in which elementary school teachers' expectations about some of their students were manipulated in a way that was intended to be beneficial to those students. In this study, teachers were led to believe that some of their students were "late bloomers" and that they would achieve at an accelerated pace sometime soon after the beginning of the school term. Actually, the students who had been labeled "late bloomers" were randomly selected from the class and were considered average to below average in terms of their intelligence.

The results from this study revealed the power of teacher expectations on student achievement. The late-blooming students improved their IQ scores dramatically compared to the other students in the class. This study suggests that teachers form expectations for their students and communicate in a manner that remains consistent with those expectations.

But how are expectations formed? What role do students' communication behaviors play in how we perceive and teach them? For years, classic studies in social psychology informed us of the role stereotyping played in how we perceive others and the problems associated with this perception process. A more contemporary study, however, suggests that teachers' perceptions and expectations for students are based not only on group stereotypes, but also on student achievement, performance, and level of motivation (Madon, Jussim, Keiper, Eccles, Smith, & Palumbo, 1998). Another classroom study found that teacher behavior is influenced more by immediate student behavior (including student communication) than by other student characteristics such as sex and age (Natriello &

Dornbusch, 1983). Both of these studies suggest that individual student behavior may play a more influential role in the formation of teacher expectations than group membership or individual characteristics.

Yet another reason for examining the influence of student communication on teachers and teaching is that teachers use student communication as information to monitor and evaluate their own teaching effectiveness. Gage and Berliner (1992) mentioned that teachers, like dancers, actors, and musicians, assess their performance by "reading" their audience. Clark and Peterson (1986) found that during instruction the greatest proportion of a teacher's thoughts deal with how well instruction is being received by students.

Why Only Nonverbal Communication?

Although students communicate using both verbal and nonverbal messages, this chapter focuses only on nonverbal messages. Researchers define nonverbal communication as the process of stimulating meaning in the minds of others through nonverbal messages, or messages that are nonlinguistic or non-language based (Richmond & McCroskey, 2000). Students convey a variety of nonverbal messages in the classroom. Some students sit upright in their chairs leaning slightly forward. They maintain direct eye contact with their instructor while simultaneously nodding their heads and uttering vocal assurances. These nonverbal messages have been shown to stimulate, in our minds, feelings of attentiveness and responsiveness. These students are a pleasure to teach. Some students, however, sit in a slouching position with their heads bobbing back and forth, eyes closed, and snoring. These students are less than a pleasure to teach. Their nonverbal messages scream boredom, lack of interest, and apathy to name just a few.

One of the reasons why we have focused this chapter on student nonverbal messages is because they remain, for the most part, unintentional and uncontrollable. Much of our nonverbal expression remains outside of our conscious awareness. Because of this, people have a tendency to trust the nonverbal message as the "real" message, especially when verbal and nonverbal messages remain incongruent. Many times we ask students if they understand a particular concept. In order not to appear ignorant in front of their peers and/or the teacher, they respond with a "yes." However, because their response (nonverbal) was delayed and because their "yes" (verbal) was conveyed in a tentative manner, an observant teacher usually interprets this discrepant message accurately using the nonverbal dimension rather than the verbal dimension of the message. In short, nonverbal messages are considered more trustworthy and authentic than verbal messages.

Another reason why nonverbal messages remain important to our communication is because they convey emotions. Some research suggests that up to 90 percent of the emotional meaning in our messages is conveyed through nonverbal behaviors (Mehrabian & Ferris, 1967). Facial and vocal cues such as eyebrows, wrinkles, and vocal inflections have been shown to stimulate the bulk of these emotional meanings in others.

To summarize, students' classroom behaviors influence the expectations we have for them and nonverbal messages have a tendency to remain more trustworthy and stimulate more of the emotional meaning in messages than verbal messages. Now, we will shift our focus to the research literature in the education and communication disciplines that examines more closely student nonverbal behavior and its influence on teachers and teaching.

Review of the Education Literature

The education research literature examines how we use specific student nonverbal behaviors to form impressions of students. The literature also suggests that we use student nonverbal messages to evaluate our teaching effectiveness and satisfaction. According to Brophy and Good (1974), student behavior ultimately conditions teacher behavior.

Teacher Impressions of Students

Brooks and Woolfolk (1987) reviewed three nonverbal cues that have been shown to influence teachers, including *proxemics* or students' use of space, student attentiveness behaviors, and *chronemics*, or students' use of time.

Proxemics.   Research indicates that proximity, or where a student sits on the first day of class (assuming student choice) affects teacher perceptions of students. Students who decide to sit closer to their teacher are perceived to be more attentive, likable, initiating, and responsive than students who decide to sit farther away. Teachers perceive students who sit closer to them as being willing to participate and those who sit farther away as avoiding classroom participation. According to Brooks and Woolfolk (1987),

> If one of the first impressions is that the student is reluctant to participate, then the teacher's reaction could be either inviting or defensive. In either case, the impression affects the teacher's response, and this response in turn affects the student's impression of the teacher. (p. 55)

Attentiveness.   Teachers perceive a student's upright posture, leaning forward position, eye contact, head nodding, and smiling as attentiveness behaviors. These behaviors are positively related to teachers' evaluations of students' competence, learning, teachability, and attitude. As student nonverbal attentiveness behaviors increase, so do teachers' perceptions of their students' competence and teachability. The reverse relationship also occurs. As students' nonverbal attentiveness decreases, so do teachers' perceptions of their students' competence, teachability, and attitudes.

Brophy and Evertson (1981) reported that teachers do not favor students who avoid eye contact. These students are perceived as being unhappy, inattentive, and/or uncooperative. In a similar attentiveness study examining children and adult behavior, Cantor and Gelfand (1974) found that adults attended more to responsive children (students who looked, smiled, and reacted enthusiastically to the adult) and gave them more help than unresponsive children. The adults also rated the children as more attractive, likable, and competent when they behaved responsively than when they were unresponsive. Cantor and Gelfand concluded that influence is bidirectional in adult-child interactions and suggests that awkward children can be trained to elicit positive reactions from adults.

Chronemics. In terms of students' use of time, research indicates that the timing of a student's interruption and the rate at which a student responds to a teacher's request impacts teacher impressions. Students who make requests at inappropriate or difficult times for the teacher are perceived negatively. Merritt and Humphrey (1979) suggest that some students are able to break classroom norms and successfully interrupt their teachers. These students get their teacher's attention by nonverbally approaching him or her and standing quietly. This allows the teacher to break away from engagement with other students when the time is appropriate. Students who were successful interrupters also avoided interrupting a teacher when the classroom was noisy or when the teacher was already overextended in terms of student engagement. Similarly, teachers appear to perceive students who respond quickly to their requests more positively than students who require more time.

These nonverbal cues and the meanings they stimulate in our minds ultimately influence reciprocal behavior that is directed back to the student.

> If a student is seen as uncooperative (as a result of his/her nonverbal behavior), teachers may interpret common behaviors such as asking for a second explanation, forgetting homework, or losing materials as hostile acts intended to cause disruption. Teachers making such interpretations may respond with criticism and punishment. (Brooks & Woolfolk, 1987, p. 56)

When this happens students react to teacher frustration and respond with their own, causing a downward spiral of mutual frustration. It is also important to remember that the opposite type of spiraling can occur with students who remain nonverbally attentive in the classroom. For example, students who remain nonverbally attentive are perceived by their teachers as competent and as possessing positive attitudes. Students react to these teacher perceptions in a positive manner causing an upward spiral of mutual satisfaction.

Teaching Effectiveness and Satisfaction

The education research suggests that student nonverbal behaviors influence how we assess our teaching effectiveness and satisfaction. Overall, teachers who remain interactive and student-centered have been shown to invest the greatest portion of their thought, while teaching, into evaluating how well their instruction is received by students. While conveying their content and interacting with students, they simultaneously assess their teaching effectiveness.

Jecker, Maccoby, Breitrose, and Rose (1964) examined how well teachers assess students' understanding of their content based on students' visual feedback cues, such as head nods and facial expressions. This research team predicted that when teacher judgments of student comprehension were based on visual nonverbal cues, misperceptions of students' comprehension would be more likely to occur than judgments based on verbal cues.

Their findings supported their prediction, and audio seemed to be the important variable. When audio was absent, teachers were significantly less able to accurately assess cognitive understanding. When audio was present, regardless of video, teachers were significantly more able to accurately assess student comprehension. Important to this study was the fact that the experience level of the teacher did not increase accuracy in perceiving student visual feedback from students.

This research suggests that since increased *verbal* feedback remains less likely to occur as classroom size continues to increase, teachers would benefit from learning more about students' *nonverbal* behaviors and how to accurately interpret such behaviors. Understanding how we decode nonverbal messages and ways to enhance the decoding process will be discussed in the final section of this chapter.

Another study by Jenkins and Deno (1969) examined whether or not students' nonverbal feedback behavior had any influence on teachers' evaluations of their performance in terms of effectiveness and satisfaction. They predicted that teachers may rely heavily on student behavior such as smiling, hand-raising, sitting straight, and behaving excitedly as ways to judge their own effectiveness. Their prediction was supported. Teachers who received positive nonverbal feedback from their students considered teaching to be more enjoyable, predicted that they would be more effective teachers, and thought that their students learned more than teachers receiving negative nonverbal feedback from students.

Review of Communication Literature

Instructional communication researchers have recently started examining student nonverbal communication and its influence on teachers and teaching. Like the education literature, communication research focuses on the role of nonverbal behavior in the perception process. The communication literature also examines nonverbal communication as a transactional process by which students and teachers mutually and simultaneously influence each other's reciprocal behaviors.

Teacher Perceptions

Over the past two decades, much has been written on teacher nonverbal immediacy and its effects on students' perceptions of teachers and learning outcomes. This research will be reviewed extensively in Chapter 6. Immediacy, for those who are unfamiliar with the concept, is defined as physical or psychological closeness (Mehrabian, 1971) and is created primarily through expressive nonverbal behaviors such as forward body leaning, purposeful gestures, and direct eye contact. In the classroom, students perceive immediate teachers as approachable and likable. Conversely, students avoid nonimmediate teachers and find them less likable.

But does student nonverbal immediacy influence teachers and their perceptions of students in similar ways? Baringer and McCroskey (2000) examined this question. They predicted that student nonverbal immediacy would be positively correlated with how teachers perceive student credibility and interpersonal attraction. In other words as teachers perceive more student nonverbal immediacy, they will also perceive their students as being more credible and more interpersonally attractive. Credibility is a perception of believability and is based on how competent and trustworthy we perceive others to be. In the classroom context, there are two forms of interpersonal attraction including task and social. We perceive others to be task attractive if they can help us meet our work objectives. When we perceive others to be outgoing, personable, and warm, we consider them to be socially attractive. Both credibility and interpersonal attraction have been shown to be important perception variables that influence teacher and student relationships.

Baringer and McCroskey (2000) also predicted that student immediacy would increase teachers' liking for students, teachers' motivation to teach, and teachers' projections of how well students will do in their courses. Their predictions were supported. Students who were immediate (compared to those who were less immediate) were perceived more positively by their teachers. They were considered more believable, task and socially attractive, and likable. Teachers were more motivated to teach the immediate students and teachers projected that immediate students would do better in the course than less immediate students.

In a study examining student nonverbal responsiveness, which is similar to immediacy, the first author of this chapter found that instructors who perceived fewer student nonverbal responsiveness cues, especially audible nonverbal cues such as vocal assurances and interrupters, evaluated more negatively both their students and the quality of the teacher–student relationship. He also found that instructors considered themselves to be less effective in the classroom and were less satisfied teaching as perceptions of student nonverbal responsiveness decreased (Mottet, 2000).

These two studies confirm for students that which previous research has learned about teachers. Not only does a teacher's nonverbal expressiveness influence positive outcomes in students, but students' nonverbal immediacy and responsiveness yield positive outcomes in teachers. The rule of reciprocity may account for much of the immediacy and responsiveness that occurs in the classroom. When teachers exhibit nonverbal immediacy, students may also become more nonverbally responsive, reinforcing teacher immediacy. Similarly, when students remain nonverbally immediate with teachers, teachers may become more responsive reinforcing students' immediacy. The reciprocity effect will be discussed in the next section.

Teachers' Reciprocal Behavior

Comstock (1999) explored the reciprocal nature of human communication in the classroom context. She tested the theory of interaction adaptation (Burgoon, Stern, & Dillman, 1995). This theory suggests that communication between people remains transactional. Unlike linear conceptualizations of communication in which teacher messages affect student messages, communication as transaction is one in which both teacher and students' communicative behavior simultaneously affects the other's. The theory of interaction adaptation suggests that both parties adapt to the other's behavior and both are responsible for relational outcomes.

Specifically, interaction adaptation theory stipulates that when people enter communication transactions with others, they have certain *requirements*, *expectations*, and *desires*. In the classroom, many teachers have *required* safety and comfort needs that influence their communication with students. Some teachers remain more structured than others and have a difficult time deviating from a lesson plan, even when a teachable moment occurs. Structure provides them with the security they require in front of their students. Experimenting with a new idea or teaching technique, in an extemporaneous manner, remains uncomfortable for them. Other teachers do not have these same security needs.

Teachers *expect* students to remain responsive to their instruction. They expect to see students paying attention and responding accordingly. They expect their students to remain on task. They expect their students to ask questions when confused. Finally, when teachers interact with students in the classroom, they hope to achieve a *desired* level of behavior. Teachers have instructional goals. They have a desire to remain on schedule and to accomplish their lesson plans. They have a desire to remain effective.

The theory suggests that future communicative behavior is determined by what is needed (required), anticipated (expected), and preferred (desired) in any given interaction. If teacher–student classroom interactions provide each other with what is needed, anticipated, and preferred, then interaction patterns are reciprocated back and forth from teacher to students to teacher. However, if the behaviors that teachers require, expect, and desire from students do not match actual student behaviors, then teachers adapt their communication to bring about their communication goals.

To illustrate this theory, we would like to walk you through three different classroom scenarios. For each of the scenarios, assume you have a *required* need for control, an *expectation* that your students will remain on task and complete their lesson, and a *desire* to establish a cooperative and democratic classroom environment. Pay attention to how you automatically adapt your communication behavior by *reciprocating*, *diverging*, or *converging* to bring about your interaction needs.

In the first classroom, students interact in such a way that allows you to maintain control. They remain on task and finish the lesson. You are able to establish and maintain a democratic classroom environment. Their behavior meets your required, expected, and desired needs. In this classroom, you adapt your behavior by *reciprocating* their on-task and cooperative communication behaviors. This is good!

In the second classroom, students interact such that you sense a lack of control. They're not on task and will not complete the lesson. Their behavior does not meet your interaction needs. Rather than reciprocating their behavior, you adapt your behavior in a *divergent* manner. You become authoritative. You become directive. You make the decisions and call the shots. In short, you interact with them in a firm manner to bring them in line with your interaction needs. This is not good!

In the third and final classroom, students remain on task, cooperative, and ahead of schedule. Their behavior not only meets your interaction needs, but exceeds them. In this classroom, you adapt your communication behavior by *converging*. In short, you increase your level of interaction with your students. You increase your level of encouragement. You reinforce their democratic decision making. You provide them with maximum freedom. This is very good!

Comstock (1999) tested interaction adaptation theory in the classroom. Based on teachers' preferences for nonverbally responsive students, she predicted that when students increase their level of nonverbal involvement in the classroom, teachers would reciprocate by increasing their own involvement. Conversely, she predicted that when students decrease and maintain a lower level of nonverbal involvement in the classroom, teachers would adapt their communication accordingly to bring about their expectations for student nonverbal responsiveness.

She found that even during a single, ten-minute class presentation to a group of students, teachers' role performances were, in part, directed by their students. "Taken together with previous research on the effects of teacher involvement behaviors on student motivation and learning, results suggest that teacher–student interaction is transactional and that teacher–student relationships involve mutual influence, with each partner partially responsible for the other's role performance and important relational outcomes" (Comstock, 1999, p. 22).

Conclusions from the Research Literature

Before discussing classroom implications and providing teachers with a few suggestions that may assist them in the classroom, let us summarize briefly some of the conclusions yielded from the research literature. These conclusions will be stated as knowledge claims or as statements reminding us of what we have learned from the education and communication research literature.

1. Teachers' pre-existing expectations for students influence how they teach students.
2. Teachers' attitudes and expectations for students are based partially on how students behave in the classroom, in addition to student attributes such as sex, race, or socioeconomic status.
3. Teachers perceive student nonverbal behaviors, and these perceptions influence their attitudes and expectations for students.
4. Students who sit closer to their teachers and engage in attentiveness behaviors are perceived more positively than students who sit farther away and students who fail to make eye contact, nod their heads, and sit upright leaning forward.
5. Students who interrupt teachers and respond to their questions in an appropriate and timely manner are perceived more positively than students who fail to notice appropriate times for interruptions and who require additional time to respond to questions.
6. Students who remain nonverbally immediate/responsive in the classroom are liked more, considered more teachable, competent, and trustworthy, and considered more interpersonally attractive by their teachers.
7. Teachers' initial attitudes and expectations for students influence how they perceive students' nonverbal behaviors. Two students may convey the same nonverbal message, but because of the teacher's existing attitude or expectation, he or she perceives one student's nonverbal message in a positive manner and the other's in a negative manner.
8. Teachers and students mutually influence each other's classroom interaction behaviors. Teachers who perceive students negatively, treat them less positively. Students react to these less-than-positive communication behaviors by reciprocating similar behaviors, which in turn reinforce the teacher's original attitudes and expectations for students.
9. Teachers remain more motivated to work with nonverbally immediate/responsive students, consider their teacher–student relationships to be of higher quality, and project that these students will do better not only in their courses but in life in general.
10. Teachers who perceive more of their students' nonverbal responsive and attentive behaviors consider themselves to be more effective as teachers and more satisfied in their teaching profession.

Now, What Are We to Do with This Information?

As a way to conclude this chapter on student nonverbal communication and its influence on teachers and teaching, we would like to discuss some classroom implications and offer a few suggestions that may help new teachers use the information presented in the chapter. Most of the suggestions that follow focus on teacher awareness. Becoming aware of how we form expectations, reciprocate nonverbal behavior, and interpret nonverbal behavior can improve our teaching (Brophy & Good, 1974).

Forming Expectations Based on Nonverbal Behavior. Teachers must guard against the natural tendency to form an expectation for a student using limited amounts of information. It is easy to take shortcuts and to prematurely form expectations, especially as classes continue to increase in size and classroom responsibilities continue to expand. We must also guard against our natural tendency to rely too heavily on nonverbal messages. What happens when students cannot regulate or control their nonverbal behavior? In some classes, students are required to sit in assigned seats. Other times, students arrive late to class for reasons beyond their control and cannot obtain a front and center seat to present a positive impression.

Some students may not be as attentive as they would like to be because of distractions caused by less concerned students whose misbehaviors go undetected by the teacher. And what happens when teachers cannot easily detect student nonverbal responsive behaviors such as in the large lecture hall or when they teach in distance education programs where their instruction is delivered via interactive television or computer? Teachers cannot assume in these nontraditional classrooms that students are less competent or teachable. (These issues will be discussed more thoroughly in Chapter 13.)

In these situations, we have a couple of suggestions for teachers. First, we encourage teachers to check their perceptions with students. Second, we encourage teachers to gather information from multiple sources and channels before solidifying expectations. To check perceptions, we suggest that teachers describe (rather than evaluate) to students what they see them doing. Then teachers need to ask for clarification to ensure that the perception is accurate. Assume you have students who appear uninterested in your class. Rather than assuming disinterest in your class, we encourage you to describe what it is you see the students doing. Then ask for clarification and be prepared for their reactions. They may not be interested in your content. Or they may be interested, but distracted. If students lack interest, then adapt your content accordingly by making it relevant to their lives. If students are interested, but distracted, then the perception-checking process may allow you to eliminate the distractions for the students.

The second suggestion is for teachers to increase the number of communication channels they use before solidifying perceptions of students. Give students additional options for communicating with you and their classmates. Many quiet students, as discussed in Chapter 3, are also nonverbally unexpressive and don't feel comfortable talking in class. Electronic mail and bulletin boards (or list serves) complement classroom interaction nicely. These instructional media give teachers additional channels from which to receive and evaluate student communication.

Reciprocating Nonverbal Behavior.   We must also guard against the natural tendency to reciprocate nonverbal behavior. This may partially explain why some teachers have been known to walk into a classroom energized and optimistic about the day's lesson but, once confronted with lethargic and apathetic students leave the classroom feeling drained and defeated. Other teachers approach the same classroom, but leave feeling more energized and successful as a teacher. In the first situation, it appears that the teacher may have been more susceptible to student nonverbal behavior and ultimately adapted to or reciprocated similar lethargic and apathetic communicative behavior. In the second situation, it appears that the teacher was not only aware of the undesirable student behavior, but adapted his or her behavior accordingly in order to stimulate appropriate student communicative behavior that was conducive to learning.

New teachers may be more susceptible to reciprocating students' nonverbal communication than more experienced teachers. We believe that novice teachers focus more on student nonverbal behavior as a way to confirm themselves rather than to determine student comprehension of course content. As a result of their need for self-validation as a new teacher, they remain susceptible to their students' nonverbal behavior. We suspect that experienced and effective teachers focus on student nonverbal behavior not for reasons of self-validation, but as a way to adapt their instructional communication to insure that they are meeting students' learning needs, expectations, and desires. These professionals may be more aware of how student behavior affects teaching behavior and have in some ways inoculated themselves against student behavior.

Suspecting that new teachers may be more vulnerable to their students' nonverbal behavior because of their need for immediate feedback, we encourage new teachers to periodically assess their teaching effectiveness by asking students for formative feedback. Unlike summative feedback assessments, where student feedback data are collected at the end of the term when it is too late for teachers to adapt their teaching to accommodate students, formative feedback assessments are collected periodically throughout the semester. This way new teachers can assess immediately how they are doing and make necessary adjustments to their teaching if necessary. Collecting student feedback data periodically throughout the semester in written form may enable new teachers the opportunity to focus less on student nonverbal behavior for self-validation and more on how well their students comprehend course content. Angelo and Cross (1993) provide some simple tips on classroom assessments and suggest ways teachers can easily assess their teaching effectiveness.

Interpreting Nonverbal Behavior.   Teachers must become more discerning in *how* they read students' nonverbal behavior. It is our belief that as teachers mature in their profession, they also become more discerning in how they interpret student messages. With experience, teachers learn which student behaviors are a reaction or a response to them or their teaching and which behaviors are a reaction or response to some other stimuli, such as a student's physiological needs.

For example, is a student's lack of responsiveness in the classroom a response to the teacher's instructional communication, or is it a response to their not getting enough sleep the night before? This type of discernment enhances how teachers respond to such student behavior.

Three ways that new teachers can improve how they interpret student nonverbal behavior is to place the nonverbal behavior in its context, interpret multiple nonverbal behaviors rather than a single behavior, and notice whether or not the verbal and nonverbal dimensions of the message remain congruent. The first author recently encountered Allison, a student in a large lecture class of 400 students, who came to lecture "under the influence." He asked a question and unfortunately Allison answered it. The context was sorority rush. The multiple cues included Allison responding to his question in an incredibly loud and slurred manner while wearing minimal clothing. Although her verbal message was partially accurate, her nonverbal message suggested that Allison was less than lucid. Her complete message remained incongruent. In fact, her sorority sisters had given her the answer and encouraged her to respond to the question. Although this example remains extreme and hopefully rare, it illustrates three ways that teachers can enhance the decoding of student nonverbal behavior.

Another way that may enhance how we interpret students' nonverbal communication is by understanding the role that our own expectations for appropriate student nonverbal behavior plays in the classroom. As long as a student does not violate our expectations, his or her behavior will not likely get our attention. However, behavior that violates our expectations will get noticed. Consider Gary for example. Gary fails to detect and follow the teacher's turn-taking hand gestures and interrupts the teacher as well as other students. As long as Gary follows appropriate turn-taking cues, no one seems to notice his behavior, but once he violates turn-taking cues, his nonverbal behavior is considered rude and disrespectful.

This interpretation process becomes a bit more complicated and confusing because we do not treat all nonverbal violators equally. When a nonverbal expectation is violated, we notice the violation and assign a positive or negative valence to the individual violating the expectation. We have a tendency to assign positive valences to individuals we like, find interpersonally attractive, and credible. Conversely, we assign negative valences to individuals we do not like, find interpersonally unattractive, and noncredible. Unlike those individuals who are negatively valenced, positively valenced individuals are granted special permission to violate nonverbal expectations.

For example, consider again the likable and intelligent Gary who failed to detect and follow his teacher's turn-taking hand gestures. Because Gary is likable and intelligent, his teacher assigns him a positive valence, which grants him special permission to interrupt the teacher. In short, the teacher does not consider his interruption rude. For a student who is less likable and perceived to be less intelligent, this type of nonverbal violation would receive a negative valence and the teacher would call the violator on his or her disrespectful and rude behavior. Same nonverbal violation, different interpretation.

It is also important for teachers to understand how their own preconceived expectations for a student or a group of students can frame how they interpret students' nonverbal messages. Research consistently reports that teachers interpret nonverbal cues in ways that are consistent with their initial expectations (Good, 1983). For example, if a student from the football team is in our class and we have a less than favorable preconceived expectation for this particular group, we may have a tendency to evaluate his nonverbal behavior in a way that fits this particular expectation. Another student may exhibit the same nonverbal behavior, but because of her or his group affiliation and our preconceived expectation for this particular group, the behavior stimulates different meanings and reciprocal behaviors.

Informing Students of Their Nonverbal Behavior.   Finally, students need to be aware of how their nonverbal behavior affects their teachers and the quality of instruction they receive in the classroom. Why should we keep this a secret? The majority of students have no idea how their own behavior influences the type and quality of instruction they receive from teachers. Many teachers mention on the first day of class that teaching and learning is a partnership and that the success of the class depends on students' classroom involvement and contributions. In many cases, these messages are ignored or not taken seriously.

Over the past several years, there has been a cultural shift to view higher education from a customer service perspective. This cultural emphasis will eventually reach the primary and secondary public school systems as taxpaying citizens demand more accountability from their alleged "substandard" educational institutions. For better or worse, viewing educational institutions from a customer service perspective is becoming a reality. Many customer service organizations spend considerable time educating their customers on how to get the most from their products and services. It's time educators do the same. Teachers need to find ways of getting students to understand or to take seriously their role in the instructional communication process. It's time for students to become partially responsible for their own learning and the quality of their educational experiences. Students can ultimately get more from the classroom experience if they engage in good student behaviors in the classroom. They must understand how their behaviors, good, bad, or indifferent, influence teacher perceptions and teaching. Students can ultimately bring out the best in most of their teachers.

R E F E R E N C E S   A N D   S U G G E S T E D   R E A D I N G S

Angelo, T. A., & Cross, K. P. (1993). *Classroom assessment techniques: A handbook for college teachers* (2nd ed.). San Francisco: Jossey-Bass.

Baringer, D., & McCroskey, J. C. (2000). Immediacy in the classroom: Student immediacy. *Communication Education, 49,* 178–186.

Brooks, D. M., & Woolfolk, A. E. (1987). The effects of students' nonverbal behavior on teachers. *The Elementary School Journal, 88,* 51–63.

Brophy, J., & Evertson, C. (1981). *Student characteristics and teaching.* New York: Longman.

Brophy, J. & Good, T. (1974). *Teacher-student relation-*

ships: Causes and consequences. New York: Holt, Rinehart, & Winston.

Burgoon, J. K., Stern, L. A., & Dillman, L. (1995). *Interpersonal adaptation: Dyadic interaction patterns.* New York: Cambridge University Press.

Cantor, N. L., & Gelfand, D. M. (1974). Effects of responsiveness and sex of children on adult's behavior. *Child Development, 48,* 232–238.

Clark, C., & Peterson, P. (1986) Teachers' thought processes. In M. Wittrock (Ed.), *Handbook of research on teaching* (3rd ed.). New York: Macmillan.

Comstock, J. (1999, November). Mutual influence in teacher-student relationships: Applying IAT to access teacher adaptation to student classroom involvement. Paper presented at the annual conference of the National Communication Association, Chicago, Illinois.

Gage, N. L., & Berliner, D. C. (1992). *Educational Psychology.* Boston: Houghton Mifflin Company.

Good, T. (1983). Research on classroom teaching. In L. Shulman & G. Sykes (Eds.), *Handbook of teaching and policy* (pp. 42–80). New York: Longman.

Jecker, J., Maccoby, N., Breitrose, H. S., & Rose, E. D. (1964). Teacher accuracy in assessing cognitive visual feedback from students. *Journal of Applied Psychology, 48,* 393–397.

Jenkins, J. R., & Deno, S. L. (1969). Influence of student behavior on teachers' self-evaluation. *Journal of Educational Psychology, 60,* 439–442.

Madon, S., Jussim, L., Keiper, S., Eccles, J., Smith,

A., & Palumbo, P. (1998). The accuracy and power of sex, social class, and ethnic stereotypes: A naturalistic study in person perception. *Personality and Social Psychology Bulletin, 24,* 1304–1318.

Mehrabian, A. (1971). *Silent messages.* Belmont, CA: Wadsworth Publishing Company, Inc.

Mehrabian, A., & Ferris, S. R. (1967). Inference of attitudes from nonverbal communication in two channels. *Journal of Consulting Psychology, 31,* 248–252.

Merritt, M., & Humphrey, F. (1979). Teacher, talk and task: Communicating demands during individualized instruction. *Theory into Practice, 18,* 298–303.

Mottet, T. P. (2000). Interactive television instructors' perceptions of students' nonverbal responsiveness and their influence on distance teaching. *Communication Education, 49,* 146–164.

Natriello, G., & Dornbusch, S. M. (1983). Bringing behavior back in: The effects of student characteristics and behavior on the classroom behavior of teachers. *American Educational Research Journal, 20,* 29–43.

Richmond, V. P., & McCroskey, J. C. (1992). *Power in the classroom.* Hillsdale, NJ: Lawrence Erlbaum Associates.

Richmond, V. P., & McCroskey, J. C. (2000). *Nonverbal behavior in interpersonal relations.* Needham Heights, MA: Allyn & Bacon.

Rosenthal, R., & Jacobson, L. (1968). *Pygmalion in the classroom.* New York: Holt.

SECTION TWO

Our Teaching Behavior

Firmly grounded in what we have learned in Section One, this section examines a number of teacher characteristics and behaviors which play an important role in students' learning and educational experience.

6 Teacher Nonverbal Immediacy

Use and Outcomes

VIRGINIA P. RICHMOND
West Virginia University

The central objective of educational systems in U.S. culture is student recognition, recall, and short- and long-term learning. The role of the teacher in educational systems is to create learning environments in which the probability of the desired achievements is enhanced. The definition of student learning varies, however. Many of the aspects that are common include mastery of certain psychomotor behaviors, acquisition of many levels of cognitive understanding, synthesis, and integration, and the development of various feelings and attitudes. Being an immediate teacher can help us meet these goals with our students.

Immediacy is a perception of physical or psychological closeness. If we use effective nonverbal and verbal behaviors with our students to increase perceptions of immediacy, our students feel closer to us. This is an important benefit of immediacy, because our job as teachers will be much easier if our students feel appropriately close to us. Over the past 20 years, research on immediacy has revealed it's connection to a variety of important learning outcomes. This chapter discusses verbal and nonverbal behaviors teachers can use to increase their students' perceptions of immediacy as well as the advantages that immediate teachers have in their classrooms. A number of important generalizations can be drawn from the large body of research on teacher immediacy:

1. Teacher immediacy behaviors can be used effectively to get students to do what we want them to do, so long as we are truly engaging immediacy behaviors and we continue to use nonverbal and verbal immediacy behaviors throughout the course.
2. Students are drawn to teachers they trust and perceive as competent and caring. Students avoid teachers that they do not trust or perceive as competent, caring, and responsive.
3. Teacher immediacy behavior gives the teacher positive forms of behavioral control, rather than using coercive or antisocial teacher strategies.

4. Immediacy in large part determines the amount power and affect (liking) that a teacher has with students.
5. Students usually will comply with, rather than resist, reasonable teacher requests, if the teacher is liked, respected, and admired by her or his students.

Mehrabian (1971) was first to advance the concept of immediacy. His immediacy concept was stated as: "People are drawn toward persons and things they like, evaluate highly, and prefer; they avoid or move away from things they dislike, evaluate negatively, or do not prefer"(p. 1). Mehrabian (1969, 1971) indicated immediacy has verbal as well as nonverbal components, and both can have an impact on learning in the classroom. Richmond, McCroskey, and their colleagues went far beyond the initial attempt of major communication scholars by viewing immediacy as a means of classroom control, as a means of building affect in the classroom, and as a means of increasing student learning that is available to educators. Richmond and McCroskey (2000a) identify ways in which people might use immediacy to increase perceptions of physical and psychological closeness, thereby developing affinity, liking, and control with others.

Within the past twenty years, researchers, scholars, and practitioners have come to realize the relevance of nonverbal communication in the classroom environment. The nonverbal component of the communication process is as important to the positive teacher–student relationship as the verbal component, and often much more important. Earlier research on communication in the classroom primarily was on the verbal interaction between student and teacher.

The author of this chapter has spent twenty years working with and training teaching assistants and teachers on how to be more effective and affective communicators in the classroom environment. The training has stressed the importance of both verbal and nonverbal communication. The author has communicated with more than 50,000 teachers, business persons, and government personnel about what usually works and does not work in the learning situation. This chapter is devoted to discussing conclusions about nonverbal immediacy communication and its impact on the teacher–student relationship.

Nonverbal Communicative Behaviors in the Classroom

We cannot always physically approach people or things we like or move away from things or people we don't like. However, we do communicate our feelings through our nonverbal behaviors. For example, if someone is saying something nice about us, we are likely to stand closer, listen more attentively, have more eye contact, perhaps even touch. On the other hand, if someone is saying something unpleasant about us, we are likely to lean away from that person, have little eye contact, remain silent, and not touch (unless it is to punch them!). Therefore, we use abbreviated forms of approach or avoidance behavior. These abbreviated forms of nonverbal behavior imply the degree of psychological closeness between

FIGURE 6.1 Avoidance–Approach Continuum

Physical Hostility → Verbal → Aggression → Neutrality → Immediacy → Intimacy
   or Violence   Hostility

people. The more forms of approach like nonverbal behavior we use, the more we are perceived as nonverbally immediate. The more we use avoidancelike behavior, the more we are perceived as nonverbally nonimmediate or unapproachable.

Behavior can be placed on a continuum from avoidance-oriented to approach-oriented (See Figure 6.1). Clearly we would like to avoid the person who wants to use physical violence or be verbally hostile or aggressive (also defined as verbal nonimmediacy) with us. We might approach or let someone approach us who display neutral behaviors, and we are very likely to approach or allow someone to approach us who uses immediacy behavior.

Thus, on the avoidance–approach continuum, most of us feel comfortable with most other people in interpersonal encounters at only one point: the immediacy point. At the avoidance end, we do not feel comfortable or want to communicate with someone who is abusive either physically or verbally. At the extreme approach end, most of us do not feel comfortable communicating on an intimate basis with more than a few people. The neutrality point also makes us uncomfortable after a while because there is very little responsiveness by the neutral person. Nonresponsiveness usually is interpreted as a negative response, so we end the conversation.

In conclusion, nonverbal behaviors that denote immediacy are those that improve and encourage interpersonal encounters and communication. Scholars suggest that some common immediacy behaviors include smiling, touching on the hand, arm, or shoulder, moving close to another, making eye contact, facing another, using warm vocals, and leaning toward someone. The remainder of this chapter reviews these and other nonverbal behaviors and how each behavior can be used to increase immediacy and improve interpersonal relations. To understand immediacy and its relationship to interpersonal communication, it is important to look at specific behaviors that express varying degrees of immediacy.

Verbal Immediacy

What people say can cause us to feel either closer or more distant from them. Increased immediacy is produced by verbally immediate or verbally effective messages that show openness to the other, friendship for the other, or empathy with the other. Such simple things as the use of the pronouns "we or us" rather than "you or you and I" can increase the feeling of immediacy. For example, when trying to denote verbal immediacy to a peer, say "we can do this together" rather than "you should try this."

Clearly, one way to communicate feelings of immediacy is through verbal messages. However, there are many nonverbal behaviors that can accomplish the same outcome. Although immediacy is communicating both verbally and nonverbally, the nonverbal component is far more important in most cases. This is because the nonverbal may exist independent of any verbal message, but verbal messages are usually accompanied by a variety of nonverbal messages. Furthermore, if a verbal message suggests immediacy while nonverbal messages are contradictory, receivers tend to disregard the verbal and respond to the nonverbal.

One of the most important ways of increasing immediacy in a relationship is sending verbal messages that encourage the other person to communicate. Such comments as "I see what you mean, Tell me more, Please continue, That is a good idea, This is a team effort, and Let's talk more about this" create increased immediacy. Contrast these statements with the following comments: "Oh, shut up, You've got to be kidding, No way, I thought of that, and that is just dumb." If you were to hear any of the latter comments, would you want to communicate more? Probably not. You would not feel very close to the person who made such comments, unless it was clear they were joking. Of course, addressing an individual by the name they prefer is more likely to denote immediacy than addressing them by another name such as "Hey You!" Mottet and Richmond (1998) have shown that in relationship development, working with verbally immediate or approach oriented communication strategies are a much more powerful communication tool in relationship formation than avoidance or verbally nonimmediate communication strategies.

In conclusion, as verbal immediacy increases so does the likelihood of a positive relationship. On the other hand, as verbal immediacy decreases the likelihood of a positive relationship decreases. Therefore, if you have not built any affinity or liking and you use verbal avoidance statements, then you have distanced yourself from the other person and virtually guaranteed that there will be no significant relationship or the relationship that exists may be a negative one.

Nonverbal Immediacy

Immediacy is the degree of perceived physical or psychological closeness between people. Several studies have been conducted looking at immediacy behaviors of teachers during instructional communication with their students. These studies have found immediacy behaviors to be associated with more positive affect as well as increased cognitive learning and more positive student evaluations of teachers (Richmond & McCroskey, 2000a). This research has suggested the appropriateness of the following communication principle:

The more communicators employ immediate behaviors, the more others will like, evaluate highly, and prefer such communicators; and the less communicators employ immediate behaviors the more others will dislike, evaluate negatively, and reject such communicators. We prefer to call this idea the "principle of immediate communication." (p. 86)

Ambady and Rosenthal (1993) completed a landmark study titled "Half a Minute: Predicting Teacher Evaluations from Thin Slices of Nonverbal Behavior and Physical Attractiveness." These researchers conducted three studies. In studies one and two, subjects were asked to rate college teachers' and high school teachers' nonverbal behavior and physical attractiveness based on ten-second silent video clips. In study three, they investigated whether strangers' ratings of teachers would predict nonverbal behavior and physical attractiveness from studies one and two if even "more thinned slices of the video" were shown. The clips were reduced from ten seconds to five and two seconds. The results were astonishing. The results revealed the following:

> There were no significant differences in the accuracy of judgments based on video clips 10s, 5s, and 2s in length. In addition, there were no significant differences in the accuracy of judgments for the two samples of teachers. . . . Moreover, judgments based on 30s exposures (three 10s clips of each teacher) were not significantly more accurate than judgments based on 6s exposures (three 2s clips of each teacher). (pp. 437–438)

Ambady and Rosenthal suggest that the human ability to form impressions is strongly supported by their studies. In fact, as has always been suggested in the nonverbal literature, impression formation takes places very early in a relationship. Often, these initial impressions determine the communication that follows. They conclude that based on molar nonverbal behaviors shown in very brief (less than 30 seconds) silent video clips, we evaluate our teachers as accepting, active, attentive, competent, confident, dominant, empathic, enthusiastic, honest, likeable, not anxious, optimistic, professional, supportive, and warm. Subjects observed specific nonverbal behavior such as symmetrical arms, frowning, head nodding, head shaking, pointing, sitting, smiling, standing, strong gestures, head touching, upper torso touching, walking, and weak gestures. They conclude the following:

> Teachers with higher ratings tended to be more nonverbally active and expressive. They were more likely to walk around, touch their upper torsos, and smile. Fewer effective teachers were more likely to sit, touch their heads, and shake rather than nod their heads. These results suggest that teachers with higher ratings showed more nonverbal expressiveness and involvement than fewer effective teachers. (pp. 436–437)

They also suggest that teachers "should be made aware of the possible impact of their nonverbal behavior and perhaps even trained in nonverbal skills" (p. 440). The researchers caution, however, that these judgments are most accurate for the affective side of teaching.

We have stated for years that the primary function of teachers' verbal behavior in the classroom is to give content to improve students' cognitive learning.

The primary function of teachers' nonverbal behavior in the classroom is to improve affect or liking for the subject matter, teacher, and class, and to increase the desire to learn more about the subject matter. One step toward that is the development of a positive affective relationship between the student and teacher. When the teacher improves affect through effective nonverbal behavior, then the student is likely to listen more, learn more, and have a more positive attitude about school. Effective classroom communication between teacher and student is the key to a positive affect toward learning. As communication improves between teacher and student, so does affect. When teachers are trained to use verbal and nonverbal communication in the classroom more effectively, student–teacher relationships improve and so do the students' affective and cognitive learning. When positive affect is present, cognitive learning increases.

The nonverbal behavior of the teacher communicates meanings to students. For example, the teacher who rarely looks at a student when talking is communicating that he or she is not very interested in that student. Students' nonverbal behavior communicates meanings to teachers. The student who is always yawning might be bored, tired, or both. The teacher should review the context and determine whether the student simply is tired or whether the teacher is so boring that he or she is putting the student to sleep.

The remainder of this chapter focuses on discussion of the various types of nonverbal behavior and how each affects the student–instructor relationship. I direct primary attention to the teacher's behavior and how this might influence communication with the student. The reason I take this approach is that it is the student's perceptions of what the teacher does that determines how effective the communication is. If a student perceives that a teacher is using coercive power, then he or she will respond in a negative fashion. If a student perceives that a teacher is using immediacy, then he or she will be more responsive to the teacher. When a student perceives that a teacher does not like her or him, the student most likely will learn to dislike the teacher. The remainder of this chapter centers on how teachers and students can use immediate nonverbal behaviors to express affect and liking. All the examples discussed can be applied to the typical classroom setting.

Instructor Appearance

Appearance sends important messages in the classroom setting. An instructor's attire influences the way students perceive that instructor. Teachers who dress very formally are seen by students as competent, organized, prepared, and knowledgeable. Teachers who dress casually or informally (not sloppy) are seen as friendly, outgoing, receptive, flexible, and fair.

We have found that when teachers dress very formally, it makes students feel as if the teacher is not receptive to their needs and not likely to communicate with them. The teacher is perceived as competent but not as receptive. The teacher who dresses casually is perceived as open, friendly, and more immediate but perhaps not as competent as the teacher who dresses more formally.

Therefore, our advice is to dress formally for a week or two or until credibility is established. Then dress more casually to project the image that one is open to student–teacher interaction. The teacher who always dresses formally may communicate that he or she does not want much student–teacher interaction, even though the dressing behavior may simply reflect the teacher's clothing preferences. Whatever the teacher's motivation, the students' perceptions are what counts in the classroom.

Gesture and Movement

Small children often use gestures and movements to explain what they cannot say verbally. As they mature, they tend to use fewer simple hand gestures and increase their use of complex hand movements. In this culture, we tend to use more gestures when we are excited or giving complex messages. On the other hand, we use fewer gestures when we are bored or transmitting a simple message. Therefore, in the early grades children are likely to use more gestures and movements than verbal messages to communicate. However, about the time children reach twelve, they should be acquiring the adult norms and using more complex gestures and a wider variety of verbal messages.

In the classroom, *adaptors* are probably the most common gesture used by students. The classroom is an anxiety-producing situation for many students. Observe a typical classroom and you will find students chewing pencils, biting their nails, picking at their desks or notebooks, pulling at their hair, smoothing their clothing, and clicking their pens. A classroom that has an inordinate amount of student adaptive behavior is one in which the anxiety level is high or the teacher is boring. Students use more adaptors in classes where they feel anxious or bored. These behaviors are often perceived as a form of misbehavior and are punished. The student who is constantly clicking her or his pen is perceived by the teacher as disruptive. Students may not even realize they are engaging in such behavior until they are reprimanded for it.

Adaptors are more prevalent during the first few days of school, near holidays, and near the end of school. Students unintentionally use more adaptive behavior at these times. Teachers also tend to use more adaptive behavior the first few days of a new school year. It is anxiety-producing for most teachers when they are meeting new classes for the first time. Teachers who use more adaptors are perceived as nervous and anxious.

There are also people (both students and teachers) who gesture very little in the classroom. Students and teachers who gesture very little might be perceived by the other as boring and unanimated. The teacher's delivery style should be animated and dynamic, and gesturing is one method of achieving this. The animated and dynamic teacher can keep the class interested in the subject for longer periods of time. Nonanimated, boring teachers put their classes to sleep.

Instructors who have an open body position communicate to their students that they are receptive and immediate, whereas teachers who fold in or keep a closed body position are perceived as nonimmediate and unreceptive. Students with similar positions are perceived in similar ways by their teachers. Students who slouch in their seats when talking to the teacher are perceived as bored, rude, or even arrogant. Teachers expect students to look interested. One of the best indicators of interest is body position.

Both students and teachers use adaptive gestures, but they should strive to decrease their reliance on such activities. Teachers should consciously work to be more animated and dynamic. This will improve student–teacher interaction and make the classroom a more exciting environment.

Facial Behavior

Teachers' facial expressions can affect how students feel about the classroom environment. The teacher who has a dull, boring facial expression when talking is perceived by the students as uninterested in them and the subject matter. This type of teacher is likely to have more classroom disruptions because students become bored with the teaching style. Teachers must have pleasing facial expressions, ones that show that they are interested not only in the subject matter, but also in their students. Pleasing facial expressions are often accompanied by positive head movements.

The teacher who uses positive head nods in response to a student's comments is perceived as friendly, concerned about the communication between teacher and student, and immediate. An instructor who rarely nods, or uses more negative head nods than positive quickly stifles teacher–student communication. Not many students volunteer to talk when they realize that their teacher will not respond in a positive or at least encouraging fashion. Positive head nods are a means of stimulating student–teacher interaction and student responses. Students who use similar head nods help promote student–teacher interaction and help the teacher know whether students have understood the content.

Smiling has long been associated with liking, affiliation, and immediacy. The teacher who smiles and has positive facial affect is perceived as more immediate and likable than the one who does not. Students react more favorably to the teacher who smiles than to the teacher who frowns a lot or does not smile much. Similarly, teachers react more favorably to the student who smiles than to the student who frowns or does not smile much. They each perceive the other as more open to communication. Therefore, the student–teacher relationship is improved by smiling. Students from kindergarten through graduate school respond better to teachers who smile.

Eye Behavior

Eye behavior of instructor and student can affect the interaction between the two. Students who look away, avoid teacher eye contact, or look down when the teacher calls on them are perceived as uninterested, shy, or unwilling to communicate. None of these are very positive perceptions. We know that people like to have eye contact when communicating with another. Eye contact might be one of the biggest indicators of student interest in the classroom environment. Students who do not have eye contact with the teacher are perceived as uninterested. Teachers are the same as other people. They want people to whom they are talking to look at them and to have eye contact with them. If that does not occur, it is taken as rejection of the content and also as a personal rejection.

Some instructors seldom have eye contact with their students. This usually suggests to the students that the teacher is not interested in them and that the teacher is not approachable. Teachers who have little eye contact with students often are very shy, and probably should not be in the classroom at all. When there is little eye contact between students and teachers, students do not know when to talk, when to ask, or how to approach the teacher. This is a common complaint on college campuses. It often is directed toward some international instructors. The students complain that the instructor never looks at them when lecturing. This behavior may be the result of the instructor's cultural upbringing. In some cultures, it is considered inappropriate for instructors and students to have direct eye contact. Regardless, this lack of eye contact inhibits effective communication in instruction.

In conclusion, eye behavior is a significant indicator of the relationship between student and teacher. Students who have eye contact with their teachers are perceived as more interested and better students. Teachers who look at their students are perceived as more animated, more interested, and more immediate.

Vocal Behavior

Recently we surveyed students to determine the nonverbal behavior that students liked or disliked most about teachers. Overwhelmingly, students felt that the monotone voice was the most objectionable behavior of a teacher. They felt that the monotone voice projected the image of boredom, noncaring, and nonimmediacy. They also said they learned less when the teacher had a dull or monotone voice. They were less interested in the subject matter and liked the class less when the teacher had a monotone voice. Students want the teacher to have a lively, animated voice.

Of all voice qualities, the monotone voice seems to draw the most negative criticism from both teachers and students. Both say that they perceive the person with the monotone voice as boring and dull. Students who use the monotone voice in class are not helping themselves at all. Instructors want students who sound interested in the class.

The author of this chapter had a professor who taught philosophy of education. He droned on and on in a monotone voice for two and a half hours every class period. The class had more than 100 people in it, and most dozed off. He was the worst model that an education department could employ to teach prospective teachers about how to be an effective and affective teacher. The most significant criticism the students had about him was not his competence, but his monotone voice.

There should be a sign placed in all classrooms that says "Laughter is encouraged in this class." Students do not get the opportunity to laugh in our classrooms. No one ever said learning had to be boring. A really good teacher laughs with the students and encourages and allows laughter when something occurs that all can enjoy. For example, the author of this chapter was lecturing one day and during the lecture she moved backwards to reach for her notes. She tripped over the garbage can behind her and fell in and got stuck. The class was stunned and then broke up laughing. She also laughed and finally some students helped her out of the garbage can. Had she not laughed, or criticized them for laughing, the class would have suffered. Laughing also allows students to release tension and to relax. Research completed more than sixty years ago by Barr studied good and poor social science teachers and found that good teachers laughed more and allowed laughter in the classroom, whereas poor teachers did not. Many things have changed since then, but it is certain that the role of laughter in the classroom has not. Teachers who laugh and encourage laughter from their students are still more immediate than those who do not.

Space

How a teacher or student uses interpersonal space with the other communicates how they perceive the other. The teacher who stands behind the desk or podium and rarely approaches students or allows them to approach her or him is perceived by students as unfriendly, unreceptive, unapproachable, and nonimmediate. This does not help improve student–teacher relationships.

The student who backs away when the teacher approaches, or will not allow a teacher to stand or sit close to them, will be perceived in a similar manner by the teacher. The student might even be perceived as uninterested in learning and hostile to the classroom environment.

Space communicates in the classroom environment. The teacher who withdraws from students is perceived as nonimmediate and noncaring. The student who withdraws from the teacher might be perceived as uninterested or hostile. We need to look beyond these perceptions to find out whether another problem is present.

Touch

Touch is a form of communication that can be very useful in establishing and maintaining an effective teacher–student relationship. Touch can be used by the instructor to reinforce a student for a job well-done. It can be used by the teacher to substitute for the verbal reprimand or control without ever saying a word. For example, the teacher who walks up and touches the child on the shoulder who is misbehaving has gotten her or his attention. The child knows that he or she should stop what they are doing. Touch should be an acceptable form of communication in the teacher–student relationship. Touching a student on the arm, hand, or shoulder should be acceptable. This type of touch can be a very effective means of communicating a message without ever uttering a word.

Teachers should remember that some students are touch-avoidant and are very uncomfortable when touched. A teacher who encounters a touch-avoidant student should leave him or her alone and not try to relax the student. In addition, some teachers are touch-avoidant and do not want to be touched. These teachers should not teach at the elementary levels. The student or teacher who is the touch-avoidant might be perceived as nonimmediate and perhaps even aloof. If a person is touch-avoidant, other nonverbal cues can be used to communicate immediacy and establish an effective student–teacher relationship.

In conclusion, teachers or students who withdraw from another's touch might be perceived as nonimmediate or touch-avoidant. Teachers and students should both be aware of the touch norms in schools and communities and be cautious about following them. Teachers should use touch as a form of reinforcement, not a punishment. Lastly, many classes such as physical education, art, and music, allow for a great deal of touch. Teachers in these classes should use appropriate touch as a form of communication.

Environment

Many classrooms are not conducive to student–teacher interaction. They have drab and dreary classrooms and very little can be done to improve the environment. Much of what I discuss here, however, can be adapted to any classroom in any school.

Attractive classrooms are much more likely to keep students and teachers attentive and reduce hostility. Many studies have revealed that ugly environments produce hostile communication among participants. Think of the worst schoolroom in which you had a class. Think of all the ugly aspects and how you felt while in that environment. It is more difficult to keep students' attention when the environment is ugly, too hot or cold, not well-illuminated, painted dingy yellow, dark brown, industrial green, battleship gray, or is unclean. These are dark, foreboding environments that say to students "don't plan on any fun here, shut up, sit, and listen."

It is a shame that in a country so affluent, many classrooms are still in the dark ages. Teachers and students usually must continue to accept this. However, many teachers redecorate their rooms at their own expense to make the environment more conducive to learning and enjoyment of learning.

There are optimal seating arrangements for different types of teaching. Traditional row and column arrangements are useful for listening, note-taking, and lecturing. Modular seating is best for student group interaction; this arrangement allows the teacher to move from group to group to give assistance. The circular, horseshoe, or open-square arrangement is particularly useful for encouraging classroom discussions between students and teachers. If a teacher can use the above arrangements in different learning situations, it will improve student interest and communication between student and teacher. Some of these classroom settings do, however, increase the noise level, which must also be considered.

Music can be used to counteract student boredom and to establish a comfortable classroom atmosphere. We have found in our research that teachers can use music as an effective reinforcer for good behavior, as a reward for completing a task, and for relaxing the students. Elementary teachers have long known the power of music in the classroom. They use it to relax students, to generate conversations, to reward, to excite, and to lull students to sleep. Teachers at any level can use music on occasion to create a better classroom environment. For example, if a teacher wants to spice up a unit on French history, he or she might play the music of the age. If a teacher wants to teach a unit on careers and employment, then he or she can play records about various positions people have held.

"The only good classroom is the quiet classroom." Unfortunately, this is the motto of many school systems. Students at any age should be encouraged to participate in classroom discussions and talk on occasion. The teaching strategy of teacher lecturing and student learning has long since lost its appeal for both segments. Teachers who allow some student talk are perceived by students as more responsive to their needs and more immediate and approachable. I do not mean that classrooms should be noisy without any purpose, but student talk is essential to student growth and development. The teacher should set up situations in which students can talk without being reprimanded. Group exercises, projects, and similar activities allow for student talk without decreasing the content. Of course, the teacher should not use such activities for content. They should be used as a means of teaching content.

Whether the students are younger or older, allowing for student–teacher interaction is an effective means of improving communication between teacher and student. Talk can also be used as a reward for good behavior. If students sit and listen, and take notes as they should, then the teacher should do a group exercise or open the class for discussion. Allowing for talk time gives students a chance to relax and release tension, and makes them feel better about the classroom environment. Those who do not want to talk, however, should not be forced to or punished for not talking.

Lighting can also influence the relationship between teacher and student. A classroom that is poorly lit or too bright can cause fatigue and eye strain. Eventually, even boredom and hostility emerge. Thompson gave three guidelines for lighting in the classroom.

> Maintain high levels of illumination. When students must expend energy just to see, they will have little left to understand what is being said. All areas of the room should be balanced in brightness. Factory and assembly-line workers have their work well illuminated. Industry has known for a long time that eye fatigue plays havoc with production schedules. To avoid sharp contrast, the visual field around the task should be only one-third as bright as the work area. No part of the visual field should be brighter than the immediate vicinity of the task. Avoid glare either from direct light sources or from reflecting surfaces. (p. 81)

Imagine sitting in a classroom and trying to absorb content when the temperature is 90 degrees with 90-percent humidity. About all you can do is sit very still and keep wiping the perspiration from your body. Many classrooms are kept too warm, both in the summer and in the winter. In the summer, they are too hot because they are not air conditioned and the humidity is high. In the winter, they are hot and dry. Both climates are disruptive to the learning and communication process between student and teacher. When a room is too hot, people become antsy and irritable. When a room is too cold, people cannot concentrate either.

The optimal classroom temperature is 64 to 70 degrees. This assumes that the room is not too dry or humid. Many classrooms do not have temperature controls, but if the room is painted a cool color, it will seem cooler. However, we know that when it's 90 degrees outside and 100 degrees inside, no one will feel cool even in a light blue room.

During the winter, humidity should not fall below 30 percent or be allowed to rise above 50 percent. As humidity moves above or below these levels, student illness and absenteeism increases. Todd-Mancillas summarize Green's (1979) results drawn from 3,600 students in grades one to eight in eleven different schools in Saskatoon, Canada:

> Results indicated that children attending schools with classrooms humidified ranging between 22% and 26% experienced nearly 13% greater illness and absenteeism than children attending schools with classrooms having humidity levels ranging between 27% and 33%. . . . (p. 85)

Green also cautions against excessive humidity, as allied research also indicates that increased respiratory infections result from humidity levels in excess of 50 percent. If teachers cannot control the temperature in their classrooms, then they should vary activities so that students do not notice the temperature as much. In other words, they should give the students plenty to do and think about other than the temperature. In cold months, if the room is too cold, they should have the students move around and talk a lot. In warmer months, if the room is too hot, they should have group discussions and activities that help direct attention away from the temperature.

The furnishings in a classroom can often determine how students feel about the environment. Ugly furnishings do not improve communication between the student and teacher. Granted, many schools do not have money to purchase new desks, chairs, equipment, and curtains. However, schools that are more attractive are generally taken better care of by the students. Teachers and students can improve the classroom by bringing in artifacts to improve the environment. "Hard architecture" often interferes with a student attention span and learning. Examples of hard architecture are hard chairs, sharp-edged tables, desks, and uncomfortable work tables. "Soft architecture" often encourages student attention and learning. Soft architecture sends signals of comfort and welcome. Examples of soft architecture are ergonomic chairs, chairs that are softer, chairs that lean back when we move, rounded tables, and comfortable looking classroom furniture.

In conclusion, the instructor who makes optimal use of the environment he or she has is likely to get along better with the students. Affect will improve for the teacher who cares about the classroom environment. Maximal use of space, seating, lighting, color, sound, noise, temperature, and furnishings improve communication between student and instructor.

Scent

The odor a person exudes can encourage others to approach or avoid that person. Teachers should avoid wearing overpowering scents in the classroom. Overpowering scents can affect student attentiveness, learning, and health. Some students have allergies and cannot be near strong scents or odors. Teachers should be sensitive to this even if other students are not.

Time

Teachers must use time to their advantage. Time can be used to reward students for good behavior, to control students, to make the classroom more interesting, and to learn about others. Teachers often spend too much time on one unit. Most adults can only listen effectively for about twenty minutes. It also is important to remember the use of time discussed in Chapter 2. Teachers should keep students' attention by using a variety of methods and activities to teach content. Students will be less likely to notice time if you keep them busy doing interesting things with the material they are learning. Keeping in mind how students learn best, it also is important to make time for previews and reviews of content.

Finally, if we as educators expect our students to take our classes seriously, we should always be ON TIME, if not a little early. By being a little early, it gives us an opportunity to interact with students as they enter the room, students who otherwise might never talk with us. If we are consistently late to our own classes, it sends the message to the students "that we are not interested in our content area or concerned about the students." Therefore, students may begin being late for our class. If this occurs, we asked for it!

Outcomes of Teacher Immediacy

Throughout this chapter, I have discussed possible teacher and student nonverbal behavior that denotes immediacy or nonimmediacy. Obviously, the immediate teacher is perceived more positively than the nonimmediate teacher. Many of the results reported here is a direct result of Richmond and McCroskey (2000a, b) and their associates. There are significant advantages to be gained from teacher immediacy in the classroom:

- Increased teacher immediacy results in increased liking, affiliation, and positive affect on the part of the student. Immediate teachers are liked far more than nonimmediate teachers.

- Increased teacher immediacy results in an increased student affect for the subject matter. Students who become motivated to learn the subject matter because of the immediate will do well in the content and continue to learn long after the teacher who motivated them is out of the picture.
- Increased teacher immediacy results in increased students' cognitive learning. Students with immediate teachers, attend more to the subject matter, concentrate more on the subject, retain more of the content, and when challenged can correctly recall more of the subject matter than students with nonimmediate teachers.
- Increased teacher immediacy results in increased student motivation. It seems that the primary way that immediacy produces learning effects may be as a function of it increasing student motivation.
- Increased teacher immediacy results in reduced student resistance to teachers' influence attempts or teachers' behavior modification attempts. Immediate teachers seem to have more referent, respect, or liking power, hence students tend to comply with or conform to the wishes of the more immediate teachers. Nonimmediate teachers have more difficulty getting students to comply with or conform to their wishes.
- Increased teacher immediacy results in the teacher being perceived as a more competent communicator, one who listens and cares. Nonimmediate teachers are usually perceived as ineffective, if not incompetent communicators.
- Increased teacher immediacy results in the teacher being able to reduce or alleviate student anxiety about the classroom situation. A more immediate teacher is perceived as a more caring, sensitive teacher, hence the student feels less apprehensive about the overall instructional environment.
- Increased teacher immediacy results in an increased student to teacher communication and interaction. Some teachers might see this aspect as a negative. It is not. If students communicate more with their teachers, then the student might get the information he or she needs.
- Increased teacher immediacy results in a reduced status differential between student and teacher. This does not mean the teacher is on the same level as the student. It simply means the student won't be so intimidated by the teacher's higher status. Therefore, the student might be more willing to ask clarifying questions about the content with no fear of the teacher.
- Increased teacher immediacy results in higher evaluations from one's immediate supervisor. While this may seem unusual at first, it is really very simple to understand. Administrators like teachers who have good classes with few problems. Immediate teachers have good classes with fewer problems than nonimmediate teachers. Hence, administrators will find immediate teachers to be the more effective teachers.

In conclusion, nonverbal immediacy behaviors are some of the most valuable communication tools instructors have available to them. These nonverbal immediacy skills can help teachers and students have happier, more productive, classroom experiences.

Potential Drawbacks of Teacher Immediacy

Immediacy has a plethora of positive results. There are a few drawbacks that teachers should know. Immediate teachers might encounter some personal or professional problems with their colleagues. They might be perceived as not having control over their classrooms. Immediate teachers have control over their classrooms. Some of their peers just do not see it.

Immediate teachers might seem as if they are pushovers to some students. Immediacy does not mean "let the students do whatever he or she wants." It means "be approachable." Immediate teachers must still be firm and have standards.

Lastly, not everyone can be immediate in the same way. Select the behaviors you are most comfortable with and use those. To be immediate, you do not have to perform all the behaviors we have identified as immediate in this chapter, but you do need some of them. If you try to use behavior that makes you uncomfortable, you will appear awkward and uncomfortable rather than immediate. False immediacy is worse than none at all.

The primary function of teachers' verbal behavior is to give content to improve students' cognitive learning. The primary function of teachers' nonverbal behavior is to improve students' affect or liking for the subject matter, teacher, and class and to increase the desire to learn more about the subject matter. In conclusion, teachers who use nonverbal immediacy behaviors with students have students who simply put learn more, both about the content and atmosphere of the classroom environment.

REFERENCES AND SUGGESTED READINGS

Ambady, N., & Rosenthal, R. (1993). Half a minute: Predicting teacher evaluations from thin slices of nonverbal behavior and physical attractiveness. *Journal of Personality and Social Psychology, 64,* 431–441.

Andersen, J. F. (1978). *The relationship between teacher immediacy and teaching effectiveness.* Unpublished doctoral dissertation, West Virginia University, Morgantown.

Andersen, J. F. (1979). Teacher immediacy as a predictor of teaching effectiveness. In D. Nimmo (Ed.), *Communication yearbook, 3* (pp. 543–559). New Brunswick, NJ: Transaction Books.

Burroughs, N. F. (1990). *The relationship of teacher immediacy and student compliance resistance with*
learning. Unpublished doctoral dissertation, West Virginia University, Morgantown.

Christophel, D. M. (1990a). *The relationships among teacher immediacy behaviors, student motivation, and learning.* Unpublished doctoral dissertation, West Virginia University, Morgantown.

Christophel, D. M. (1990b). The relationships among teacher immediacy behaviors, student motivation, and learning. *Communication Education, 37,* 323–340.

Chesebro, J., & McCroskey, J. C. (1998). The relationship of teacher clarity and teacher immediacy with students' experiences of state receiver apprehension. *Communication Quarterly, 46,* 446–456.

Frymier, A. (1994). A model of immediacy in the

classroom. *Communication Quarterly, 42,* 133–144.

Green, G. H. (1979). Ah-choo! Humidity can help. *American School and University, 52,* 64–65.

Kearney, P., Plax, T. G., & Wendt-Wasco, N. J. (1985). Teacher immediacy for affective learning in divergent college classes. *Communication Quarterly, 3,* 61–74.

McCroskey, J. C. (1997). Self-report measurement. In Daly, J. A., McCroskey, J. C., Ayres, J., Hopf, T., & Ayres, D. M.(Eds.). (2nd ed.) (pp. 191–216). *Avoiding communication: Shyness, reticence, and communication apprehension.* Cresskill, NJ: Hampton Press.

McCroskey, J. C., Richmond, V. P., Sallinen, A., Fayer, J., & Barraclough, R. (1995). A cross-cultural and multi-behavioral analysis of the relationship between nonverbal immediacy and teacher evaluations. *Communication Quarterly, 44,* 281–291.

McCroskey, J. C., Sallinen, A., Fayer, J. M., Richmond, V. P., & Barraclough, R. A. (1996). Nonverbal immediacy and cognitive learning: A cross-cultural investigation. *Communication Education, 45,* 200–211.

Mehrabian, A. (1969). Some referents and measures of nonverbal behavior. *Behavioral Research Methods and Instrumentation, 1,* 213–217.

Mehrabian, A. (1971). *Silent messages.* Belmont, CA: Wadsworth.

Mottet, T., & Richmond, V. P. (1998). An inductive analysis of verbal immediacy: Alternative conceptualization of relational verbal approach/avoidance strategies. *Communication Quarterly, 46,* 25–41.

O'Mara, J., Allen, J. L., Long, K. M., & Judd, B (1996). Communication apprehension, nonverbal immediacy, and negative expectations for learning. *Communication Research Reports, 13,* 109–128.

Plax, T. G., Kearney, P., McCroskey, I. C., & Richmond, V. P. (1986). Power in the classroom VI: Verbal control strategies, nonverbal immediacy, and affective learning. *Communication Education, 35,* 43–55.

Richmond, V. P. (1990). Communication in the classroom: Power and motivation. *Communication Education, 39,* 181–195.

Richmond, V. P. (1997a). *Nonverbal communication in the classroom: A text and workbook and study guide.* Acton, MA: Tapestry Press.

Richmond, V. P. (1997b). Quietness in contemporary society: Conclusions and generalizations of the research. In Daly, J. A., McCroskey, J. C., Ayres, J., Hopf, T., & Ayres, D. M.(Eds.). (2nd ed.) (pp. 257–268). *Avoiding communication: Shyness, reticence, and communication apprehension.* Cresskill, NJ: Hampton Press.

Richmond, V. P., & Hickson III, M. (in press). *Going public: A basic guide to public talk.* Boston, MA: Allyn & Bacon.

Richmond, V. P., & McCroskey, J. C. (1992). Power in the classroom: Communication, control, and concern. (Eds.). *Power in the classroom: Communication, control, and concern.* Hillsdale, NJ: Lawrence Erlbaum.

Richmond, V. P., & McCroskey, J. C. (1998). *Communication apprehension, avoidance, and effectiveness.* (Chapter 6). (5th ed.). Boston, MA: Allyn and Bacon.

Richmond, V. P., & McCroskey, J. C. (2000a). *Nonverbal behavior in interpersonal relationships.* Boston, MA: Allyn and Bacon.

Richmond, V. P., & McCroskey, J. C. (2000b). The impact of supervisor and subordinate immediacy on relational and organizational outcomes. *Communication Monographs, 67,* 85–95.

Richmond, V. P., Gorham, J., & McCroskey, J. C. (1987). The relationship between selected immediacy behaviors and cognitive learning. In M. L. McLaughlin (Ed.), *Communication yearbook, 10* (pp. 574–590). Newbury Park, CA: Sage.

Richmond, V. P., McCroskey, I. C., Kearney, P., & Plax, T. G. (1987). Power in the classroom VII: Linking behavior alteration techniques to cognitive learning. *Communication Education, 36,* 1–12.

Richmond, V. P., McCroskey, I. C., Plax, T. G., & Kearney, P. (1986). Teacher nonverbal immediacy training and student affect. *World Communication, 15,* 181–194.

Richmond, V. P., Heisel, A., Smith, R. S., & McCroskey, J. C. (1998). The impact of communication apprehension and fear of talking with a physician on perceived medical outcomes. *Communication Research Report, 15,* 344–353.

Richmond, V. P., Smith, R.S., Heisel, A., & McCroskey, J. C. (2000). *Nonverbal immediacy and physician/patient communication.* Paper presented at the Eastern Communication Association, Pittsburgh, April, 2000.

Sanders, J. A., & Wiseman, R. L. (1990). The effects of verbal and nonverbal teacher immediacy on perceived cognitive, affective, and behavioral learning in the multicultural classroom. *Communication Education, 39,* 341–351.

Todd-Mancillas, W. R. (1982). Classroom environments and nonverbal communication. In L. L.

Barker (Ed.), *Communication in the classroom: Original essays* (pp. 77–97). Englewood Cliffs, NJ: Prentice-Hall.

Thompson, J. J. (1973). *Beyond words: nonverbal communication in the classroom.* New York: Citation Press.

Thweatt, K., & McCroskey, J. C. (1996). Teacher nonimmediacy and misbehavior: Unintentional negative communication. *Communication Research Reports, 13,* 198–204.

Thweatt, K., & McCroskey, J. C. (1998). The impact of teacher immediacy and misbehaviors on teacher credibility. *Communication Education, 47,* 348–358.

Wrench, J., & Richmond, V. P. (2000). *The relationship between teacher humor assessment and motivation, credibility, verbal aggression, affective learning, perceived learning, and learning loss.* Paper presented at the National Communication Association Conference, Seattle, November.

7 Making Content Relevant to Students

ANN BAINBRIDGE FRYMIER

Miami University

A question that students bring to the classroom, but rarely explicitly ask the instructor is, "What's in this for me?" Students want to know how the material relates to them personally and why they should bother to learn what the teacher is presenting. Since we teachers typically choose to discuss in class what we believe to be the "most important" topics and concepts, everything seems relevant to us. This brings up a very important aspect of the relevance concept—it is a perception. Therefore, something that I perceive as relevant to me, you may see as completely irrelevant. Relevance is a perception the receiver has of the message and, as such, is influenced by message characteristics, personal characteristics of the receiver, and source characteristics. So if relevance is a receiver perception of a message that can vary from person to person, how is the teacher supposed to make the content relevant to everyone? Making content relevant to every student sitting in class (particularly large classes) is generally an unrealistic expectation. However, a teacher can utilize several strategies to increase the likelihood that more students will perceive the content as personally relevant. The focus of this chapter will be on issues involved in perceiving something as relevant, and strategies for increasing perceptions of relevance. These concepts will be discussed in terms of Keller's ARCS model of motivation, expectancy value theory, and Petty and Cacioppo's elaboration likelihood model.

Keller's ARCS Model

If something is relevant, it is related and it is pertinent. Keller (1983) defines relevance as a perception of personal needs being met by instructional activities or as a highly desired goal being perceived as related to instructional activities. In other words, we perceive something as being relevant if we perceive it is related to our personal needs (e.g., needs for affiliation, control, achievement) or our personal goals (e.g., career goals). Relevance, however, is only one component of Keller's (1983, 1987) ARCS model of motivation. ARCS stands for *attention,* relevance, confidence, and satisfaction. According to this model, before classroom instruction can be made relevant, the teacher must first gain students' attention. As mentioned in Chapter 2, it is clear that students' attention is a necessary precursor to learning. If students do not pay attention, they will not be involved nor put forth an effort to learn. The second step is to make the content relevant, which satisfies students' needs. Building positive expectancies, which Keller refers to as *confidence* is the third step. Confidence can be developed by communicating to students what is expected of them and that they can succeed at the task. The last condition necessary for students' motivation is satisfaction. Students need to feel satisfied with the outcomes of their effort in order to continue to be motivated. Satisfaction is facilitated by both intrinsic and extrinsic rewards.

Expectancy-Value Theory

The ARCS model and specifically the relevance component, draw heavily on expectancy value theory. Expectancy value theory proposes that individuals will be motivated to perform behaviors that are perceived to be personally satisfying and have a positive expectancy for success (Atkinson, 1978; Wong, 1998). Both a positive expectation for success and a positive value for the task are necessary for motivation to occur according to expectancy value theory. Students will be unmotivated to perform a task if they find the task to be unimportant (low value) or if they expect to fail at the task. To be motivated, a student must believe that he or she has the ability to perform the task successfully, that his or her effort will result in some outcome (e.g., grade, learning), and that the outcome has value. The concept of relevance is primarily related to the value component of expectancy value theory. When students perceive a concept or task as relevant, they see it as valuable, as having importance. Therefore, making content relevant to students is an instructional strategy that contributes to student motivation, however, alone it is not sufficient. As outlined in Keller's ARCS model, there are other factors that contribute to motivation. Making content relevant must be combined with other instructional strategies that gain students' attention, help them to feel confident, and help them feel satisfied with the class. The other chapters in this book provide numerous instructional strategies that help accomplish these goals.

Elaboration Likelihood Model

Relevance is also discussed in Petty and Cacioppo's (1986) delineation of the elaboration likelihood model. Petty and Cacioppo use the terms relevance and personal involvement somewhat interchangeably. According to the elaboration likelihood model, the extent to which a persuasive message is personally relevant influences whether a person will be motivated to elaborate on the message (carefully think about the message). Elaboration is a key factor in long-term attitude change according to this model. Similar to Keller's model, Petty and Cacioppo view relevance as a component of motivation. When people perceive something as being relevant, they perceive it as having value, and worthy of their effort.

Relevance and Learning

There has been little research on the nature of relevance or its relationship to learning. However, relevance has frequently been discussed as an important aspect of teaching. One reason that relevance has rarely been empirically examined is because it is so inherently logical that making content relevant for one's audience enhances retention. The research that does exist indicates, for the most part, that relevance does make a difference in learning.

In one of the earlier studies, Newby (1991) observed first-year elementary school teachers and their classrooms over a 16-week period of time. The teachers' motivational strategies and students' on-task behaviors were recorded. Teachers' motivational strategies were classified as attention gaining, emphasizing relevance, confidence building, or imposing rewards or punishments. Relevance strategies were infrequently used, only making up 7.49 percent of the total motivational strategies, however it was the only motivational strategy to be positively associated with students' on-task behavior. Presumably, the relevance strategies helped students (who were in kindergarten through sixth grade) understand why they needed to perform a task and why it was important. They were given a reason for the task and were therefore willing to perform the task.

In a different line of research, Frymier and Shulman (1995) developed a relevance scale that measured the frequency with which teachers used relevance strategies while teaching. The scale consists of twelve items and is shown in Figure 7.1. Students indicated how frequently their teachers used each of the strategies in the scale. What Frymier and Shulman found was that when teachers used the relevance strategies more frequently (as perceived by students), students felt more motivated to study for the class. Additionally, relevance accounted for variance in students' stated motivation to study after teacher use of verbal and nonverbal immediacy was taken into consideration. In other words, making content relevant contributed to student motivation beyond the contribution of teacher immediacy to motivation. (See Chapter 6 for a more thorough discussion of teacher immediacy.)

In a second study, Frymier, Shulman, and Houser (1996) found relevance to again be positively associated with motivation to study and found a positive relationship with affective learning and learning behaviors. Frymier et al. also found perceptions of relevance to be associated with student reports of feeling empowered. Students who felt their teachers made content relevant also felt empowered in those classes. Empowerment is a motivationally based concept, so it is very logical that making content relevant would be associated with feelings of empowerment. Affective learning refers to students' attitudes toward the course and its content. So students who value the content and think the subject matter is

FIGURE 7.1   Frymier and Shulman's (1995) Relevance Scale

Directions: Read each statement and use the following scale to indicate how frequently your teacher performs each of the behaviors. There are no right or wrong answers.

Never = 0   Rarely = 1   Occasionally = 2   Often = 3   Very Often = 4

1. ___ Uses examples to make the content relevant to me.

2. ___ Provides explanations that make the content relevant to me.

3. ___ Uses exercises or explanations that demonstrate the importance of the content.

4. ___ Explicitly states how the material relates to my career goals or my life in general.

5. ___ Links content to other areas of content.

6. ___ Asks me to apply content to my own interests.

7. ___ Gives assignments that involve the application of the content to my career interests.

8. ___ Helps me to understand the importance of the content.

9. ___ Uses own experiences to introduce or demonstrate a concept.

10. ___ Uses student experiences to demonstrate or introduce a concept.

11. ___ Uses discussion to help me understand the relevance of a topic.

12. ___ Uses current events to apply a topic.

important, would be said to have achieved affective learning. Chapter 1 in this book provides a more thorough discussion of affective learning.

In Frymier et al.'s (1996) study, students who felt their teachers were using relevance strategies valued the content more. Additionally, Frymier et al. found relevance to be associated with a variety of learning indicators. Learning indicators were measured by asking students to report how frequently they engaged in nine behaviors that were related to learning (e.g., I see the relationship of the course content from one day to the next throughout the semester). (See Frymier & Houser, 1999, for a full discussion of the learning indicators scale.) As teachers used more relevance strategies, students reported engaging in more learning behaviors. These three studies together lead us to the conclusion that relevance pays off. Making content relevant to students facilitates their learning. However, two experimental studies did not find a relationship between making content relevant and learning.

Based on Frymier and Shulman's (1995) findings, Frymier and Houser (1998) hypothesized that relevance would only enhance motivation and learning when accompanied by teacher immediacy. They believed that immediacy served to gain attention (Kelley & Gorham, 1988), and that if content were made relevant in low-immediacy conditions, it would not enhance motivation because students would not be paying attention. They expected student motivation and learning to be the highest under conditions of high immediacy and high relevance. Frymier and Houser did not find support for their hypothesis. Student motivation and learning increased under high-immediacy conditions, but relevance had no impact on student motivation and learning. Frymier and Houser had difficulty manipulating relevance without changing the content and admitted that they may not have really manipulated relevance. It is impossible to know from this study whether the results were due to methodology or to the nature of relevance itself.

In a follow-up to Frymier and Houser's work, Behrens (1999) compared three relevance strategies suggested by Keller (1987) to a low-relevance condition. The three strategies were to link content to the present situation, past experiences, and one's future. Behrens manipulated the relevance of a short lecture on a topic that students would have little prior knowledge of (jungle survival) and little initial relevance to the class students were to imagine themselves in (this study was conducted before the TV show "Survivor" aired). Students were to imagine that they were in a class called "Peoples and Cultures of Latin America" and that the lecture they were to read was being given by the professor (no sex or rank for the professor was given). After reading the lecture, students were asked to complete scales measuring their learning and motivation. Behrens (1999) found no differences in learning or motivation among the four relevance conditions. The perceived relevance of all four conditions was very close to the midpoint of the scale. Students did not perceive the information in any of the conditions to be completely irrelevant (even though that was the goal of the low-relevance condition). One possible interpretation of these results is that the students perceived at least moderate relevance because a professor presented the information. Behrens suggests that students may assume that the content presented in class is important and therefore relevant. Future research needs to address both message and source characteristics that lead to perceptions of relevance.

The results of these last two studies may lead you to question the importance of making content relevant to students. However a close look at the studies indicates that the problems are more likely due to measurement and manipulation issues rather than to conceptual issues. Frymier and Houser (1998) probably did not sufficiently manipulate relevance. In all likelihood, relevance did not effect learning because the manipulation was too subtle to have an impact. Behrens also had trouble manipulating relevance, however in post-hoc analyses he reports students' perceptions of relevance (two different measures of relevance) were correlated with both motivation to study ($r = .41$ and $r = .52$) and with affective learning ($r = .61$ and $r = .45$). When students perceived the material as relevant they reported being more motivated and having greater affective learning. The problem was that he could not reliably manipulate relevance. Both Frymier and Houser (1998) and Behrens (1999) tried to manipulate relevance by changing message characteristics. Other factors such as source characteristics, environment, and student characteristics may also influence relevance. Future research needs to examine these other factors in relation to relevance perceptions.

Strategies for Enhancing Relevance

Keller (1987) provides six types of strategies for enhancing content relevance, which includes experience, present worth, future usefulness, need matching, modeling, and choice. One thing all of these strategies have in common is that they require teachers to have some knowledge and understanding of their students. This is particularly true for the experience strategies. Experience strategies include, "State explicitly how the instruction builds on the learner's existing skills," "Use analogies familiar to the learner from past experience," and "Find out what the learners' interests are and relate them to the instruction" (Keller, 1987, p. 4). These strategies require a teacher to know something about the students' past experiences, skills, and interests. There are some classroom situations where this is quite possible and maybe even fairly easy to accomplish. Small classes that are somewhat homogenous are best suited for relating content to students' existing skills, past experiences, and interests. For example, if you are teaching an advanced organizational communication course where everyone in the class has had the same prerequisites and is in the same major, these students have some common experiences that can be related to the content.

The future usefulness strategies are well-suited for a class where students have similar career goals or reasons for taking the class. These two strategies are "State explicitly how the instruction relates to future activities of the learner" and "Ask learners to relate the instruction to their own future goals" (Keller, 1987, p. 4). For example, business majors enrolled in a required public speaking class would likely have similar career goals. Using examples showing the relevance of public speaking skills to the business world would likely be effective for a majority of the students.

The more diverse the classroom, the more difficult it is to choose a strategy that will help all students perceive the content as relevant. In highly diverse classrooms, the choice strategies may be highly effective. There are two choice strategies, "Provide meaningful alternative methods for accomplishing a goal" and "Provide personal choices for organizing one's work" (Keller, 1987, p. 4). By giving students choices in how to achieve a learning goal, students can find their own connections between the content and their personal needs or goals. This brings us to a broader strategy not discussed by Keller.

One general approach is to have students determine why and how content is relevant to them. Giving students choices in completing assignments encourages them to make the content relevant to their own needs and interests. For example, if a learning objective for your class is to learn a particular theory such as Baxter's (1990) dialectic theory, an assignment could involve students applying the theory to a relationship of their choosing. In completing the assignment, students have to relate the theory to a situation that is important to them. The student generates the relevance in this situation. One important note: Teachers need to take care to help students apply the theory to appropriate situations, so that the theory is indeed useful and relevant to the situation.

Keller (1987) also discusses the strategies of present worth, need-matching, and modeling. Present worth is basically telling students why the content is relevant and important. Need-matching involves attempting to link the content to specific student needs such as the need for affiliation, need for power, and the need for achievement. The strategy of modeling involves using individuals such as alumni or tutors to demonstrate or model the value and relevance of the content. Keller also suggests that the instructor model enthusiasm for the content. To learn more about relevance strategies and the ARCS model as a whole, see Keller (1987).

Another way teachers can encourage students to make content relevant to their own needs and goals is to ask students to do so. First, present the content you want students to learn such as Monroe's motivated sequence. Once the concept has been defined, ask students why it is important to know this or how this information could be used. The teacher can also play devil's advocate and ask, "Why should anyone care about this? What difference does it make?" Such questions require students to justify for the teacher, themselves, and their classmates why the content is important and relevant. This strategy pushes students to figure out for themselves how the content relates to their own needs, goals, and interests. Students may also be more willing to accept the reasons given by their peers than the reasons given by the instructor.

Difficulties with Relevance

The primary difficulty with the concept of relevance is that it is a perception. This is a problem because it is so easy to assume that others perceive things the same as we do. As teachers we tend to see what we teach as being very important and relevant. We may even believe that what we teach is relevant to everyone regardless of his or her position in life. When we are this enthusiastic about our courses, it is easy to forget that others may not see the relevance of what we teach. We have to continually remind ourselves of this fact and make an effort to employ strategies that will help students see the relevance of what we teach.

Another related difficulty with relevance is that students' goals and needs change over time. The strategies and assignments used one semester to make content relevant may not be very useful one or two semesters later. This is particularly true if you draw on current events to demonstrate relevance. Not only do we need to continually update the content in our courses, but we also need to update our knowledge of how the content relates to a variety of people. Being knowledgeable about student concerns, lifestyles, and interests is important to the task of making content relevant, and this information is constantly changing.

It is a whole lot easier to avoid thinking about whether students see the relevance of what we are teaching, however it is a whole lot more satisfying when students believe our class is really important.

Improving Your Teaching

Where does relevance fit into the bigger picture of teaching? I previously stated that relevance alone was insufficient, that it needed to be combined with other instructional strategies. We can use Keller's ARCS model as a guide to understanding additional instructional strategies we should use to be effective teachers. The first step in Keller's model is attention. Verbal and nonverbal immediacy behaviors are very effective means for gaining students' attention (see Chapter 6). It is difficult not to pay attention when the teacher is making eye contact, smiling at us, calling us by our first name, and using vocal variety. Using appropriate humor (see Chapter 10) is another useful strategy. However, as Wanzer points out in Chapter 10, if humor does not come naturally to you, you should probably avoid using this strategy.

The second component of Keller's model is *relevance* and the third is *confidence.* Confidence refers to developing positive expectations among students. Recall that in the expectancy value theory, motivation occurs when students value the activity and expect to succeed at the task. So strategies that help students feel that success is likely are important. This does not mean that you need to make your class easy or give everyone a good grade. Students need to feel a sense of control, that they have the necessary tools to successfully complete a task. Being clear (see Chapter 8) is important so that students understand what is expected of them. Clarity also facilitates understanding of the content so that it is used correctly in assignments. While immediacy is useful in gaining attention, it is also useful in building confidence. Highly immediate teachers are approachable. Students feel more comfortable asking questions of immediate teachers. When students feel free to ask questions, they are likely to clarify assignments and content, which makes them more confident in their ability to complete assignments successfully.

The last component of Keller's model is satisfaction. This component focuses on how to maintain and increase students' motivation. If students' hard work and accomplishments go unnoticed, or worse, punished, motivation will wane. It's easy to recognize and reward students who do well. It's much more difficult to find appropriate ways to recognize and reward students who are less successful. First of all, it is important to remember that grades are not the only rewards that teachers have to offer. Everyone likes to hear the words, "Good job" or having one's improvements noticed. Even silly things like stickers, smiley faces, or "Good Job!" at the top of a paper can make students feel good about their efforts.

Our success in enhancing satisfaction lies largely in our ability to give constructive feedback, nonverbal and verbal, oral and written. The general rule of thumb is to always find something positive to say about a student's performance. Sometimes this is a real challenge, but we need to make the effort to find something positive to say. Second, remember that receiving feedback makes people feel vulnerable. People respond differently to vulnerability, but a common response is to be defensive. Be prepared to deal with this response and avoid becoming defensive yourself. Earlier, I said you need to be clear to help build positive expectations. Being clear in your grading criteria is also important. In addition to being clear, you need to be specific in how and why the student did not meet those criteria. Receiving negative feedback is less frustrating if we understand exactly what we did wrong. A fourth suggestion is to focus on behavior and not on personal characteristics. Describe the behavior and avoid making inferences about the student's motivation, ability, or personality, i.e., "You had two false starts and lost your place three times during the speech" versus "You weren't prepared for your speech." Lastly, communicate to students your desire for them to succeed. If students believe you are pulling for them, they are more likely to view your feedback as constructive and be less defensive. If students feel you are against them, they are likely to blame you for the poor grade, rather than take responsibility themselves. While giving feedback to students is probably one of the most tedious and difficult aspect of teaching, it is also very important if you really want to help students learn.

Teaching is a complex activity that involves many skills and abilities and is constantly being influenced by the students and the classroom. Keller's ARCS model provides a useful framework for assessing our teaching. I have identified a variety of communication behaviors that can be used to improve teaching. These behaviors can be used and adapted in a variety of ways. There is not a single model or set of behaviors that make up "effective teaching." Good teachers come in many flavors. Strategies such as relevance, immediacy, and humor can be used in many different ways to facilitate student motivation and learning.

Conclusion

When students perceive course content and activities as relevant to them, their motivation is likely to increase. When students are motivated learners, they put forth more effort and in most situations will learn more. When teachers take the time to learn about their students and then find ways to link students' needs, goals, and interests to the content, a greater number of them will perceive the content as relevant and important. As suggested in Chapter 2, it is often necessary to use a variety of strategies, since some students will respond to some strategies but not to others.

Making content relevant is an important component of effective teaching, but it is only a single component. Using relevance strategies with verbal and non-verbal immediacy behaviors gains students' attention, enhances perceptions of relevance, and helps build confidence. Being clear in presentations and handouts also helps students feel confident with the material. Finally, it is important to give special attention to the feedback you offer students. If they feel there is no chance of succeeding in your class, it doesn't really matter how relevant you make the material or how many times you smile and make eye contact—they won't be motivated learners. When giving feedback find something positive to say, be descriptive, be clear and specific, and be supportive.

REFERENCES AND SUGGESTED READINGS

Atkinson, J. W. (1978). The mainsprings of achievement-oriented activity. In J. Atkinson & J. Raynor (Eds.), *Personality, motivation and achievement* (pp. 11–39). New York: Halsted.

Baxter, L. A. (1990). Dialectical contradictions in relationship development. *Journal of Social and Personal Relationships, 7,* 68–88.

Behrens, F. H. (1999). *Do relevance strategies affect a student's motivation to learn?* Unpublished master's thesis, Miami University, Oxford, Ohio.

Frymier, A. B., & Houser, M. L. (1998). Does making content relevant make a difference in learning? *Communication Research Reports, 15,* 121–129.

Frymier, A. B., & Houser, M. L. (1999). The revised learning indicators scale. *Communication Studies, 50,* 1–12.

Frymier, A. B., & Shulman, G. M. (1995). "What's in it for me?": Increasing content relevance to enhance students' motivation. *Communication Education, 44,* 40–50.

Frymier, A. B., Shulman, G. M., & Houser, M. (1996). The development of a learner empowerment measure. *Communication Education, 45,* 181–199.

Keller, J. M. (1983). Motivational design of instruction. In C. M. Reigeluth (Ed.), *Instructional design theories: An overview of their current status* (pp. 383–434). Hillsdale, NJ: Lawrence Erlbaum.

Keller, J. M. (1987). Strategies for stimulating the motivation to learn. *Performance and Instruction, 26* (8), 1–7.

Kelley, D. H., & Gorham, J. (1988). Effects of immediacy on recall of information. *Communication Education, 37,* 198–207.

Newby, T. J. (1991). Classroom motivation: Strategies of first-year teachers. *Journal of Educational Psychology, 83,* 195–200.

Petty, R. E., & Cacioppo, J. T. (1986). The elaboration likelihood model of persuasion. In L. Berkowitz (Ed.), *Advances in experimental social psychology* (Vol. 19, pp. 123–205). New York: Academic Press.

Wong, P. T. P. (1998). Academic values and achievement motivation. In P. T. P. Wong & P. S. Fry (Eds.), *The human quest for meaning.* Mahwah, NJ: Lawrence Erlbaum.

8 Teaching Clearly

JOSEPH L. CHESEBRO
State University of New York at Brockport

Most students can recall, typically with some frustration, encountering the type of teacher who is an expert in a subject, even brilliant in a field, but cannot teach that information to others. In other words, the person cannot teach clearly. Instead, they use advanced terminology, teach at a fast pace, and wonder why students are not "getting it." They fail to realize that clarity is essential to good teaching.

One of the main objectives of teaching is for the teacher to enable students to develop the same understanding of the material as he or she has. In other words, the goal is to have students accurately understand the information. In fact, this is how students are tested. Tests are graded based on the extent to which students have the correct answers, or the answers that agree with the teacher's understanding of the subject. Therefore, clear teaching is fundamental to good teaching. If students fail to learn information correctly, they will not be able to use it reliably when it really counts—after they are out of school. Therefore, it is important that teachers learn about clear teaching and make an effort to teach their students clearly.

Research on clarity from a variety of perspectives serves as further evidence of the importance of clear teaching. In a review of aspects of effective teaching, Rosenshine and Furst (1971) listed clarity as an important part of good teaching. Smith, Land, and colleagues have demonstrated that presentations by teachers who exhibit indicators of unclear teaching, such as vocalized pauses ("um's") and mazes (losing students by failing to stay on track: "what I'm trying to say is . . . actually, that's not it . . . well, yes it is,") inhibit student achievement regardless of grade level and subject matter. Cruickshank, Kennedy, and colleagues have identified a number of teacher behaviors that students find important for clear teaching. Follow-up research in which students encountered teachers exhibiting these different behaviors demonstrated that students of the clear teachers (as opposed to unclear teachers) were more satisfied with their teachers and achieved more. My own research has taken three different approaches. First, students reported about a hypothetical teacher and indicated that they preferred the one who exhibited clear teaching behaviors. Second, reporting on actual teachers they have had, students reported that they liked clear teachers more and believed that they learned more from clear teachers (and their beliefs have been found to be a good indicator of the extent to which they actually have learned). Finally, of students who were taught by clear and unclear teachers, the students of clear teachers performed much better than those of unclear teachers. Regardless of how clarity has been defined and researched, the results are consistent: students of clear teachers like their teachers more and more importantly, learn more. Therefore, it is in almost every teacher's interest to teach as clearly as possible. This chapter synthesizes the various avenues of clarity research by identifying important components of clear teaching and provides suggestions for ways in which teachers can teach with greater clarity.

Components of Clear Teaching

Clear teaching involves a number of aspects. Though teacher immediacy and content relevance are not considered part of clear teaching, it is necessary to mention their importance. Immediate teaching sets a positive tone in the classroom and helps gain students' attention, and students are more likely to attend to relevant information. Without students' attention, even very clear teaching is likely to be ignored or "missed" by students who are attending to other things. Therefore, it is important to be complete and not just focus solely on immediacy or relevance or clarity and assume that good teaching involves only one of the three.

Because research on clear teaching has been conducted by a number of research teams in the fields of communication and educational psychology, several separate yet important aspects of clarity have been identified. They can be grouped into two general categories: verbal clarity and structural clarity. Verbal clarity involves being a fluent speaker (few "ums" and "uhs" as vocalized pauses), explaining concepts clearly, and using examples that help clarify and are not confusing. Structural clarity involves good organization and staying "on task" (not losing students by getting off the topic), the use of previews, reviews, and transitions, and sometimes blank outlines which are given to students to guide their notetaking (skeletal outlines).

Verbal Clarity

Fluency.   The aspects of verbal clarity listed above make sense, but they also look deceptively simple. It can be quite difficult for a teacher to concentrate on all of these at once. Just being fluent can be difficult at times. While trying to use clear examples and explain complex concepts, a teacher may notice that some students have a confused look on their faces and realize that the explanation is not working. In the process of trying to think of a better explanation (while facing a group of students who are confused), it can be difficult to remain fluent and not stammer and sound something like "what I mean to say is . . . uh, nevermind, um, ah, a better way to um look at this ah is to kind of sort of think of this as. . . ." It would be unrealistic to expect teachers to be completely fluent and never sound like this at times. However, to a group of students who are already confused and trying hard to understand the teacher, phrases like this can become frustrating if they persist throughout the entire class period. To curb a bad habit of stammering, having vocalized pauses, and false starts, teachers should learn to be comfortable with silence. Specifically, teachers should practice pausing until they have a clear idea of what they want to say or try to pause in the middle of sentences rather than filling that space with "um" and "uh." Again, this sounds easy but can be difficult when facing a class full of students who expect the teacher to be saying something reasonably intelligent. To improve, teachers should work on silence when they are comfortable by adding pauses in sentences and pausing longer between thoughts. Though complete fluency should not be expected, improved fluency is likely to enable teachers to teach more clearly.

Explanations and Examples.   In addition to fluency, the use of examples to explain concepts also is an important aspect of verbal clarity. For guidance on how to approach explanations and examples one need look no further than the second chapter in this volume. Teachers wishing to explain concepts effectively first should consider their students' schemas for the material. In other words, when explaining something teachers should remember their students' experiences, existing knowledge of the topic, and in general, their points of view. Teachers who consider these things are in a much better position to explain and provide examples than those who are unaware of their students' perspectives. Doing this enables teachers to approach the topic at the appropriate level and not talk "above" or "below" their students. It also is important for teachers to take this approach so that they use the appropriate language when explaining concepts to their students and avoid using terminology that is too advanced or that students have not yet encountered. For example, it would have been a mistake to discuss schemas in this chapter if the concept of schema had not been explained earlier in this chapter or in previous chapters. In one sense, it is a simple point, but students typically can provide abundant examples of teachers whose explanations were poor due to confusing terminology or to a failure to understand students' points of view. Therefore, teachers should attempt to explain concepts in "students' language" or from a student perspective to ensure that students will find the explanations clear and be able to integrate them into their schemas.

Given that this is a chapter on clarity, it should be recognized that the above discussion of "students' language" is somewhat abstract and possibly unclear. The problem is that it is missing clear, concrete, and relevant examples of "students' language." One familiar example of the importance of considering the "student's language" involves the typical trip to the physician. When offering diagnoses, physicians are in a position similar to that of teachers: They are experts on a subject that they are trying to explain to nonexperts. When speaking to other physicians or nurses, doctors can be free to use terminology like gastrointestinal disorder because their listeners are likely to have a schema for that terminology. However, because most patients do not have a schema involving that terminology, they would not understand a physician's explanation that they are suffering from a gastrointestinal disorder. However, if the physician explains the diagnosis in the "student's language" by explaining that the patient has a stomach virus or stomach flu, the patient is much more likely to understand the physician. Just like physicians, teachers must be responsive to their students' points of view when explaining concepts.

In addition to providing a more concrete explanation of the concept of "students' language," the above example demonstrates the importance of using examples to strengthen one's explanation of a concept. It is a useful example for a number of reasons. First, it is concrete rather than abstract in that it discusses something tangible that people actually do (visiting a physician). Second, it is relevant to the audience's experiences in that most people can relate to the experience of receiving both clear and confusing information from physicians. Third, it improves the explanation by demonstrating the tangible benefits of taking a listener-centered approach. In other words, it helps the teacher make the point that the teacher is trying to make. An explanation that once was a bit too abstract now has been strengthened with a clear example.

Teachers should realize that they have different types of examples at their disposal (McCroskey, 1997). They can compare two things using an analogy, just as the roles of physicians and teachers were compared above. Teachers also may create hypothetical examples to have their students imagine certain situations and envision how they would handle those situations. A hypothetical example to illustrate the concept of recognizing the listener's perspective might begin "imagine you're trying to give directions to someone who is completely unfamiliar with the area." Teachers also may use factual examples to make a point. This approach often can be effective because it enables students to see an actual application of a concept. Teachers also should consider the value of using stories or narratives as examples. Students tend to enjoy stories and they often can help teachers make their point more clearly than other types of examples. In the past when I have taught public speaking, my students responded much more to my story about "drawing a blank" and forgetting my speech as I was trying to begin it than they did to my comments about the importance of being prepared. The personal story made a much more vivid example and my point was made stronger because of it.

A final type of example, which strays somewhat from the verbal clarity category, is the in-class activity. Though activities may not be considered a traditional type of example, they can be used with great success to explain and clarify concepts. When teaching units like ethics, activities which pit classmates against each other and force students to make ethically-based choices might help a teacher make his point much more than a class discussion. In public speaking classes, students often fail to use transitions to link two main points to each other. Compared to simply discussing transitions and their importance, an activity in which each student must create transitions to link two totally unrelated topics (e.g., baseball and computers) would be a much more vivid and memorable way for students to learn about transitions. Teachers should keep in mind the value of conducting in-class activities. In addition to gaining a clearer understanding of a topic through activities, students tend to enjoy activities and are likely to appreciate the variety as well as the break from the lecture or discussion.

The importance of the verbal component of clarity is evident. To learn effectively, students need teachers who speak clearly and who can explain concepts clearly. However, it is important for teachers to understand the ways in which structural clarity is just as important for student success. Each of the elements of structural clarity is concerned with presenting class content in a clearly organized and ordered manner.

Structural Clarity

Previews.   Elements of structural clarity include previews, reviews, transitions, organization, and the use of visual aids or skeletal outlines. Each of the elements of structural clarity involves the attempt to enable students to develop a clear schema for course material. Teachers begin courses with a clear schema for the material and much of their job is devoted to enabling students to build their own schemas for the material. As each class period begins, teachers should preview that day's material with what researchers have called an advance organizer (Ausubel, 1963). An advance organizer is when the teacher identifies the day's major topic and two or three of the main points that will be discussed. If the lesson was on structural clarity, the day might begin like "today we are going to discuss structural clarity, which involves (1) previews, (2) reviews, (3) transitions, (4) organization, and (5) skeletal outlines," much like this paragraph began. Previews like this are important because they help students focus on the material that will be covered in addition to giving them the framework of the topic. As opposed to just starting to talk about previews, taking the time to provide an advance organizer helps students activate the relevant part of their schemas so that they are ready follow the lecture. Without the preview, students may be confused and wonder "where is this coming from?"

Organization.   Once the preview has been completed, it is important that the lecture is organized in a reasonable way and that there are only a few main points. At this point students are trying to develop their schema, so they will benefit from an organized class session. Rather than trying to cover a large number of main points, teachers should cover relatively few (three to five). At first, it may seem that too little is being covered. However, when time is made for previews, reviews, discussions, activities, and other participation, teachers will realize that their class sessions will be more successful if they try to teach just a few concepts very well rather than merely addressing a large number of concepts. Students will be more likely to develop strong schema for the material if they are allowed to focus on just a few main points but are able to elaborate greatly on those points.

Once teachers have organized their material, they should be sure that they follow it with relatively few tangents. In other words, teachers should stay on task. This is not to say that all tangents are bad. Students may find somewhat off-topic stories interesting and being flexible will help keep the class session spontaneous and lively. However, students will get confused and possibly frustrated if teachers frequently stray too far off the topic. If done more than occasionally, these tangents will inhibit students from clearly forming a schema for the material in their mind.

Transitions.   Even when teachers do stay on task, it is important that teachers develop transitions between their main points. Teachers should remember that they have an advantage in that they already have a schema for the material. They know how all of the topics or ideas are linked and as they are discussing a main point, they know how it links to the next point. However, students are not able to see all of these connections and may quickly become lost if teachers do not make these connections clear. Had there been no previews and transitions in this chapter, the change in focus from verbal clarity to structural clarity would have been abrupt and confusing. The previews and transitions were necessary to help readers visualize the connections between the different types of clarity. Teachers should remember the value of transitions when preparing their classes and be sure to make connections between points clear to their students.

Reviews.   At this point, the importance of providing previews, good organization, and transitions has been discussed. However, one more ingredient is needed for teachers to clarify their class sessions even further—reviews. Reviews are useful because they give students a second chance to solidify their schema for the new material they are encountering. They give students a chance to pause and examine the way in which the topic is organized. They also can enable the student to identify areas of confusion and ask for clarification. Finally, reviews are repetitious. If material has been previewed, discussed, and reviewed, students have at least three chances to remember it. Additionally, because of primacy and recency effects (discussed in Chapter 2), students tend to remember information that is presented first and last, which is an argument both for previews and reviews.

The beginning of the previous paragraph is an example of a review. It is useful because it synthesizes a small number of main points while "setting the stage" for the next main point. Teachers should utilize reviews at lease two different times: the beginning of a class session and the end of a class session (they also may wish to review after complex main points). Before previewing the day's session, it is important to review that which had been covered on the previous few days. Doing this helps focus students' attention and ready them for new material that will be covered. Teachers may wish to use this review period to gain feedback on the extent to which the previous material was taught clearly. Rather than saying "yesterday we talked about . . ." a teacher might gain feedback by asking "what three main things did we talk about yesterday . . . " and then ask students to explain each of the points and subtopics. By doing this, the teacher can gain an idea of areas in which students may be struggling.

In addition to reviewing at the beginning of class, teachers should review at the end of class. This helps provide closure to the class session and helps students see the progress that they have made. Again, teachers may review using questions to gain feedback about which aspects of the class were clear and which were unclear. Keeping in mind that the goal of the session is for students to develop their schemas for the material, teachers may review by having students draw and compare concept maps for the unit. Concept maps involve the use of pictures and shapes to represent a large amount of information in an organized manner. They can be useful because they essentially are a visual schema drawn by the students themselves (for more on concept maps, see Rose & Nicholl, 1997).

Although end-of-class reviews are a useful teaching tool, teachers should be aware of the difficulty of reviewing at the end of the class. As soon as they begin reviewing and students sense that there is no more "new" material, they will begin to "pack up" and prepare to leave class (and expect to do so very soon!). Because this can be distracting, teachers might just end class there. However, doing this essentially rewards students ("all we have to do is begin packing and the teacher will let us go"). The key to keeping students focused on the class is to give them a reason to focus. Teachers should highlight important information and keep students attention, possibly by asking questions or requiring other types of participation. Regardless of the specific tactic, teachers should be sure that students know that class will not end until they have participated in the review process. (Hint: If students consider the end of class a reward, then reward good behavior like their attention or participation in review by ending class after they have participated rather than rewarding their "packing up" behavior by ending right after they have packed up. The key is to end class right after the desirable behavior and not the undesirable behavior. It will not work overnight, but it will after a few class periods!)

It should be evident by now that teachers must devote a good amount of effort in order to be structurally clear in their teaching. They must review the previous few days, preview the current day, have an appropriate number of main points and link them clearly with solid transitions, and then successfully review the day's session. If teachers consistently do this, their students will benefit greatly. Students will be able to reliably develop their schema for the material and develop a clear understanding of the topic. Because of the small number of main points and all of the repetition, students will be more likely to remember the material. As an added bonus, they probably will appreciate your ability to present material clearly!

Skeletal Outlines. In addition to the things teachers can do to increase structural clarity during a class session, teachers also may find it useful to provide their students with skeletal outlines of each unit. A skeletal outline has each important point on it as well as subpoints, all of which are followed by space in which the students can place their notes. Kenneth Kiewra, an educational researcher, has devoted much time to the study of skeletal outlines and their instructional benefits. Skeletal outlines can facilitate clarity for a number of reasons. First, all of the important points are on the page, so students are not likely to miss something important. Second, the points are organized as the teacher intends them to be organized, so errors in interpretation are less likely. In other words, each student's notes will have the same organizational pattern, while their notes probably would vary considerably without a skeletal outline. Third, for students who are trying to develop their schema for new material, skeletal outlines function as a "head start" by providing a solid framework into which information can be integrated. It is important to note that skeletal notes might not be best for all instructional situations. Some students may find them confining, and others may become too dependent on them and have difficulty taking notes without them. Also, if they are not used carefully, skeletal outlines may lead teachers to just cover information point by point and not exhibit variety, conduct activities, and explore some points in greater detail. Still, given all of their advantages, skeletal notes are worth considering.

Visual Aids.   In order to enhance structural clarity, teachers also should consider using some type of visual aid to present important points. This is not the forum to debate whether PowerPoint is a better visual aid than traditional overheads or the very traditional blackboard. Instead, the advantages shared by each of the three are worth noting. They enable teachers to make previews, reviews, and organizational patterns very clear. As the class session progresses, teachers can point to important ideas, or to the next topic, so that students know the precise information on which they should be focusing. The use of a visual aid also means that students will be getting their information both audibly and visually, which helps increase their chances of clearly receiving the information. Regardless of the type of aid used, teachers should strongly consider using a visual aid to help their students, especially those who learn more visually than through hearing.

Fluency, explaining, examples, activities, previews, reviews, organization, staying on task, transitions, visual aids or skeletal outlines—it is evident that being clear demands great effort from teachers. Some teachers may believe that simply going in the classroom and "getting through" the material is good enough. However, based on the way students attend to and process messages, much more is needed to effectively assure that students clearly receive our messages. Adding reviews, previews, transitions, and visual aids may seem like repetition, overkill, or a waste of time, but each serves an important function to enable students to learn and should be considered important by teachers.

It is worth noting that there may be classes, topics, or units for which clarity is not desirable. Ambiguity may be preferred for advanced students, or for assignments or classes that require greater flexibility or creativity. In these situations, too much clarity may restrict students' options or act as a crutch that narrows their thinking. These types of situations notwithstanding, teachers should recognize the value of clarity as a key component of effective teaching. With this in mind, the following section outlines a number of things teachers can do to improve the clarity of their teaching.

Preparing to Teach Clearly

Think immediacy. Though immediacy is not an actual aspect of clarity, it should be considered almost a necessary precursor to clear teaching. It functions to gain students' attention and in general helps create a positive atmosphere in the classroom. While immediacy alone is not enough to guarantee effective teaching, it is an important factor that should not be overlooked.

Make content relevant. One of the few times all students visibly are paying attention is when teachers say "this is on the test." When students know that content is relevant to their needs or interests, they will take notice. Like immediacy, relevance is not a part of clarity but should be considered almost a necessary precursor. One way to make content relevant is to begin each class session with an example, story, activity, and so on, that will make students want to learn more about the subject.

Consider students' prior knowledge. What are their backgrounds and experiences? What do they already know about the subject and what do they need to know? To borrow from a well-known phrase, teachers should "put themselves in their students shoes" when preparing a class session and consider how their messages will be received by students. Doing this will help teachers be more effective when completing the following steps.

Organize the session carefully. Try to limit each session to three to five main points so that it has focus. Try arranging the material in different ways and consider which way makes the most sense, is the most interesting, and is most clear. Be sure to consider possible transitions that will lead students from one point to the next.

Develop explanations. Once the session is organized, examine the material before class for things that may be difficult to explain or that students may find unclear or difficult to understand. This approach is better than tentatively trying to develop explanations in class with a group of expectant and possibly confused students watching and waiting. Explanations will be more fluent if they are developed ahead of time.

Develop examples. In addition to developing explanations, this is a good time to develop two to three examples of any important concepts that will be taught. While one example might be enough, additional examples will increase the likelihood that students will understand the material clearly. Remember the value of using in-class activities as additional examples.

Review. When in class, review the previous class session or two. The repetition is good for students' memory and it helps focus students' attention and schemas on the class material. It also indicates the progress they have made in the class. Remember that the review can be made more interactive by asking students questions about what was discussed previously.

Preview. After reviewing previous classes, preview the current session. This will help students "pick up" where they "left off" on the previous session.

Teach with variety. Remember to do more than just lecture. Questions, discussions, and activities often can help students gain a clearer understanding of the material than lecturing alone. Be mindful of the 20-minute rule of thumb from

Chapter 2 and remember that after encountering a certain amount of lecturing, students' attention is likely to fade.

Clarify visually. Material can be made even more clear through the use of the board, PowerPoint, overheads, or skeletal outlines.

Review again. At the end of class, review the main points. This helps clarify the main points and the repetition is good for students' memory. Remember to use questions or make the review important to students by requiring their participation in some way so that they don't spend this time putting their books away in preparation to leave the class.

Ask students for feedback. After a few weeks, ask the students to anonymously evaluate your teaching. This allows you to get feedback on any specific aspect of your teaching. Students probably will be pleasantly surprised that their teacher wants their input.

View quizzes and tests in a new way. Though everyone recognizes quizzes and tests as evaluations of student work, teachers also can use them as feedback on their teaching. Examine quizzes and tests for questions that most or all students missed. When most students are missing a question, the problem may be that it was a poor question, but it could mean that they never understood the material clearly in the first place. This may be important feedback that the material needs to be taught differently next time.

Given all of the elements of clarity, it is important to point out that clear teaching takes time and practice. We learn by mistakes and are bound to find ourselves in situations in which we feel unable to offer a clear explanation. However, it gets easier over time, and as it does, you will find that your time has been well spent and that your students appreciate the clarity in your teaching.

REFERENCES AND SUGGESTED READINGS

Alexander, L., Frankiewicz, R., & Williams, R. (1979). Facilitation of learning and retention of oral instruction using advance and post organizers. *Journal of Educational Psychology, 71,* 701–707.

Ausubel, D. P. (1963). *The psychology of meaningful verbal learning.* New York: Grune and Stratton.

Avtgis, T. A. (2000). *Affective learning, teacher clarity, and student motivation as a function of uncertainty reduction.* Paper presented at the annual Eastern Communication Association Conference, Pittsburgh, PA.

Bush, A., Kennedy, J., & Cruickshank, D. (1977). An empirical investigation of teacher clarity. *Journal of Teacher Education, 28,* 53–58.

Chesebro, J. L. (1999). The effects of teacher clarity and immediacy on student learning, receiver apprehension, and affect. Unpublished manuscript.

Chesebro, J. L., & McCroskey, J. C. (2001). The relationship of teacher clarity and immediacy with student state receiver apprehension, affect, and cognitive learning. *Communication Education, 50,* 59–68.

Chesebro, J. L., & McCroskey, J. C. (1998). The relationship between teacher clarity and immediacy and students' experiences of state receiver apprehension when listening to teachers. *Communication Quarterly, 46,* 446–455.

Civikly, J. M. (1992). Clarity: Teachers and students making sense of instruction. *Communication Education, 41,* 138–152.

Cruickshank, D. R., & Kennedy, J. J. (1986). Teacher clarity. *Teaching & Teacher Education, 2*(1), 43–67.

Cruickshank, D. R., Myers, B., & Moenjak, T. (1975). *Statements of clear teacher behaviors provided by 1009 students in grades 6–9.* Unpublished manuscript, The Ohio State university.

Hines, C., Cruickshank, D., & Kennedy, J. (1985). Teacher clarity and its relationship to student achievement and satisfaction. *American Educational Research Journal, 22,* 87–99.

Kallison, J. M., Jr. (1986). Effects of lesson organization on achievement. *American Educational Research Journal, 23,* 337–347.

Kendrick, W. L., & Darling, A. L. (1990). Problems of understanding in classrooms: Students' use of clarifying tactics. *Communication Education, 39,* 15–29.

Kennedy, J., Cruickshank, D., Bush, A., & Myers, B. (1978). Additional investigations into the nature of teacher clarity. *Journal of Educational Research, 72,* 3–10.

Kiewra, K. A. (1985). Investigating notetaking and review: A depth of processing alternative. *Educational psychologist, 20,* 23–32.

Kiewra, K. A., Benton, S. L., Christensen, M., Kim, S., & Risch, N. (1989). *The effects of notetaking format and study technique on performance.* Paper presented at the annual meeting of the American Educational Research Association, San Francisco, CA.

Kiewra, K. A., Dubois, N. F., Christian, D., & McShane, A. (1988). Providing study notes: A comparison of three types of notes for review. *Journal of Educational Psychology, 80,* 595–597.

Kiewra, K. A., Dubois, N. F., Christian, D., McShane, A., Meyerhoffer, M., & Roskelley, D. (1991). Note-taking functions and techniques. *Journal of Educational Psychology, 83,* 240–245.

Land, M. (1979). Low-inference variables and teacher clarity: Effects on student concept learning. *Journal of Educational Psychology, 71,* 795–799.

Land, M., & Smith, L. (1979). The effect of low inference teacher clarity inhibitors on student achievement. *Journal of Teacher Education, 31,* 55–57.

McCroskey, J. C. (1997). *An introduction to rhetorical communication* (7th ed.). Boston: Allyn & Bacon.

Powell, R. G., & Harville, B. (1990). The effects of teacher immediacy and clarity on instructional outcomes: An intercultural assessment. *Communication Education, 39,* 369–379.

Rose, C., & Nicholl, M. J. (1997). *Accelerated learning for the 21st century.* New York: Dell Publishing.

Rosenshine, B., & Furst, N. (1971). Research on teacher performance criteria. In B. O. Smith (Ed.). *Research in teacher education* (pp. 37–72). Englewood Cliffs, NJ: Prentice-Hall.

Sidelinger, R. J., & McCroskey, J. C. (1997). Communication correlates of teacher clarity in the college classroom. *Communication Research Reports, 14,* 1–10.

Simonds, C. J. (1997). Classroom understanding: An expanded notion of teacher clarity. *Communication Research Reports, 14,* 279–290.

Smith, D. G. (1977). College classroom interactions and critical thinking. *Journal of Educational Psychology, 69,* 180–190.

Smith, L., & Cotten, M. (1980). Effect of lesson vagueness and discontinuity on student achievement and attitudes. *Journal of Educational Psychology, 72,* 670–675.

Smith, L., & Land, M. (1981). Low-inference verbal behaviors related to teacher clarity. *Journal of Classroom Interaction, 17,* 37–42.

9 Socio-Communicative Style and Orientation in Instruction

Giving Good Communication and Receiving Good Communication

VIRGINIA P. RICHMOND
West Virginia University

In school systems throughout the nation, the call has been for·effective and communicatively competent educators. When we refer to someone as "communicatively competent," we are suggesting that the person has "adequate ability to make ideas known to others by talking or writing" (McCroskey, 1984, p. 263). This is communication competence at its most basic level. It ignores feelings, attitudes, and behavior—focusing simply on being understood.

Basic communication competence depends on at least three elements: (1) a cognitive understanding of the communication process, (2) the psychomotor capacity to produce necessary communication behaviors, and (3) a positive affective orientation toward communication. In order to achieve basic communication competence, you must develop an understanding of what you need to do, develop the physical behaviors required to do it (learn to write, articulate words, and so forth), and want to do it.

Unfortunately, basic communication competence is not enough. Many educators do not simply want to be understood by students. We also want our students to like us, we want to build relationships with them, and frequently we want to influence them. In short, we want to be *instructionally* and *interpersonally* communicatively competent. Interpersonal communication competence rests on a foundation of general communication competence. In addition, the instructionally–interpersonally competent communicator exhibits competent communication styles.

Instructors exhibit trait differences in their basic communication styles. These communication styles have been examined under such labels as communicator style (Norton, 1983), personal style (Merrill & Reid, 1981), social style (Lashbrook, 1974), and *psychological androgyny* (Bem, 1974; Wheeless & Dierks-Stewart, 1981). These various approaches to communication style are rooted in Jungian psychology. This work has its best-known manifestation in the Myers-Briggs personality inventory. All of these approaches are based on the assumption that trait differences in communication behavior are produced by an individual's temperament of personality.

Components of SCO and SCS

"Communicating effectively with different people on different topics and at different times requires flexible communication behaviors" (Richmond & McCroskey, 1992, p. 86). The constructs of socio-communicative style (SCS) and socio-communicative orientations (SCO) are based on these earlier research programs (Cole & McCroskey, 2000; Richmond & McCroskey, 1990; Thomas, et al., 1994). See Boxes 9.1 and 9.2 for measures. The two constructs are essentially the same. However, SCS is the perception others have of that individual—presumably based on her or his regular communication behavior patterns (e.g., students' perception of a teacher). SCO, on the other hand, represents the way one perceives oneself. It is that person's image of his or her own trait behavior pattern (e.g., teacher's perception of her or his socio-communicative orientation. The SCS and SCO need not be highly correlated, because individual teachers may not be particularly perceptive of their own behaviors, and/or may behave quite differently with different students. Because both sources and receivers make many decisions based on their perceptions of themselves and others with whom they communicate, both SCO and SCS are seen as very important for understanding communication behavior whether it is in the classroom, in the organization, or in individual dyads (McCroskey & Richmond, 2000; Richmond & McCroskey, 2000; Wanzer & McCroskey, 1998). The communication style-based approaches typically identify two or three dimensions of an individual's style that are assumed to produce different communication behaviors. The two primary dimensions commonly are labeled *assertiveness* (called *masculinity* by Bem) and *responsiveness* (called *femininity* by Bem) and are presumed to represent the core elements in style. The third dimension usually is called *versatility* or *flexibility* and represents the degree to which the teacher is capable of adapting her or his style to varying situational constraints.

Assertiveness. When people stand up for themselves and do not let others take advantage of them, without taking advantage of others themselves, they are acting assertively. It is also acting assertively to speak up for oneself, whether that is making a request or expressing a feeling. Assertive communicators are also able to initiate, maintain, and terminate conversations, according to their interpersonal goals (McCroskey & Richmond, 1996, 2000; Richmond & McCroskey, 2001). Assertive communicators talk faster and louder, use more gestures, make more eye contact, and lean forward more in interactions. Assertiveness focuses on the

BOX 9.1   **Socio-Communicative Style**

The questionnaire below lists 20 personality characteristics. Please indicate the degree to which you believe each of these characteristics applies to your _____ (e.g., primary mentor) by marking whether you (5) strongly agree that it applies, (4) agree that it applies, (3) are undecided, (2) disagree that it applies, or (1) strongly disagree that it applies. There are no right or wrong answers. Work quickly; record your first impression.

____ **1.** Helpful

____ **2.** Defends own beliefs

____ **3.** Independent

____ **4.** Responsive to others

____ **5.** Forceful

____ **6.** Has strong personality

____ **7.** Sympathetic

____ **8.** Compassionate

____ **9.** Assertive

____ **10.** Sensitive to the needs of others

____ **11.** Dominant

____ **12.** Sincere

____ **13.** Gentle

____ **14.** Willing to take a stand

____ **15.** Warm

____ **16.** Tender

____ **17.** Friendly

____ **18.** Acts as a leader

____ **19.** Aggressive

____ **20.** Competitive

Items 2, 3, 5, 6, 9, 11, 14, 18, 19, and 20 measure assertiveness. Add the scores on these items to get your assertiveness score. Items 1, 4, 7, 8, 10, 12, 13, 15, 16, and 17 measure responsiveness. Add the scores on these items to get your responsiveness score.

task dimension of relationships (Wheeless & Lashbrook, 1987). Many of these assertive behaviors are considered to be masculine behaviors (Bem, 1974), but this does mean that these behaviors are limited only to men. Both men and women can display assertive behaviors.

Assertiveness is one of several aggression traits identified by Infante (1988), who early on argued that "Aggressiveness occurs in physical or symbolic forms

BOX **9.2** **Socio-Communicative Orientation**

The questionnaire below lists 20 personality characteristics. Please indicate the degree to which you believe each of these characteristics applies to YOU, as you normally communicate with others, by marking whether you (5) strongly agree that it applies, (4) agree that it applies, (3) are undecided, (2) disagree that it applies, or (1) strongly disagree that it applies. There are no right or wrong answers. Work quickly; record your first impression.

____ 1. Helpful

____ 2. Defends own beliefs

____ 3. Independent

____ 4. Responsive to others

____ 5. Forceful

____ 6. Has strong personality

____ 7. Sympathetic

____ 8. Compassionate

____ 9. Assertive

____ 10. Sensitive to the needs of others

____ 11. Dominant

____ 12. Sincere

____ 13. Gentle

____ 14. Willing to take a stand

____ 15. Warm

____ 16. Tender

____ 17. Friendly

____ 18. Acts as a leader

____ 19. Aggressive

____ 20. Competitive

Items 2, 3, 5, 6, 9, 11, 14, 18, 19, and 20 measure assertiveness. Add the scores on these items to get your assertiveness score. Items 1, 4, 7, 8, 10, 12, 13, 15, 16, and 17 measure responsiveness. Add the scores on these items to get your responsiveness score.

which are either constructive or destructive. Constructive elements produce satisfaction and improve the interpersonal relationship while destructive forms produce dissatisfaction and deteriorates the relationship" (p. 6). Infante points out that "the constructive facets are assertiveness and argumentativeness . . . and the destructive facets of the aggressive dimension of personality are hostility and verbal aggression" (p. 7). Infante points out that behaviors of an aggressive personality are: verbal or nonverbal hostility, irritability, negativism, resentment, and suspicion. Additionally, Infante points out verbally aggressive messages attack the self-concept of another person, include negative statements about the other person, and reveal the source's extremely high need to control or "put the other person" in her or his place. He concludes by stating that, "All verbal aggression is hostile, but not all hostility involves attacking the self-concepts of other people" (p. 7). More recently, Rancer (1998) and Wigley III (1998) have continued to confirm Infante's early research.

McCroskey and Richmond (1996) argued that aggressiveness could be considered as "assertiveness plus." In other words, the aggressive person acts similarly to the assertive person in that both will speak up to demand what is rightfully theirs, but the aggressive person will attempt to be successful, many times forcing others to yield their own rights. The assertive person does not hinder others' chances of being successful, whereas the aggressive person has a "win-at-all-costs" orientation. Another distinction is that the assertive person makes requests while the aggressive person makes demands. Although either assertive or aggressive behavior can lead to goal achievement, assertive behavior is more likely to lead to long-term effectiveness while maintaining good relationships with others. Aggressive people might win in the short term, but they probably burn a few bridges along the way (McCroskey & Richmond, 1996; Richmond & Martin, 1998; Richmond & McCroskey, 2001).

Responsiveness. Responsiveness involves being other-oriented, in other words, the responsive person is sensitive to others. The responsive individual considers others' feelings, listens to what others have to say, and recognizes the needs of others (McCroskey & Richmond, 1996). Words that are commonly used to describe the responsive communicator include *friendly, compassionate, warm, sincere,* and *helpful.* The responsive communicator is able to be empathic and immediate when interacting with others. Responsive communicators speak with greater inflection, use open body gestures, and show animated facial expressions. Responsiveness focuses on the relational dimension of relationships. Many of these responsive behaviors are considered to be feminine (Bem, 1974). This does not imply that only women can be responsive. Just like there are men and women who are assertive, there are men and women who are responsive.

Being responsive does not mean that a person always complies with the wishes and demands of others. There is an important difference between being submissive and being responsive. Submissive people yield their rights to others, even when yielding their rights goes against their own goals or needs. Submissive communicators sacrifice their own goals in order to benefit others. On the other hand, although the responsive communicator is considerate of others' needs, the responsive communicator also pays attention to her or his own goals. Responsive people recognize and consider other people's needs and rights, but do this without sacrificing their own legitimate rights. McCroskey and Richmond (1996) noted that being submissive or responsive will probably produce short-term liking from another person, however, responsive communicators are able to maintain liking in a relationship and still reach their own interpersonal goals.

Submissive persons will rarely reach their goals because they spend much of their time meeting the goals of other people. Submissive persons will "give in" to more dominant personalities.

Versatility. Because communication takes place in a given context, it is difficult, if not impossible, to identify communication behaviors that are appropriate and effective in all situations. Thus, the third dimension of SCO is versatility (McCroskey & Richmond, 1996; Richmond & McCroskey 2001). Other terms that are used for versatility include *adjustability, accommodating, adaptability* and *flexibility* (e.g., Oprah Winfrey, Maya Angelou). Words that demonstrate a lack of versatility include *rigid, bossy, arrogant, domineering, harsh, inflexible, dogmatic, intolerant, imperious, uncompromising, unyielding,* and *often abusive of other persons* (e.g., Bobby Knight, Judge Judy). The importance of versatility is that in addition to being assertive and responsive, individuals must be versatile. Therefore, people such as educators need to know when to be assertive and when to be responsive. Similarly, teachers need to also know when not to be assertive and when not to be responsive. The idea behind versatility is that people such as educators and supervisors need to be able to adapt their behavior within a situation and from one communication context (teaching a large lecture class) to another communication context (advisement of students).

Categories of SCO/SCS and Styles

Because SCO and SCS are based in part on the work of Merrill and Reid (1981), it is useful to examine the way they interpret various combinations of scores on measures of assertiveness and responsiveness. Merrill and Reid indicated that social style is a collection of observable communication behaviors that impact one's effectiveness in interpersonal and organizational relationships. They argued that people are creatures of habit and by identifying their own and others' social style, people could have more beneficial and satisfying relationships. Depending on whether people are high or low in assertiveness and high or low in responsiveness, Merrill and Reid would classify these persons into one of four categories: *amiable, analytical, driver,* and *expressive.*

Amiables (who also often are labeled as "submissive") are considered relationship specialists and are high on responsiveness and low on assertiveness. Merrill and Reid (1981) stated that amiables seem "to be most comfortable working in environments where they can provide services and be supportive and helpful in their relationships with others" (p. 149). We will often find these people in "careers such as teaching, personnel management, social work, psychology, and other helping professions" (p. 149). The terms used to describe the amiables are as follows: supportive, respectful, willing to help, accommodating, willing to listen, dependable, agreeable, conforming, dependent and pliable.

Although amiables are likely to be found in professions such as teaching that is not to say that all, or even most, people in a given profession will be of a single socio-communicative style. For example, the special education or kindergarten teacher is likely to be amiable. The college professor heavily involved in laboratory research is more likely to be analytical. The teacher who becomes principal and has to be "in charge" of running the school may be more of a driver. The drama teacher or cheerleading coach might be an expressive. You can find the various styles in all walks of life, but some professions are likely to attract higher numbers of certain social styles than others.

Drivers (who often are referred to as "aggressive") are low in responsiveness but high in assertiveness. The drivers are considered to be control specialists. The terms used to describe drivers are as follows: *strong-willed, independent, practical, decisive, efficient, pushy, high risk takers, severe, harsh, tough,* and *dominating.* Merrill and Reid (1981) stated that "drivers know what they want and they do whatever it takes in order to accomplish their given goals." These individuals are action-oriented and are not very patient. Drivers initiate action, are power driven, and are often very independent thinkers. These people might be in careers such as small business owners, top management, production managers, administrative personnel, politics, and other decision-making management positions. "Because of their ability to take responsibility and direct others, top management often puts these individuals into positions of control" (pp. 149–150). Again, there can be drivers in many other professions. The ones listed are only indicators of where drivers are most likely to be found.

The analyticals (who often are referred to as "noncompetent") are considered technical specialists and are low in responsiveness and low in assertiveness. The terms used to describe the analyticals are as follows: *critical, indecisive, stuffy, picky, cold, aloof, industrious, persistent, serious, exacting, orderly,* and perhaps even *unenthusiastic.* Merrill and Reid (1981) noted that analytically driven people have a "show me" attitude; these people often do not make decisions based on personal relationships, but instead make decisions on evidence and experience. Although analyticals might be slow in making a decision or in being persuaded, once a decision is made, analyticals tend to stand by it because the decision was arrived at in a rational manner. Merrill and Reid suggest that professions such as science, engineering, construction work, accounting, computer tech, and certain aspects of the law often have a high proportion of this style. Again, there could be other styles in these professions. Some research suggests that analyticals are more likely to be apprehensive about communication and, as a result, be more withdrawn and quiet. Thus, analyticals may be less effective communicators than those with the other styles and more resistant to attempts to interact with them.

Expressives (who also often are labeled as "competent") are considered social specialists and are high in responsiveness and high in assertiveness. "Persons with expressive behavior are often found in sales, entertainment, advertising, art, music, and writing" (Merrill & Reid, p. 150). Richmond and McCroskey (2001) believe that many educators at all levels and in all disciplines need to have some expressive tendencies in their nature in order to be more instructionally–interpersonally competent communicators. Merrill and Reid (1981) suggested that expressive individuals value relationships, but at the same time, are very goals-focused, and many times may use their relationships in order to attain personal goals. Like drivers, expressive are very action-oriented. The terms used to refer to expressives are as follows: *enthusiastic, friendly, ambitious, stimulating, manipulative, excitable, dramatic, creative, imaginative, future-oriented, adaptable, status-oriented,* and somewhat *undisciplined.* Expressives do not have high needs for regularity in their routines and are quite flexible in their behaviors.

SCO and Other Communication Variables

Investigating the relation between various communication variables provides additional validity for the constructs (or identifies weaknesses in the constructs) and allows for studying how communication variables often interact with one another to achieve various relational outcomes. Several studies have used the SCO measure to study how communicator style is related to other communication variables. Some of these studies are briefly reported here.

In looking at students' perceptions of their teachers, Thomas et al. (1994) found that teacher immediacy was positively related to assertiveness and responsiveness. Although immediacy and the two other variables were moderately correlated, the correlation between assertiveness and responsiveness was not significant. This is meaningful, according to Thomas et al., because others had proposed that immediacy was just another name for being responsive. Their results demonstrated, however, that producing perceptions of immediacy involved both assertive and responsive behaviors. Thomas et al. alluded to the fact that teachers would also need to be versatile in order to adapt their assertive and responsive behaviors in order to be effective in the classroom.

Also looking at students' perceptions of their teachers, Wooten and McCroskey (1996) found that when students perceived their instructors as high in assertiveness and responsiveness, they had higher interpersonal trust with those instructors. This relationship was strongest with assertive students. When assertive students perceived their teachers as assertive and responsive, there was a higher level of trust between student and instructor. In this case, communicating assertively and responsively leads to a stronger relationship between the two parties.

Martin and Anderson (1996) reported on the relation between SCS with the communication traits of argumentativeness and verbal aggressiveness. In defining these two aggressive communication traits, Infante (1987) stated that argumentativeness could be considered a subset of assertiveness and that verbal aggressiveness involves a lack of responsiveness toward others. Based on how each of these constructs are defined, Martin and Anderson expected that assertive communicators would be more argumentative whereas responsive communicators would be lower in verbal aggressiveness. These hypotheses were supported; people with the competent and aggressive communicator styles were more argumentative whereas those people with the competent and submissive communicator styles were less verbally aggressive.

Several studies have considered the relation between SCO and nonverbal communication behaviors (McCroskey & Richmond, 2000; Richmond & McCroskey, 2000). Myers and Avtgis (1996) reported that people differ in their nonverbal immediacy behaviors depending on their communicator style. Competent (expressives) communicators were more nonverbally immediate; competent communicators were less tense, smiled more, and moved more than submissive and aggressive communicators. Communicator style was also found to make a difference on individuals' tendency to be touch avoidant. Martin and Anderson (1993) reported that aggressive communicators were more same-gender touch avoidant than the other types of communicators, whereas non competing communicators were more opposite-gender touch avoidant than the three other types of communicators. The results from both of these studies provide further support for the importance of possessing both assertive and responsive behaviors.

Which Style Is Best? *NONE*

Communication styles are all different and they all have positive and negative characteristics. Merrill and Reid (1981) argued that each style has value and that no one style is necessarily better than the others. In addition, one can be dominant in one of the four styles and have the tendencies of another style. For example, one might be an expressive with some driver tendencies or an analytical with some amiable tendencies. The key is that you need to recognize those with whom you are communicating and adjust your style to be compatible with orientation, particularly if you want communication to be successful. Salespersons have known for years that they have to be versatile in order to succeed.

Merrill and Reid (1981), McCroskey and Richmond (2000), and Richmond and McCroskey (2001) also pointed out the need for versatility: Individuals need to be able to change and adapt their communication styles and behaviors according to the situation. The key to much of this success is being versatile, regardless of your primary style. "Versatility is the dimension of behavior that indicates the extent to which others see us as adaptable, resourceful, and competent. It is behavior that earns their social endorsement of us because it accommodates their preferences" (Merrill & Reid, p. 44). As educators we need to know when to be assertive, when to be responsive, when to push, when to back off, when to listen to our students, and when to "put our students on hold" (e.g., the overly dominant student who tries to control the class). As educators, we have to understand that working with students who have different styles is going to be required of us, and to be successful we need to see possible conflict areas and adapt. For example, an amiable teacher might perceive the driver student as too pushy, impersonal, unfriendly, and dominating. The analytical teacher might see the expressive students as too talkative and outgoing. The driver teacher might perceive the amiable student as too easy, soft, pliable, and malleable. The expressive teacher might perceive the analytical student as too exacting, precise, critical, quiet, and very stuffy and picky about details.

The Ideal Teacher

There have been volumes written on the most desirable characteristics of communicatively competent educators. But what are the critical characteristics: competence? intelligent? talkative? outgoing? sensitive? immediate? clarity? power? affinity? Take your pick. There is research completed that indicates that any or all of the above characteristics are critical characteristics for instructionally–interpersonally communicatively competent educators.

Regardless of the communicator style or social style employed by educators, it is clear that all educators need to have two major characteristics: versatility and consistency. In other words, for students to have any chance of working with us successfully, we must be able to adapt to the needs of our students while at the same time making predictable, consistent decisions, regardless of the students involved. For example, on the versatile dimension, there is a need to realize when to be an expressive, analytical, driver, or amiable and when not to use a certain style. On the consistency dimension, as educators, we need to be predictable and consistent in our communication and decision making so students know how to communicate with us. There is nothing worse for the student or instructor than trying to communicate with a moody person or an unpredictable, inconsistent person. Richmond and McCroskey (2001) suggest that you might be reading the above statements and saying "One cannot be both versatile and consistent—it seems like an oxymoron" (p. 105). No, it isn't. As educators, we can adapt to situations and students while at the same time being firm and predictable on decisions (e.g., most course syllabi have standard guidelines that we expect all students to follow). As teachers we also have to do the same for our co-workers and employers. We need to be more versatile and predictable so students and our employers know what to expect from us and how to communicate with us in an instructionally communicatively competent style.

REFERENCES AND SUGGESTED READINGS

Anderson, C. M., & Martin, M. M. (1995). Communication motives of assertive and responsive communicators. *Communication Research Reports, 12*, 186–191.

Bem, S. L. (1974). The measurement of psychological androgyny. *Journal of Consulting and Clinical Psychology, 42*, 155–162.

Buchholz, S., Lashbrook, W. B., & Wenberg, J. R. (1976). *Toward the measurement and processing of social style.* Paper presented at the annual meeting of the International Communication Association, Portland, OR.

Chesebro, J. L. (1999). *The effects of teacher clarity and immediacy on student learning, apprehension, and affect.* Doctoral dissertation, West Virginia University, Morgantown, WV.

Christophel, D. M. (1990). The relationship among teacher immediacy behaviors, student motivation, and learning. *Communication Education, 39*, 323–340.

Cole, J. G., & McCroskey, J. C. (April, 2000). *Temperament and socio-communicative orientation.* Paper presented at the annual convention of the Eastern Communication Association, Pittsburgh, PA.

Dolin, D. (1995). *Ain't misbehavin': A study of teacher misbehaviors, related to communication behaviors, and student resistance.* Doctoral dissertation, West Virginia University, Morgantown, WV.

Frymier, A. (1992). *The impact of teacher immediacy and affinity-seeking on students' motivation and learning.* Doctoral dissertation, West Virginia University, Morgantown, WV.

Heisel, A. D. (2000). *Strategic verbal aggression: Attacking the self-concept to enhance motivation in the classroom.* Doctoral dissertation. West Virginia University, Morgantown, WV.

Infante, D. A. (1987). Aggressiveness. In J. C. McCroskey & J. A. Daly (Eds.). *Personality and interpersonal communication* (pp. 157–194). Newbury Park, CA: Sage.

Infante, D. A. (1988). *Arguing constructively.* Prospect Heights, IL: Waveland.

Kearney, P. (1984). Perceptual discrepancies in teacher communication style. *Communication, 13,* 95–105.

Kearney, P., Plax, T. G., Smith, V. R., & Sorensen, G., (1988). Effects of teacher immediacy and strategy type on college student resistance to on-task demands. *Communication Education, 37,* 54–67.

Lashbrook, W. B. (1974). *Toward the measurement and processing of the social style profile.* Eden Prairie, MN: Wilson Learning Corporation.

Martin, M. M., & Anderson, C. M. (1996). Argumentativeness and verbal aggressiveness. *Journal of Social Behavior and Personality, 11,* 547–554.

McCroskey, J. C. (1984). Communication competence: The elusive construct. In R. N. Bostrom (Ed.). *Competence in communication.* Beverly Hills: Sage.

McCroskey, J. C. (2001). *An introduction to rhetorical communication* (8th ed.). Boston: Allyn and Bacon.

McCroskey, J. C., & Richmond, V. P. (1996). *Fundamentals of human communication: An interpersonal perspective.* Prospect Heights, IL: Waveland Press.

McCroskey, J. C., & Richmond, V. P. (2000). Applying reciprocity and accommodation theories to supervisor/subordinate communication. *Journal of Applied Communication Research, 28(3),* 278–289.

Merrill, D. W., & Reid, R. H. (1981). *Personal styles & effective performance.* Radnor, PA: Chilton.

Mottet, T. P. (1998). *Interactive television instructors' perceptions of students' nonverbal responsiveness and effects on distance teaching.* Doctoral dissertation. West Virginia University, Morgantown, WV.

Myers, S. A., & Avtgis, T. (1996). *The impact of socio-communicative style and relational context on perceptions of nonverbal immediacy.* Unpublished manuscript, Kent State University, OH.

Norton, R. (1983). *Commentator style: Theory, applications, and measures.* Beverly Hills, CA: Sage.

Rancer, A. S. (1998). Argumentativeness. In J. C. McCroskey, J. A. Daly, M. M. Martin, & M. J. Beatty (Eds.). *Communication and personality: Trait perspectives* (pp. 149–170). Cresskill, NJ: Hampton Press.

Richmond, V. P. (1990). Communication in the classroom: Power and motivation. *Communication Education, 39,* 181–195.

Richmond, V. P., & Martin, M. M. (1998). Socio-communicative style and socio-communicative orientation. In J. C. McCroskey, J. A. Daly, M. M. Martin, & M. J. Beatty (Eds.). *Communication and personality: Trait perspectives* (pp. 133–148). Cresskill, NJ: Hampton Press.

Richmond, V. P., & McCroskey, J. C. (1990). Reliability and separation of factors on the assertiveness-responsiveness measure. *Psychological Reports, 67,* 449–450.

Richmond, V. P., & McCroskey, J. C. (1998). *Communication: Apprehension, avoidance and effectiveness* (5th ed.). Boston: Allyn and Bacon.

Richmond, V. P., & McCroskey, J. C. (2000). The impact of supervisor and subordinate immediacy on relational and organizational outcomes. *Communication Monographs, 67(1),* 85–95.

Richmond, V. P., & McCroskey, J. C. (2000). *Nonverbal behavior in interpersonal relations* (4th ed.). Boston: Allyn and Bacon.

Richmond, V. P., & McCroskey, J. C. (2001). *Organizational communication for survival: Making work, work.* (2nd ed.). Boston: Allyn and Bacon.

Richmond, V. P., & Roach, K. D. (1992). Power in the classroom: Seminal studies. In V. P. Richmond & J. C. McCroskey (Eds.). *Power in the classroom: Communication, control, and concern.* (47–67). Hillsdale, NJ: Lawrence Erlbaum.

Robinson, R. Y. (1994). *Affiliative communication behaviors: A comparative analysis of the interrelationships among teacher nonverbal immediacy, responsiveness, and verbal receptivity on the prediction of student learning.* Doctoral dissertation. West Virginia University, Morgantown, WV.

Robinson, R. Y., & Richmond, V. P. (1995). Validity of the verbal immediacy scale. *Communication Research Reports, 12,* 80–84.

Rocca, K. A. (2000). *Attendance and participation in the college classroom: The role of the instructor.* Doctoral dissertation. West Virginia University, Morgantown, WV.

Thomas, C. E. (1994). *An analysis of teacher socio-communicative style as a predictor of classroom communication behaviors, student liking, motivation, and learning.* Doctoral dissertation, West Virginia University, Morgantown, WV.

Thomas, C. E., Richmond, V. P., & McCroskey, J. C. (1994). The association between immediacy and socio-communicative style. *Communication Research Reports, 11,* 107–115.

Thweatt, K. S., & McCroskey, J. C. (1998). The impact of teacher immediacy and misbehaviors on teacher credibility. *Communication Education, 47,* 348–358.

Wanzer, M. B. (1995). *Student affinity-seeking messages and teacher liking: Subordinate initiated relationship building in superior-subordinate dyads.* Doctoral dissertation, West Virginia University, Morgantown, WV.

Wanzer, M. B., & McCroskey, J. C. (1998). Teacher socio-communicative style as a correlate of student affect toward teacher and course material. *Communication Education, 47(1),* 43–52.

Wheeless, V. E., & Dierks-Stewart, K. (1981). The psychometric properties of the Bem Sex-Role Inventory: Questions concerning reliability and validity. *Communication Quarterly, 29,* 173–186.

Wheeless, V. E., & Lashbrook, W. B. (1987). Style. In J. C. McCroskey & J. A. Daly (Eds.). *Personality and interpersonal communication* (pp. 243–274). Newbury Park, CA: Sage.

Wigley III, C. J. (1998). Verbal aggressiveness. In J. C. McCroskey, J. A. Daly, M. M. Martin, & M. J. Beatty (Eds.). *Communication and personality: Trait perspectives* (pp. 191–214). Cresskill, NJ: Hampton Press.

Wooten, A. G., & McCroskey, J. C. (1996). Student trust of teacher as a function of socio-communicative style of teacher and socio-communicative orientation of student. *Communication Research Reports, 13,* 94–100.

10 Use of Humor in the Classroom

The Good, the Bad, and the Not-So-Funny Things That Teachers Say and Do

MELISSA WANZER

Canisius College

After turning in a less than stellar first year in college, my father and I had a heated conversation one summer evening about my grades. He asked me why my grades were so poor and I told him that, among other things, my attendance was not always perfect. Before he could ask why I was having problems attending class regularly, I quickly explained that many of my professors were boring and did not have a sense of humor. My father quickly retorted, "professors are not supposed to be funny" and something else about my ability to generate excuses for my irresponsible behavior. At the time of this conversation I remember thinking that my father was probably correct. Later in my college career I encountered several professors who used humor effectively and, as a result I enjoyed their classes, learned more, and my attendance improved dramatically! While there are many other reasons for my significant improvement in class attendance (e.g., maturity, improved study skills) and grades (e.g., potential loss of funding from parents), I do feel that if students view professors as boring they may be more likely to skip their classes. In my experiences as both a student and teacher, use of humor is one way to stimulate interest in subject matter.

Humor is one instructional tool that teachers can use in the classroom to increase their effectiveness. This chapter provides a fairly detailed overview of research on humor in the classroom as well as practical suggestions for teachers who want to use humor more effectively. There are many benefits associated with use of humor in the classroom, however, teachers need to first understand why and how humor works as an instructional tool.

Positive Outcomes of Teacher Humor Use

When teachers use humor effectively in the classroom it can result in a number of benefits for teachers and students alike. For example, when teachers use humor they may receive more positive student evaluations (Bryant, Crane, Cominsky, & Zillmann, 1980) and find that students are more willing to participate in their classes. Additionally, when students take courses from teachers who use humor they may become more motivated to do well in the class (Gorham & Christophel, 1992). While there are a number of benefits that teachers derive from using humor in the classroom, the most significant reason to study teacher humor is to better understand its relationship to student learning. A number of studies have identified a positive relationship between teachers' use of humor and student learning.

Explanations for the Humor–Learning Relationship

Why does teachers' use of humor increase student learning? One theoretical explanation for the humor-learning relationship is based on the attention-gaining and holding power of humor (Ziv, 1979). The theory holds that, similar to teacher immediacy (Kelly & Gorham, 1988), humor is arousing, which is related to gaining and keeping students' attention, which is related to memory, which in turn is related to learning outcomes (see Chapter 2 for a review of this process). The attention-gaining model advanced initially by Ziv (1979) has been the main theory used to explain the humor-learning relationship in the classroom (Wanzer & Frymier, 1999; Ziegler, 1998).

Teacher use of humor may also serve as a powerful means of gaining liking and establishing a rapport with students. If teachers use humor in the classroom they are often doing so to reduce tension, to facilitate self-disclosure, to relieve embarrassment, to save face, to disarm others, to alleviate boredom, to gain favor through self-enhancement, to convey good will, or to accomplish some other prosocial goal (Gorham & Christophel, 1990, p. 58). Teachers may be using humor primarily as a means of gaining liking and a residual effect may be increased student learning. More specifically, if students like humorous professors more they may attend class more frequently, pay attention during class, and work harder to learn the subject matter. It is a well-known fact that we are more likely to comply with requests that are made by those individuals we like (Cialdini, 1993). In sum, if students like the teacher they will be more willing to comply with a wide range of teacher requests which ultimately can result in greater learning outcomes.

Other professions may use humor as a means of generating positive affect. Primary care physicians who used humor with their patients were less likely to have malpractice suits brought up against them (Levinson, Roter, Mullooly, Dull, & Frankel, 1997). Managers who use humor are liked more and perceived as more effective by their employees (Rizzo, Wanzer, & Booth-Butterfield, 1999). Doctors, managers, and teachers may all utilize humor as a means of increasing liking. The benefits of humor clearly extend beyond the classroom context.

Explanations for Mixed Support of the Humor–Learning Relationship

Does a teacher's use of humor always promote learning in the classroom? The answer to this question is *not* an unequivocal yes. Some humor researchers may be reluctant to recommend humor as an instructional tool because of mixed study results. One problem with the humor–learning line of inquiry may be that other teacher attributes such as immediacy or socio-communicative style interact with humor to facilitate learning. That is, humor does not work alone to facilitate learning but instead works in tandem with other teacher communication traits.

Another explanation for the mixed study results may be problems with the ways that researchers have tested the humor–learning relationship. According to Ziv (1988), who summarized some of the research investigating humor and learning, 11 studies found a positive direct or indirect relationship between humor and learning while 7 studies failed to identify any significant relationship. There may be several reasons why early studies did not find a positive relationship between humor and learning. One potential explanation for the failure to show support for the humor learning effect was the length of the early studies (Ziv, 1988). In several of these studies exposure to humorous materials may have been too short for information to be retained (e.g., ten-minute exposure to stimuli may have been too short to impact retention). Additionally, participants may not have perceived the humorous stimuli as funny thus negating the ability to be aroused into an attentive state. Finally, many of the earlier studies were conducted in artificial experimental settings that did not resemble true classroom situations (Ziv, 1988).

Other researchers have identified various problems with the experimental procedures used to test the humor–learning relationship. For example, Gorham and Christophel (1990) noted that in many of the early studies testing the relationship between humor and learning, similar research procedures were utilized. Very often participants were tested for recall following lectures in which humor was introduced in the experimental condition and omitted in the control. It is somewhat difficult to generalize conclusions across many of the humor studies because different types of humor (cartoons versus jokes) and placement of humor (humor placed at key points in the presentation versus random placement) could elicit varied rates of retention. Another possible explanation for the inconsistent findings may be the different types of channels used to send the humorous messages. Some researchers delivered humor through use of audiotapes while others used lectures or video clips. It is difficult to compare these study results when the researcher is using different types of humor, placement of humor, and channels to communicate humor. In sum, differences in study results may be a function of study design as well as the ways in which humor was operationalized.

Teacher Humor Orientation and Student Learning

A more recent trend in studying the relationship between humor and learning has been to examine how teachers who differ in humor orientation may impact learning (see for example, Wanzer & Frymier, 1999). What is humor orientation (HO)? Humor orientation is a communication based personality trait measured by the HO scale (Booth-Butterfield & Booth-Butterfield, 1991), which assesses an individual's predisposition to use humor frequently and in a number of different situations as well as their self-perceived effectiveness in producing humorous communication. Individuals scoring high on the HO scale are perceived as funnier and more socially attractive than individuals scoring low on the HO scale (Booth-Butterfield & Booth-Butterfield, 1991; Wanzer, Booth-Butterfield, & Booth-Butterfield, 1995, 1996). Also, students reported learning more from professors perceived as high in HO. Student perceptions of teacher HO was positively associated with their affective and cognitive learning. When comparing the best match in the classroom between teachers and students in regards to HO researchers concluded that the high HO students learned the most from high HO instructors. Not surprisingly, the least amount of learning occurred when a low HO instructor taught a high HO student.

Student perceptions of teacher HO are also related to perceptions of instructor immediacy. Teacher immediacy, also discussed in Chapter 6, refers to a teacher's use of verbal and nonverbal behaviors to facilitate perceptions of physical and psychological closeness. When students view their professors as using humor frequently and effectively, they also view them as more immediate. This finding is not surprising because many of the same behaviors used to be funny (e.g., smiling, gestures, changing our voice, and so on) are the exact ones that we use to be immediate. Finally, while HO is related to learning it may not be as powerful as immediacy in explaining differences in student learning. If teachers cannot use humor effectively, they can still increase learning outcomes in the classroom through verbal and nonverbal immediacy behaviors. This conclusion will be discussed further in the remaining sections of the chapter.

What if you are not a high HO and humor use does not come naturally to you? What if you do not know about the types of humor to use (and avoid) in the classroom? Several researchers have examined the types of humor that teachers use in the classroom and identified those behaviors deemed the most and least appropriate by students.

Types of Humor Used by Teachers: The Good and the Bad

Bryant, Crane, Cominsky, and Zillmann (1980) had undergraduate students tape record their instructors' lectures and then analyze the content of the tapes for humorous incidents. Based on this research, six different categories of humorous teacher behavior were identified: jokes, riddles, puns, funny stories, humorous comments, and an "other" category. The incidents were further analyzed to determine whether the humor was spontaneous or prepared, was sexual, hostile, or nonsensical, what characters were involved (teacher, student, other), was self-disparaging, or student-disparaging, and whether the humor distracted from the content or contributed to it. Interestingly, sex differences were found with male teachers being perceived as more free to use humor than female teachers. The results of this study imply that the type of humor was not as important as was the sex of the person using it. This study was the first to identify the types of humor that teachers used in the classroom.

Subsequent research on types of humor in the classroom attempted to identify an exhaustive and representative classification scheme of humorous teacher behaviors. Gorham and Christophel (1990) recognized humor as a high-inference variable which included a mix of both verbal and nonverbal behaviors. They researched the relationship between student perceptions of teacher immediacy in relationship to humor use. First they had undergraduates complete immediacy and learning scales on instructors. Next, they asked students to record and observe their instructors' use of humor while teaching over five different class sessions. The student observations of teacher humor were content analyzed and thirteen different categories of humor were identified. Some examples of the humor categories included: brief tendentious comment directed at an individual student, the class as a whole, or the department or university, personal anecdote related to the subject matter, personal anecdote that is not related to the subject matter, jokes, and physical or vocal comedy.

The Gorham and Christophel (1990) study examined correlations between one item of the verbal immediacy scale, "uses humor in class," and the number of humorous incidents reported by students. The researchers noted that the total number of humorous incidents was positively associated with this single item. They also concluded that students do not find teachers' use of self-deprecating humor and humor directed at individual students effective ways to increase learning. Additionally, students indicated that their instructors' use of tendentious humor was not effective in generating affect. In sum, not all types of humor were viewed as equally appropriate or effective in the college classroom.

Finally, Gorham and Christophel (1990) noted that the amount and the type of humor influenced learning but not to the same extent as immediacy. Based on this data, they felt that the relationship between teachers' use of humor in the classroom and learning is best understood when considered along with teacher immediacy. Humor is one type of immediacy behavior that teachers can capitalize on in the classroom.

But just how appropriate are the categories of humor presented by Gorham and Christophel? In another humor study, high school teachers indicated that most of the humor categories were appropriate to use in the classroom. Two items were perceived by teachers to be marginally inappropriate for the classroom. These items were: "The teacher tells a personal anecdote or story not related to the subject/topic" and "The teacher tells a general anecdote or story not related to the subject/topic." High school teachers indicated that related humor was the most effective type of humor to use in the classroom. Additionally, teachers did not perceive self-deprecating humor and humor directed at individual students as inappropriate for the classroom. Thus, students and teachers may not see eye to eye on the types of humor that are most appropriate for the classroom (Neuliep, 1991).

The studies mentioned thus far have helped to clarify some of the types of humor that students and teachers deem appropriate for the classroom but what seems to be missing from the literature on humor in the classroom are examples of highly inappropriate or ineffective classroom humor. Teachers need to understand the types of humor that will not work in the classroom and may actually detract from learning. Wanzer and Frymier (1999) conducted exploratory work in this area and asked students to generate examples of inappropriate and appropriate teacher humor. The categories of appropriate teacher humor were very similar to many of those identified in the Gorham and Christophel study. Appropriate classroom humor included: related humor, unrelated humor, impersonation, nonverbal behaviors, disparaging humor, humorous props, sarcasm, and unintentional humor.

Interestingly, two of the inappropriate humor categories were also identified as appropriate for the classroom. For example, sarcasm and irrelevant/unrelated humor were both identified as appropriate and inappropriate types of teacher humor. We speculate that the differences in perceptions of teacher humor may stem from the type of teacher who is using the humor as opposed to the type of humor being used. For example, high HO teachers may be able to get away with using both sarcasm and unrelated humor and still be viewed as highly effective. On the other hand, low HO teachers may not be able to use any type of humor effectively in the classroom.

Other categories of inappropriate humor included: making fun of students, humor based on stereotypes, failed humor, sexual humor, swearing to be funny, joking about serious issues, and personal humor. A number of students indicated that it was very inappropriate to make fun of or pick on a student. Students felt that teachers should not single students out in class and make fun of them. Many commented that it was *never* appropriate to make fun of a student in class. Students also indicated that humor directed at certain groups and based on stereotypes should not be used in the classroom. The third most frequently recognized type of inappropriate humor, failed humor attempts, may be very difficult to monitor. How does a teacher know for certain when his or her humor attempts are going to fail? This data seems to indicate that students feel that teachers need to be in tune with what students may or may not find funny. Why do humor attempts fail? One explanation may be differences in interpretations of humor based on age, culture, sex, or life experience differences. If, for example, I refer to a funny episode of "Saturday Night Live" with the Mr. Bill character and no one has ever heard of him, they may perceive my humor as a failed attempt.

Suggestions for Using Humor
Effectively in the Classroom

Using humor in the classroom can be very challenging. In the final sections of this chapter a number of practical suggestions for using humor in the classroom are advanced. The suggestions offered are based on humor research, personal teaching experiences, and discussions with students and colleagues about their perceptions of appropriate and inappropriate classroom humor.

First, teachers should probably refrain from using humor that singles out or belittles a particular student. If students feel "picked on" or "belittled" they may be less likely to participate or attend class. One student commented that when observing a student getting made fun of by a professor he or she may laugh at the humorous attempt but later feels very sorry for the student who was singled out. Students also indicated that when the professor targets a particular student repeatedly the students in the class often view this behavior as verbally aggressive. According to Gorham and Christophel (1990), even highly immediate teachers should refrain from picking on students in an effort to be funny because this is viewed as behavior that is out of character.

While both related and unrelated humor can be effective in the classroom it is probably a good idea to link the humor to the subject matter when possible. Humorous examples, jokes, and stories can help the student recall the material later. If a student can recall the humor, he or she may also be able to recall the concept or theory that the professor was attempting to illustrate. I have seen some of my students years after having them in class and many will say that they remember a humorous story as well as the theory or concept that I was explaining at the time. While unrelated humor can also be effective in the classroom as an icebreaker or affinity-seeking strategy, it does not have the advantages of related humor. Unrelated humor can be distracting while humor that is integrated into the message content is easier to understand. In sum, the receiver does not have to struggle to "get" the related humor or make a mental detour to interpret the joke and then come back to the message (Gass & Seiter, 1999).

A number of researchers have noted that teachers use self-disparaging or self-deprecating humor in the classroom in an attempt to be funny. Teachers may feel that this type of humor is safe because they are the targets of the humor. However, realize that self-disparaging humor, while viewed as appropriate in the classroom, could damage one's credibility. The research examining the effects of self-disparaging humor on persuasion has elicited mixed results. At times self-disparaging humor can enhance persuasiveness while at other times it can negatively affect perceptions of speaker persuasiveness. Some advice to follow when using self-disparaging humor is to avoid it if you feel that you have low credibility in the classroom. If, however, you feel that you possess a moderate to high amount of credibility in the classroom then "making light of your human frailties might make you appear more likeable and less pretentious" (Gass & Seiter, 1999, p. 275). Be sure to use self-disparaging humor in moderation because repeatedly putting yourself down could damage perceptions of your competence.

If you know that you are a low HO, or cannot tell a funny joke or story to save your life, then by all means do not attempt to tell funny jokes or stories in the classroom. If you are someone who has poor timing or delivery, or is unable to recall the punch line of jokes then do not use this type of humor. Remember that funny jokes and stories are only two of many types of humor that you have at your disposal.

Contemplate the type of humor that you are going to use in the classroom and make sure that it will be perceived as both funny and nonoffensive by your audience. Students indicated that sexual humor and humor based on stereotypes were inappropriate for the college classroom. We recommend that people refrain from using these types of humor in the classroom. Sexual humor and humor based on stereotypical behaviors of women could both be related to sexual harassment complaints from students. Conduct an audience analysis before choosing humorous messages. Be sure to realize that age, culture, gender, and life experiences of your audience will all influence interpretations of your humor. If you are using humorous examples from television shows or movies be sure that most of the students can identify the examples or characters that you are referring to in your lecture. If students do not understand the humor they will view it as a failed attempt and may be distracted from your lecture.

If you do not have any ideas about the kinds of humor to use in the classroom, observe a faculty member that uses humor regularly and effectively. Perhaps this colleague is a high HO and you can get some great ideas about different ways to incorporate humor into your repertoire of teaching behaviors. Generate discussions on humor in the classroom with colleagues, students, and researchers who study humor in an effort to understand why some types of humor may or may not work in the college classroom.

If you do not feel comfortable as the source of humor then use other types of humorous content in your teaching. Teachers can use humorous props which include cartoons, funny tapes or videotapes, handouts, disguises or hats, and which even direct students to humorous Web sites. Any type of humor incorporated into your teaching may be appreciated by students and viewed as a means of facilitating enjoyment of the classroom material.

If you are a high HO or someone who regularly uses humor in their teaching, realize that there is a saturation point. Students do not want their teachers to use excessive amounts of humor in their teaching. Too much humor can have a negative impact on learning. As Gorham and Christophel (1990) noted, "students might enjoy Joan Rivers as a teacher but put little stock in what she teaches them" (p. 59). Additionally, other researchers point out the fact that award-winning instructors use moderate amounts of humor (Downs, Javidi, & Nussbaum, 1988).

Finally, if you do not feel comfortable with any of the suggestions offered in this chapter and would never be the type of person to use humor in the classroom, then use verbal and nonverbal immediacy behaviors with your students as often as possible. Use of verbal and nonverbal immediacy behaviors can facilitate learning in the classroom. As stated previously, many of the behaviors that teachers use when they are being immediate (e.g., smiling, laughing, vocal variety, gestures) are the same ones that people use when they are being funny.

Final Remarks Related to
Humor Use in the Classroom

There is a substantial body of literature devoted to the use of humor in educational settings. Those who study and write about humor in educational settings are quick to identify a myriad of benefits associated with teachers' humor use. For example, when teachers use humor their students learn more (Davies & Apter, 1980; Gorham & Christophel, 1990; Wanzer & Frymier, 1999; Ziv, 1979, 1988), evaluate their teachers more positively (Bryant, Crane, Cominsky, & Zillman, 1980), are more willing to participate in class (Korobkin, 1988), and report less anxiety (Long, 1983; Ziv, 1976). Additionally, teacher humor has been recognized as an effective classroom management tool with the power to establish or dissolve boundaries of a group, encourage creativity, motivate individuals, control conflict, and relieve stress (Wallinger, 1997). While there are numerous benefits to using humor in the classroom, it is important to note that not all teachers should be encouraged to immediately "jump on the humor bandwagon." First, before utilizing humor as an instructional tool, it is important to understand more about how humor operates in the classroom. This chapter provided an overview of research on humor in the classroom as well as practical suggestions derived from this substantial body of literature.

R E F E R E N C E S   A N D   R E C O M M E N D E D   R E A D I N G S

Booth-Butterfield, M., & Booth-Butterfield, S. (1991). Individual differences in the communication of humorous messages. *Southern Communication Journal, 56*, 32–40.

Bryant, J., Comisky, P., & Zillmann, D. (1979). Teachers' humor in the college classroom. *Communication Education, 28*, 110–118.

Bryant, J., Crane, J. S., Cominsky, P. W., & Zillmann, D. (1980). Relationship between college teachers' use of humor in the classroom and students' evaluations of their teachers. *Journal of Educational Psychology, 72*, 511–519.

Chapman, A. J., & Crompton, P. (1978). Humorous presentations of material and presentations of material: A review of the humor and memory literature and two experimental studies. In M. M. Grunneberg & P. E. Morris (Eds.). *Practical aspects of memory.* London: Academic Press.

Christophel, D. M. (1990a). *The relationships among teacher immediacy behaviors, student motivation, and learning.* Unpublished doctoral dissertation, West Virginia University, Morgantown.

Christophel, D. M. (1990b). The relationship among teacher immediacy behaviors, student motivation, and learning. *Communication Education, 37*, 40–53.

Cialdini, R. B. (1993). *Influence: Science and Practice* (3rd ed.). New York: HarperCollins.

Curran, F. W. (1972). *A developmental study of cartoon humor and its use in facilitating learning.* Unpublished doctoral dissertation, Catholic University of America.

Davies, A. P., & Apter, M. J. (1980). Humor and its effect on learning in children. In P. E. McGhee & A. J. Chapman (Eds.). *Children's humor* (pp. 237–254). New York: Wiley.

Dickmeyer, S. G. (1993). *Humor as an instructional practice: A longitudinal content analysis of humor use in the classroom.* Paper presented for review to the Instructional Practices Section: Eastern Communication Association.

Downs, V. C., Javidi, M., & Nussbaum, J. F. (1988). An analysis of teachers' verbal communication within the college classroom: Use of humor, self-disclosure, and narratives. *Communication Education, 37*, 127–141.

Gass, R. H., & Seiter, J. S. (1999). *Persuasion, aocial*

influence, and compliance gaining. Boston: Allyn and Bacon.

Gilland, H., & Mauritsen, J. (1971). Humor in the classroom. *Reading Teacher, 24,* 753–756.

Gorham, J. (1988). The relationship between verbal teacher immediacy behavior and student learning. *Communication Education, 37,* 40–53.

Gorham, J., & Christophel, D. M. (1990). The relationship of teachers' use of humor in the classroom to immediacy and student learning. *Communication Education, 39,* 46–62.

Gorham, J., & Zakahi, W. R. (1990). A comparison of teacher and student perceptions of immediacy and learning: Monitoring process and product. *Communication Education, 39,* 354–368.

Gruner, C. R. (1967). Effects of humor on speaker ethos and audience information gain. *Journal of Communication, 17,* 228–233.

Gruner, C. R. (1976). Wit and humor in mass communication. In A. J. Chapman & H. C. Foot (Eds.). *Humor and laughter: Theory, research, and applications.* London: Wiley.

Hauck, W. E., & Thomas, J. W. (1972). The relationship of humor to intelligence, creativity, and intentional and incidental learning. *Journal of Experimental Education, 40,* 52–55.

Javidi, M. N., & Long, L. W. (1989). Teachers' use of humor, self-disclosure, and narrative activity as a function of experience. *Communication Research Reports, 6,* 47–52.

Kaplan, R. M., & Pascoe, G. C. (1977). Humorous lectures and humorous examples: Some effects upon comprehension and retention. *Journal of Educational Psychology, 69,* 61–65.

Kelley, D. H., & Gorham, J. (1988). Effects of immediacy on recall of information. *Communication Education, 37,* 198–207.

Kennedy, A. J. (1972). *An experimental study of the effects of humorous message content upon ethos and persuasiveness.* Unpublished doctoral dissertation, University of Michigan.

Kilpela, D. E. (1961). *An experimental study of the effect of humor on persuasion.* Unpublished master's thesis, Wayne State University.

Korobkin, D. (1988). Humor in the classroom: Considerations and strategies. *College Teaching, 36,* 154–158.

Lashbrook, W. B. (1974). *Toward the measurement and processing of the social style profile.* Eden Prairie, MN: Wilson Learning Corporation.

Levinson, W., Roter, D. L., Mullooly, J. P., Dull, V. T., & Frankel, R. M. (1997). The relationship with malpractice claims among primary care physicians and surgeons. *The Journal of the Ameri-can Medical Association, 277,* 553–559.

Long, H. B. (1983). *Adult learning: Research and practice.* New York: Cambridge.

Markiewicz, D. (1972). *The effects of humor on persuasion.* Unpublished doctoral dissertation. Ohio State University.

Neuliep, J. W. (1991). An examination of the content of high school teachers' humor in the classroom and the development of an inductively derived taxonomy of classroom humor. *Communication Education, 40,* 343–355.

Rizzo, B., Wanzer, M. B., & Booth-Butterfield, M. (1999). Individual differences in managers' use of humor: Subordinate perceptions of managers' humor orientation, effectiveness, and humor behaviors. *Communication Research Reports, 16*(4), 370–376.

Tamborini, R., & Zillmann, D. (1981). College students' perception of lecturers using humor. *Perceptual and Motor Skills, 52,* 427–432.

Taylor, P. M. (1964). The effectiveness of humor in informative speeches. *Central States Speech Journal, 5,* 295–296.

Terry, R. L., & Woods, M. E. (1975). Effects of humor on the test performance of elementary school children. *Psychology in the Schools, 12,* 591–610.

Wakshlag, J. J., Day, K. D., & Zillman, D. (1981). Selective exposure to educational television programs as a function of differently placed humorous inserts. *Journal of Educational Psychology, 73,* 27–32.

Wallinger, L. M. (1997). Don't smile before Christmas: The role of humor in education. *NASSP Bulletin, 81,* 27–34.

Wanzer, M., Booth-Butterfield, M., & Booth-Butterfield, S. (1995). The funny people: A source orientation to the communication of humor. *Communication Quarterly, 43,* 142–154.

Wanzer, M., Booth-Butterfield, M., & Booth-Butterfield S. (1996). Are funny people popular? An examination of Humor Orientation, loneliness, and social attraction. *Communication Quarterly, 44,* 42–52.

Wanzer, M. B., & Frymier, A. B. (1999). The relationship between student perceptions of instructor humor and student's reports of learning. *Communication Education, 48,* 48–62.

Weinberg, M. D. (1973). *The interactional effect of humor and anxiety on academic performance.* Unpublished doctoral dissertation, Yeshiva University.

Youngman, R. C. (1966) *An experimental investigation of the effect of germane humor versus nongermane humor in an informative communication.* Unpublished master's thesis, Ohio University.

Zeigler, J. B. (1998). Use of humour in medical teaching. *Medical Teacher, 4*(20), 341–348.

Zillmann, D., & Bryant, J. (1983). Uses and effects of humor in educational ventures. In P. E. McGhee & J. H. Goldstein (Eds.), *Handbook of humor research, Volume II: Applied studies* (pp. 173–194). New York: Springerverlag.

Ziv, A. (1976). Facilitating effects of humorous atmosphere on creativity. *Journal of Educational Psychology, 68,* 318–322.

Ziv, A. (1979). *L'humor en education: Approche psychologique.* Paris: Editions Social Francaises.

Ziv, A. (1984). *Personality and sense of humor.* Tel Aviv: Yahdav.

Ziv, A. (1988). Teaching and learning with humor: Experiment and replication. *Journal of Experimental Education, 57,* 5–15.

11 Understanding Student Reactions to Teachers Who Misbehave

PATRICIA KEARNEY

TIMOTHY G. PLAX

TERRE H. ALLEN

California State University, Long Beach

Terre Allen began her career as a high school English teacher. While teaching students a unit in Classical Literature, she noticed that they were completely uninterested and uninvolved in the material. After thinking long and hard about how to motivate her students to love the subject, she decided to develop a lesson plan around a popular movie. Sure enough, the strategy worked: Students found the material exciting and entertaining. At one point during class discussion, one student asked Terre, "Do you really go to the movies?" When she replied, "Yes, of course I do," the class echoed their disbelief. Apparently, students assume that teachers don't do what other normal people do, like attend movies, grocery shop, and dine out at restaurants. Students in this class imagined that Terre spent of all her time reading Shakespeare, diagramming sentences, and uncovering hidden meaning in poetry.

Terre's experience illustrates that students have clear and precise expectations of how teachers are supposed to behave, both in and out of the classroom. Students tend to view teachers in terms of the teacher role, rather than perceiving them as unique individuals who have lives beyond the classroom. Students hold expectations regarding the way teachers should look, dress, think, and behave. Not unlike teachers who have expectations for appropriate student behavior in the classroom, students, too, have expectations for appropriate teacher behaviors. When teachers violate those expectations in positive ways, as in our example with Terre, students are likely to respond favorably. However, not all teacher role violations are positive. In fact, an entire line of research examines the dark side of teaching by focusing on what teachers say and do that students do not like. This chapter discusses the research that concentrates on those *teacher misbehaviors*.

Examining teacher misbehavior is important for a variety of reasons. If asked what person in your life had the most significant, but *negative* impact on you, all of us are likely to be able to name a teacher. In fact, you may not be able to recall all of your teachers' names, but you should have no trouble identifying a teacher by name who had significantly humiliated or embarrassed you.[1] In this chapter, then, we argue that what we do as teachers to hurt or demotivate our students is as important as what we do to help or motivate them. This chapter begins by discussing two underlying assumptions that guide the research on teacher misbehaviors.

Teachers Don't Misbehave—or Do They?

The research on teacher misbehavior departs from a century of traditional approaches which overlook teachers themselves as a potential source of problems in the classroom. When you consider the fact that researchers are typically teachers, too, it is not surprising that researchers failed to consider teachers as a problem source. Departing from that tradition, Kearney, Plax, Hayes, and Ivey (1991) initiated a program of research grounded in two assumptions: (1) teachers themselves may misbehave and (2) these misbehaviors can become potential sources of student demotivation, dissatisfaction, and resistance.

With our first assumption, we recognize that teachers can and occasionally do misbehave. Paralleling an earlier conceptualization of student misbehavior, Kearney et al. (1991) defined teacher misbehaviors as those teacher behaviors that interfere with instruction and thus, learning. Repeatedly letting students out of class early, returning papers late, providing nonspecific evaluations on homework assignments, making tests too hard (or too easy) all interfere with instruction and learning, and thus, are considered to be teacher misbehaviors.

The second assumption contends that when teachers misbehave, students are likely to become demotivated, dissatisfied, and resist teacher attempts to keep them on task. A large body of literature documents a relationship between what teachers say and do with students' behaviors. Teacher behaviors are known to influence student achievement, time spent on task, compliance, affect, work habits, motivation, the development of social skills, and a number of other student reactions. We know, then, that what teachers say and do can significantly affect how students think and behave.

How Do Teachers Misbehave?

Kearney et al. (1991) asked students to think back over their college career and to recall specific instances where teachers had said or done something that had irritated, demotivated, or substantially distracted them in an aversive way during a course. Students were then asked to provide brief written descriptions of as many teacher misbehaviors as they could and to be as specific in their depictions as possible. Of the 250 students sampled, almost 2,000 descriptions of teacher misbehaviors emerged. These descriptions were then content-analyzed and coded into 28 different categories of misbehavior. Box 11.1 provides that list. Across all the misbehaviors coded, the five most frequently cited types of misbehaviors for college teachers were:

1. Sarcasm or putdowns
2. Early dismissal
3. Strays from the subject
4. Unfair testing
5. Boring lectures

Underlying these 28 categories are 3 groupings or dimensions of teacher misbehavior that can be profiled as: incompetence, offensiveness, and indolence. In explanation, *incompetent* teachers engage in a cluster of misbehaviors that indicate to students that they don't care about either the course or the student. These teachers don't bother to learn their students' names, make their tests too difficult, and are unable or unwilling to help their students succeed. Above all, incompetent teachers are simply bad lecturers: They either bore or confuse their students; some overload them with too much information; and still others mispronounce words or engage in accented speech that the students cannot understand.

Offensive teachers are mean, cruel, and ugly. They humiliate students, play favorites, intimidate, and are generally condescending, rude, and self-centered. Offensive teachers can be sarcastic, verbally abusive, arbitrary, and unreasonable. Finally, *indolent* teachers are reminiscent of the absent-minded professor. They sometimes fail to show up for class and often arrive late when they do, forget test dates, neglect to grade homework, constantly readjust assignments, and underwhelm students by making their classes and tests too easy.

This research goes a long way toward identifying and clarifying what constitutes teacher misbehaviors. We also know how these individual misbehaviors cluster together to form three distinct teacher profiles. Obviously, no one teacher fits any of those profiles exactly; they serve instead as prototypes of ineffective, misbehaving teacher types. Based solely on students' perceptions, then, we know what behaviors we, as teachers, should avoid.

Why Do Teachers Misbehave?

The literature is rife with reasons why students might misbehave. Among those reasons are low motivation to learn, laziness, poor socioeconomic background, absent or apathetic parents, and so on. Only recently have we begun to understand why teachers misbehave. One thing we know is that new teachers are often eager to do a good job and to be the best teacher they can be. Most new

BOX **11.1**   Teacher Misbehavior Categories with Sample Descriptions

Absent
Does not show up for class, cancels class without notification, and/or offers poor excuses for being absent.

Tardy
Is late for class or tardy.

Keeps Students Overtime
Keeps class overtime, talks too long or starts class early before all the students are there.

Early Dismissal
Lets class out early, rushes through the material to get done early.

Strays from Subject
Uses the class as a forum for her or his personal opinions, goes off on tangents, talks about family and personal life and/or generally wastes class time.

Confusing/Unclear Lectures
Unclear about what is expected, lectures are confusing and vague, contradicts himself or herself, jumps from one subject to another and/or lectures are inconsistent with assigned readings.

Unprepared/Disorganized
Is not prepared for class, unorganized, forgets test dates, and/or makes assignments but does not collect them.

Deviates from Syllabus
Changes due dates for assignments, behind schedule, does not follow the syllabus, changes assignments, and/or assigns books but does not use them.

Late Returning Work
Late in returning papers, late in grading and turning back exams, and/or forgets to bring graded papers to class.

Sarcasm and Putdowns
Is sarcastic and rude, makes fun of and humiliates students, picks on students, and/or insults and embarrasses students.

Verbally Abusive
Uses profanity, is angry and mean, yells and screams, interrupts and/or intimidates students.

Unreasonable and Arbitrary Rules
Refuses to accept late work, gives no breaks in three-hour classes, punishes entire class for one student's misbehavior, and/or is rigid, inflexible and authoritarian.

Sexual Harassment
Makes sexual remarks to students, flirts with them, makes sexual innuendos and/or is chauvinistic.

Unresponsive to Students' Questions
Does not encourage students to ask questions, does not answer questions or recognize raised hands, and/or seems "put out" to have to explain or repeat himself or herself.

Apathetic to Students
Doesn't seem to care about the course or show concern for students, does not know the students' names, rejects students' opinions and/or does not allow for class discussion.

Inaccessible to Students Outside of Class
Does not show up for appointments or scheduled office hours, is hard to contact, will not meet with students outside of office time and/or doesn't make time for students when they need help.

Unfair Testing
Asks trick questions on tests, exams do not relate to the lectures, tests are too difficult, questions are too ambiguous, and/or teacher does not review for exams.

Unfair Grading
Grades unfairly, changes grading policy during the semester, does not believe in giving A's, makes mistakes when grading and/or does not have a predetermined grading scale.

Boring Lectures
Is not an enthusiastic lecturer, speaks in monotone and rambles, is boring, too much repetition, and/or employs no variety in lectures.

Information Overload
Talks too fast and rushes through the material, talks over the students' heads, uses obscure terms and/or assigns excessive work.

Information Underload
The class is too easy, students feel they have not learned anything, and/or tests are too easy.

Negative Personality
Teacher is impatient, self-centered, complains, acts superior and/or is moody.

Negative Physical Appearance
Teacher dresses sloppily, smells bad, clothes are out of style, and cares little about his or her overall appearance.

Does Not Know Subject Matter
Doesn't know the material, unable to answer questions, provides incorrect information, and/or isn't current.

Shows Favoritism or Prejudice
Plays favorites with students or acts prejudiced against others, is narrow-minded or close-minded, and/or makes prejudicial remarks.

Foreign or Regional Accents
Teacher is hard to understand, enunciates poorly, and has a strong accent that makes it difficult to understand.

Inappropriate Volume
Doesn't speak loudly enough or speaks too loud.

Bad Grammar/Spelling
Uses bad grammar, writes illegibly, misspells words on the exam (or on the board) and/or generally uses poor English.

teachers want to be at least as good as their best teacher and to avoid any resemblance whatsoever to their worst teacher. Since teachers begin with so much determination to succeed, why would they ever misbehave? This question can be answered in one of three ways. First, some teachers misbehave because of what appear to be the more obvious reasons: They may grow bored, fail in their efforts to teach, decide they don't like their profession after all, become outdated, develop expectations which are too high, fixate on things they don't like about their school, department or colleagues, or suffer from burnout, overload or stress.

Second, some teachers misbehave for less obvious reasons: They work too hard at trying to impress their students and themselves. New and inexperienced teachers spend an inordinate amount of time worrying about issues such as: Will the students think I'm smart? What if I can't answer their questions? Will they know how inexperienced I am? To compensate for those concerns, new teachers often engage in *professoritis*. They work hard at trying to impress, rather than to teach. In their efforts to ensure that students find them credible, competent, and intelligent, these teachers often assign too much homework, overload students with information, and make their tests too hard. Research shows that new teachers need to be socialized over time to focus primarily on their students, rather than on themselves (Staton & Hunt, 1992). Therefore, teachers sometimes engage in misbehaviors because they are too self-focused, worrying excessively over whether or not they come across as credible. Over time, successful teachers learn to balance their concern for themselves with their concern for their students.

A third reason why teachers misbehave is simply because they feel justified in doing so. While being late for class or missing office hours may be perceived as teacher misbehaviors by students, teachers may find perfectly acceptable reasons for engaging in such behaviors. Correspondingly, students may blame a teacher for returning homework late, delivering a less than entertaining lecture, or asking difficult questions—all of which may be easily excused and explained by the teacher. One word of caution for those who rely on this third reason: Unless students similarly justify the teacher's behavior violation, it's likely to be perceived as a misbehavior and, importantly, those misbehaviors can have devastating consequences.

How Are Misbehaving Teachers Perceived?

Research indicates that students perceive their teachers who misbehave in a variety of negative ways. First of all, students seem to equate teachers who are nonimmediate with teachers who misbehave. As you will recall from Chapter 6, immediacy behaviors are those that communicate closeness and warmth, whereas, nonimmediacy behaviors communicate distance and detachment. In an experimental simulation, Thweatt and McCroskey (1996) tested the link between teacher misbehavior and teacher immediacy. The results of their experiment indicate that nonimmediacy is viewed by students as a type of teacher misbehavior. In fact, they found that nonimmediacy appeared to overwhelm the impact of other good teacher behaviors. That is, nonimmediate teachers who "behaved appropriately" were often perceived unfairly as also misbehaving.

Second, students are likely to perceive misbehaving teachers as less credible than teachers who conform to their role expectations. In a follow-up study, Thweatt and McCroskey (1998) examined the combined impact of teacher immediacy and misbehavior on teacher credibility. Teacher credibility refers to students' perceptions of teacher competence, trustworthiness, and caring. As might be expected, the immediate teacher who did not misbehave was perceived to be the most credible. The least credible teacher was both nonimmediate and misbehaved. However, it was teacher immediacy and not misbehavior, that appeared to be most closely associated with students' perceptions of teacher credibility. Apparently, when the teacher was immediate, the impact of other negative teacher misbehaviors became less important.

Third, students perceive teachers who misbehave as both unassertive and unresponsive. Wanzer and McCroskey (1998) examined the relationships among teacher assertiveness and responsiveness, teacher misbehaviors, and student liking or affect toward the teacher and the course. Assertiveness is the ability to use effective and appropriate communication to stand up for one's rights, but not at the expense of others'. Assertive teachers are task-oriented and demonstrate some degree of authority and independence in the classroom. Responsiveness refers to the degree of warmth, friendliness, and compassion that one expresses. Responsive teachers are understanding, social, and sensitive.

Wanzer and McCroskey (1998) found that teachers who are assertive are also perceived to misbehave less than teachers who were nonassertive. Similarly, responsive teachers are less likely to be seen as engaging in misbehaviors than their nonresponsive counterparts. In other words, both responsive and assertive teachers were perceived to misbehave less than unresponsive and unassertive teachers.

This research would suggest, then, that teachers who misbehave are likely to be perceived as unfriendly and nonimmediate. They are also likely to be seen as uncaring, untrustworthy, and incompetent. And, they come across as unassertive and unresponsive to students. Regardless of the reasons why teachers misbehave, justifiably or not, students are likely to judge them harshly.

How Do Teacher Misbehaviors Influence Student Outcomes?

The consequences of negative teacher behaviors on students' instructional outcomes are problematic. The first two negative consequences are associated directly with student learning. Beginning with student affective learning, we know that misbehaving teachers are associated with decreased levels of student affect. Two studies support this relationship. In the same study reported earlier, Wanzer and McCroskey (1998) also found that teachers who misbehave are less liked by their students and, correspondingly, students are less apt to like the course. Similarly, Dolin (1995) determined that teacher misbehaviors are negatively associated with students' affect toward the teacher, the course content, taking additional classes, and engaging in behaviors or skills recommended in the course.

Next, students report that they learn less from misbehaving teachers. Only one study has examined this relationship. Dolin (1995) argued that misbehaving teachers who let students out early, are tardy to class, and stray from the subject are likely to contribute to students' diminished time on task. Thus, misbehaving teachers interfere with students' learning. Relying on student estimates of their own learning, Dolin found support for her reasoning: Teachers who misbehaved were also associated with decreased levels of student learning.

Finally, teacher misbehaviors are known to influence learning in more indirect ways. In a seemingly unrelated line of research on student motivation, Gorham and Christophel (1992) asked college students to list those teacher behaviors that motivated and demotivated them to do their course work. Interestingly, as demotivators, these students listed many of the same characteristics that were defined earlier as teacher misbehaviors (e.g., boring or confusing lectures, dissatisfaction with grading and assignments, and poor organization of the course or learning material). Thus, teacher behaviors identified as demotivating are also those characterized as teacher misbehaviors.

Apparently, teachers are relatively unaware of how their own misbehaviors can demotivate students. When college teachers were asked how students were motivated or demotivated to learn (Gorham & Millette, 1997), their lists overlapped substantially with students' lists. However, for some teachers, particularly those with low personal motivation themselves, students' demotivation was attributed more to student factors and less to their own teacher misbehaviors. In other words, these teachers perceived student demotivation to be the students' fault and responsibility—and not their own.

Overall, this research suggests that teacher misbehaviors have a considerable impact on students. The more teachers misbehave, the less students learn and the less they like and appreciate the process of learning. Moreover, it appears that what students define as teacher misbehaviors are also a significant source of their demotivation to learn. Teacher misbehaviors, then, may actually encourage students to derail the learning process and prompt or encourage students themselves to misbehave.

How Do Students Explain and Cope with Teachers Who Misbehave?

In an effort to determine how students manage to deal with teachers who misbehave, we began by looking at those explanations or attributions that students assign to misbehaving teachers (Kelsey, Kearney, Plax, & Allen, 2000). Recall that earlier research indicated that teacher immediacy seemed to overwhelm or neutralize the impact of teacher misbehaviors on students' perceptions (Thweatt & McCroskey, 1996). Because that investigation relied on scenarios of hypothetical teachers, we re-examined this relationship with real teachers. We wanted to know if and how teacher immediacy mediated students' attributions of actual teachers who misbehaved.

Attribution theory (Heider, 1958) provided the basis for helping us understand how students make sense of their teachers when they misbehave. According to this theory, when a perceiver is faced with the necessity of interpreting the behavior of another, the perceiver chooses among three possible alternative explanations: the situation, chance, or a person's disposition. When situation is used as an explanation, the perceiver attributes the cause of another's behavior to environmental factors. With chance, the perceiver attributes cause to fate, accidents, or mistakes. With disposition, the perceiver assigns cause to the other's personality characteristics or traits. These explanations or attributions of another's behavior fall into one of two general categories: external attributions and internal attributions. Both situational and chance causes are external types of attributions which are often considered to be unintentional and outside the individual's control; whereas, disposition is an internal type which is normally considered to be intentional and controllable by the individual.

Applied to the classroom context, for example, a teacher may misbehave by failing to show up for class. Students may explain or interpret that misbehavior to either external or internal causes. Externally, the student may decide that the teacher's failure to attend was simply because of some family emergency or a car accident. Internally, the student may attribute cause to some persistent trait or characteristic unique to that teacher, like laziness, apathy, or thoughtlessness.

Following this thinking, we asked 400 college students to indicate how likely their teacher would engage in each of the 28 different kinds of misbehaviors. From their responses, students' teachers were then categorized according to one of three misbehaving profiles: indolent, incompetent or offensive. We also asked them to complete scales assessing their attributions of their teachers' misbehaviors (internal/external), how routinely their teacher engaged in those behaviors, as well as their teacher's level of immediacy.

Results of this study were fascinating and, to some extent, unexpected. First of all, regardless of the particular teacher misbehavior profiled, students attributed internal, not external, causes in explaining their teachers' misbehaviors. This was true for teachers who were offensive, incompetent, and indolent. Second, the more routinely or consistently the teacher was believed to engage in those misbehaviors, the greater the assignment of internality. That is, the more a student perceives the teacher's misbehavior as a normal part of how that teacher acts, the more likely the student will be to attribute that behavior to internal or personal dispositions of that teacher. Third, as you might expect, teachers high in immediacy were perceived to misbehave less than teachers moderate or low in immediacy—and moderates were perceived to misbehave less than those low in immediacy. What was unexpected, however, was the role of teacher immediacy. With this sample, immediacy failed to neutralize the impact of teacher misbehavior on students' attributions. Specifically, only teacher misbehavior, not immediacy, proved to be a predictor of students' attributions, and then, only for internal attributions. Regardless of teacher level of immediacy, then, students assigned blame to their teachers whenever they misbehaved.

What does all this mean? Students explain or make sense out of their teachers' misbehaviors by assigning some internal, dispositional teacher trait or characteristic. In other words, they believe that when their teachers misbehave, the teachers are doing it on purpose. This is true for teachers who are incompetent, offensive, and indolent. This is also true for teachers who are high, moderate, or low in immediacy. In other words, students don't give teachers a break when it comes to attributions about the teachers' misbehaviors. This is a perfect example of what has been called *the fundamental attribution error*. According to this principle, individuals tend to overestimate the influence of personal characteristics (internal attributions) and underestimate the influence of situational factors (external attributions) when explaining other people's behavior—particularly when that behavior is negative. For teachers who misbehave, then, we can expect students to accuse and assign them blame and make little or no effort to understand or justify other potential situational causes.

Given that students are quick to assign blame when their teachers misbehave, we then asked how students managed to cope with their teachers when they misbehave. In a related study, we examined this question, relying on Expectancy Violation Theory and the research on Imagined Interactions (IIs) to provide us with direction (Berkos, Allen, Kearney, & Plax, 2000). Recall that students have expectations about how their teachers should behave. According to Expectancy Violation Theory (Burgoon, 1978; LePoire & Burgoon, 1994), when teachers violate those expectancies by misbehaving, students are likely to search for and assign meaning. That's where *imagined interactions* come in.

Imagined interactions (Edwards, Honeycutt, & Zagacki, 1988) are those processing mechanisms that people use to evaluate others' behavior and make decisions about how to respond. Imagined interactions should be particularly useful for students who view their teachers' misbehaviors as norm violations. Specifically, IIs are a type of conversational daydream in which individuals imagine what they might say to another person, or reflect on what they should have said in a conversation that has already taken place. Imagined interactions serve three primary functions: They help us to rehearse what we'll say in future encounters, release built-up emotions and tension, and analyze and clarify our thinking. Importantly, IIs are useful as coping mechanisms and strategies.

Perhaps then, we reasoned, students would use IIs to cope with teacher expectancy violations. The misbehavior or the violation should stimulate students' cognitive processing in their efforts to cope with the violation. Rather than using IIs to help them rehearse how to respond to the teacher, however, we predicted that students would rely on IIs primarily as a substitute for interacting with or confronting their misbehaving teacher. Recognizing that actual confrontation may thwart their objectives for passing the course or getting a good grade, students may use IIs as a vehicle for coping with frustrations resulting from teacher violations or misbehaviors.

In order to test these relationships, we gave 250 students one of three teacher misbehavior profiles. We then asked them to recall and provide us with an example of a college teacher they knew who fit that profile. Box 11.2 provides sample descriptions that students provided of actual teachers who were offensive, incompetent, or indolent. Students also completed scales assessing their use of imagined interactions in dealing with that target teacher and their likelihood of actually confronting the teacher or relying instead on IIs.

Our results indicated that students were able to recall vivid examples of teachers who fit each of the misbehavior profiles. Moreover, they indicated that they would, in fact, use IIs, but would be even more likely to do so with an offensive teacher and least likely to do so with an indolent one. As predicted, rather than interacting with or confronting their misbehaving teacher, students reported a greater reliance on IIs as a way to deal with their teachers. Apparently, students prefer to use IIs as a substitute for and a means of avoiding actual contact with their teachers who misbehave. This is particularly true with offensive teachers who are characterized as aggressive, mean, and authoritarian. As evidenced by the teacher descriptions in Box 11.2, offensive teachers appear to be, understandably, the most difficult for students to approach.

In response to our question, then, "How do students explain and cope with teachers who misbehave," the answer is fairly simple. Students explain their teacher misbehaviors by assigning blame to the teachers themselves. According to students, when teachers misbehave, they do so willfully and intentionally. Regardless of how teachers may rationalize or justify what they do, students just don't see it that way. When it comes to students' efforts to cope with misbehaving teachers, apparently students choose to avoid interacting with or confronting their teachers. Instead, they react to the norm violation by rehearsing an imagined encounter they are not likely to have. These imagined interactions allow students to analyze the teacher misbehaviors, make attributions, and cope with violations outside their control.

What are the Implications of
Teacher Misbehaviors for the Classroom?

This chapter reflects a departure from traditional discussions of teaching because we have explored how teachers can serve as a potential source of problems in the classroom. We explained that, in the same ways that teachers have expectations regarding students' behavior, students hold expectations for how teachers should behave. In interpreting our findings for the classroom, teachers must recognize that there are certain attitudes and behaviors that students expect teachers to display. Many of these attitudes and behaviors can be displayed through classroom communication, however, some behaviors are not related directly to communication. Effective teaching involves both "show and tell." In other words, teachers must show or demonstrate certain behaviors and tell or communicate certain attitudes that reflect students' expectations. The following section offers some

BOX **11.2**   **Students' Characterizations of the Three Teacher Misbehavior Profiles**

Offensive Teacher

"He only tells them their way of doing work is wrong. He said things like 'don't bother coming to class because you are doing terrible anyway.'"

"She would always talk down or belittle those she did not like, by using sarcastic or rude comments."

"My teacher was offensive because he was constantly promoting his religion while putting others down. This was very inappropriate, especially for an anatomy class."

"Using cursing for emphasis and being very aggressive in discipline. His in-your-face teaching style did spur some to work harder but some rebelled and did not complete the work."

"He used pick-up lines on pretty female students."

Incompetent Teacher

"Actually he didn't lecture, but he read us material from the book. In many cases, lectures were like, 'Open the page . . . and so on . . . on the bottom part is a definition you need to know.' He never demonstrated any interest in students."

"The teacher would talk too fast and tried to cover too much material. The teacher would assign too much homework and never would allow time for students' questions."

"He just gave homework and tests and didn't lecture or teach—at all."

"He told us that the next test was going to be too difficult to pass."

"Talked and lectured to herself. Did not want to be asked questions."

Indolent Teacher

"She never stuck to due dates and was very lax in grading. The entire semester was basically spent reading a newspaper while she was at her desk. When we finally got our assignments back, they were so tardy the corrections were no longer helpful."

"Totally unprepared for class and also was consistently late. Sometimes he never showed up. The teacher lost our homework."

"Consistently 5–10 minutes late, blaming traffic! Repeated topics already lectured."

"He missed a lot of class and would play videos."

"Encouraged group work, even on exams. We didn't have to take the final."

"Never got our assignments back."

practical recommendations that stem from the research on teacher misbehaviors in order to enhance our teaching and classroom communication skills.

Recommendation #1: Communicate commitment, caring, and concern to your students. Recall that students' characterizations of teacher misbehaviors are profiled in one of three ways: incompetence, indolence, and offensiveness. Even though students are able to differentiate among the three, these profiles share commonalities. For instance, both incompetence and indolence reflect a lack of teacher commitment to helping students succeed. While incompetent teachers appear to be unwilling or unable to help their students learn, indolent teachers fail to prioritize students by neglecting to grade homework or by missing class. Offensiveness easily stands out as a particularly devastating teacher misbehavior profile. Even so, offensive teachers also reflect a lack of concern or caring for students.

Recommendation #2: Don't misbehave. Teachers do misbehave but we recommend avoiding misbehaviors as much as you can. Students recognize when we do and they don't like it. We cannot assume that students will overlook it when we do misbehave. Students are not forgiving and they have long memories. Students are not naive; they are capable of making astute observations about what teachers should and should not do.

Recommendation #3: If you must misbehave, offer students a reasonable explanation. Our research suggests that students assign internal attributions and intentionality to teachers who misbehave. This is true even for immediate teachers who are, presumably, well liked by their students. Unless we offer a thoughtful justification for missing office hours or losing students' papers, students are likely to assign some internal, negative motive for our indolence.

Recommendation #4: If you do misbehave, apologize to students. A sincere apology can be a powerful tool for creating affect with our students. In effect, we can turn around what began as negative attributions associated with a misbehavior to those that are more positive and affect-gaining toward us and the course. Teachers who do not apologize when they misbehave only confirm students' negative attributions.

Recommendation #5: When you misbehave, be sure to indicate to students that your violation is highly unusual and uncharacteristic. All teachers misbehave from time to time, but not all teachers routinely do so. If a teacher's misbehaviors are habitual and reoccurring, he or she clearly falls within one of the three profiles described in this chapter. For those of us who make mistakes and unintentionally misbehave from time to time, we must clearly communicate to our students that it is abnormal for us to behave this way and we will work hard at not letting it happen again.

Recommendation #6: Check students' perceptions and expectations of your behavior regularly. We, as teachers, do not always know when we misbehave or violate students' expectations of us. Our research suggests that college students are not likely to confront us or tell us when we do misbehave. We may not learn that students disapprove of what we say and do until it is too late. Too often, students rely on end-of-the-term teaching evaluations as a means of communicating passively to us their complaints. Consequently, we recommend the use of mini-evaluations throughout the term as a perception-checking device. In fact, you can devise your own mini-evaluations that can be used for a variety of purposes, including early assessment of targeted learning outcomes.

ENDNOTE

1. Kearney recalls her sixth-grade teacher, Mrs. Mildred Stone, as the teacher who caused her great embarrassment during her science presentation to the class. Plax names his first-grade teacher, Mrs. Hayden, who humiliated him in front of the others by washing his mouth out with soap. And, Allen recalls her third-grade teacher, Mrs. Marilyn Embry, who said, "Terre, you aren't as smart as people think you are. You aren't anything special. I hate little prissy girls like you!"

REFERENCES AND SUGGESTED READINGS

Berkos, K. M., Allen, T. H., Kearney, P., & Plax, T. G. (2000). *When expectations are violated: Using imagined interactions to cope with norm violations.* Manuscript submitted for publication.

Burgoon, J. K. (1978). A communication model of personal space violations: Explication and initial test. *Human Communication Research, 4,* 129–142.

Dolin, D. J. (1995). *Ain't misbehavin: A study of teacher misbehaviors, related communication behaviors, and student resistance.* Unpublished doctoral dissertation, West Virginia University, Morgantown.

Edwards, R., Honeycutt, J. M., & Zagacki, K. S. (1988). Imagined interactions as an element of social cognition. *Western Journal of Speech Communication, 52,* 23–45.

Gorham, J., & Christophel, D. M. (1992). Students' perceptions of teacher behaviors as motivating and demotivating factors in college classes. *Communication Quarterly, 40,* 239–252.

Gorham, J., & Millette, D. M. (1997). A comparative analysis of teacher and student perceptions of sources of motivation and demotivation in college classes. *Communication Education, 46,* 245–261.

Heider, F. (1958). *The psychology of interpersonal relations.* New York: Wiley.

Kearney, P., Plax, T. G., Hays, E. R., & Ivey, M. J. (1991). College teacher misbehaviors: what students don't like about what teachers say or do. *Communication Quarterly, 39,* 309–324.

Kelsey, D., Kearney, P., Plax, T. G., & Allen, T. H. (2000). *Immediacy as a mediator of students' attributions of teacher misbehaviors.* Manuscript in preparation.

LePoire, B. A., & Burgoon, J. K. (1994). Two contrasting explanations of involvement violations: Expectancy violations theory versus discrepancy arousal theory. *Human Communication Research, 20,* 560–591.

Staton, A. Q., & Hunt, S. L. (1992). Teacher socialization: Review and conceptualization. *Communication Education, 41,* 109–137.

Thweatt, K. S., & McCroskey, J. C. (1996). Teacher nonimmediacy and misbehavior: Unintentional negative communication. *Communication Research Reports, 13,* 198–204.

Thweatt, K. S., & McCroskey, J. C. (1998). The impact of teacher immediacy and misbehaviors on teacher credibility. *Communication Education, 47,* 348–358.

Wanzer, M. B., & McCroskey, J. C. (1998). Teacher socio-communicative style as a correlate of student affect toward teacher and course material. *Communication Education, 47,* 43–52.

12 Teacher Behavior and Student Motivation

DIANE M. MILLETTE
University of Miami

JOAN GORHAM
West Virginia University

There are only three things of importance to successful learning: motivation, motivation, and motivation . . . any fool can teach students who want to learn.

—Sir Christopher Ball[1]

What Is Motivation?

Motivation is a force or drive that influences behavior to achieve a desired outcome. In the classroom, teachers consider motivated students those whose goals match theirs. "Motivated" students want to learn. In achieving that goal, they are "motivated" to attend and prepare for class, turn in assignments, study for exams, ask questions, please the instructor, understand the material, and receive good grades. Such students are active, excited, persistent, optimistic, challenged, focused, and task-oriented. "Unmotivated" students are apathetic, helpless, defensive, anxious, unprepared for, or absent from class. In reality, all students are motivated. Apathetic, defensive, and unprepared students are simply responding to drives not in concert with your goals as their teacher.

Compliance-gaining strategies can be used by teachers to get students to do what we want them to do, that is, to engage in behaviors that we believe will result in students achieving our goals for the course. (See Richmond and McCroskey, 1992, for a comprehensive discussion of this approach.) These power-based control strategies used to manage students may include teacher's messages such as "If you don't do it by the deadline, you'll get a lower grade" (punishment) or "I will give you extra credit if you do this assignment" (reward). Some argue that the result of behavior instigated by the teacher's use of external punishment and reward strategies thus "motivates" students to engage in on-task behaviors, as does the teacher's legitimate power ("You must do as I ask because I am the teacher"). More commonly, however, motivation is conceptualized as an internal drive. As such, it is more likely to be nurtured and strengthened by teachers' use of referent power ("You want to work with me because you like and respect me") and expert power ("You trust that I have knowledge that will serve your needs"). Motivation has both direction and valence, or degree of intensity. In other words, students can be motivated to avoid a task as strongly as they can be motivated to complete it successfully, and they can differ in the relative intensity of their motivational response. *Student motivational style*—the consistent pattern of motivational responses within a given situation—can be adaptive or maladaptive; it can help students learn or act as an obstacle to learning.

If use of compliance gaining strategies is a push, then motivation is a pull. The stronger the pull, the less push is required to direct students' behavior. In the quotation which heads this chapter, Sir Christopher Ball states "any fool can teach students who want to learn." While overly simplistic and not quite accurate, Ball's observation recognizes that motivation to learn will frequently result in students' accommodating to significant obstacles in the path to that goal. Some educators believe the primary challenge we face as teachers is convincing students to buy what we're selling—education. In reality, students in our university classes are motivated by a variety of forces. Some are associated with the goal of education, such as desire to earn good grades, to get into graduate or professional school, or to understand a particular topic. Others are not. Our challenge as teachers is to develop rapport with students, then persuade them to move toward our educational goals. To the extent that persuasion implies internalization (e.g., a student complies because it is intrinsically rewarding and consistent with the way he or she thinks or behaves), you as a teacher can, in fact, have some degree of influence on your students' motivation.

The interests, needs, and motivations of any student are more a matter of emotions than of intellect. As early as 1924, when education systems still commonly ascribed to a "spare the rod and spoil the child" philosophy, Dreaver clearly identified the importance of the emotions learners bring with them to the learning process:

> The fact must be emphasized once more that an individual's tendencies are educationally and socially more important than his capabilities, however important the latter may be and despite the contrary belief on the part of the man in the street. In school, and in life no less, it is the driving power that counts in the long run. (cited in Kidd, 1973, p. 94)

The practical task at hand is understanding what motivates students to behave a certain way and how to create a motivational climate that maximizes on-task behavior. This chapter focuses on those issues, summarizing research and offering suggestions to help you, as a teacher, cultivate a productive learning environment.

What Motivates Students?

Research characterizes the path of motivation to learning as a sequential process in which a student who is able to act (student energy) makes a choice (volition) that includes a certain purpose (direction) followed by continuation (involvement). In other words, a student makes a purposeful choice to pursue a goal and persists until the goal has been successfully attained. In a university classroom, students will differ in the degree to which they possess a general predisposition toward and valuing of learning (trait orientation) and they will differ in the degree to which they are motivated to engage in the particular class (state orientation). State orientation is modifiable in the context of a particular class. Your students may thus be more or less motivated in your class than they are in other classes.

Freud believed that a person's motives for acting, as well as the meaning behind those acts, are often unknown on a conscious level. Maslow (1954) described a hierarchy of organismically based needs in which each higher level builds on the satisfaction of the preceding levels. Thus, motivation to address bodily needs (food, water, sleep, sex) will eclipse a shift of energy to other goals until those needs are reasonably satisfied. Attention at the next level is to safety, insurance against pain and danger, the need for stability, and a predictable and orderly society. This is followed by the need for acceptance and belonging; then by need for self-esteem, self-respect, self-confidence, feeling of strength and adequacy; and, finally, by need for self-actualization or self-fulfillment "to be the most one is capable of being" through the full engagement of talents, capacities, and potentialities. These are unlearned, primary motivational dispositions.

Secondary motivation is associated with drives that have been learned. They are most commonly associated with the way an individual manages the pressures of social living. The strength of secondary motives is dependent on their relationship with primary, unlearned drives. Students may respond to the same external stimulus differently, depending upon the drives present at the time.

Secondary motivation may be extrinsic or intrinsic. *Extrinsic motives* arise from sources outside of students. Students do something (work for grades, practice the piano) because someone else wants them to (parents or teachers) or because of some value associated with the activity (winning a piano competition). It is believed that over time extrinsic rewards and constraints decrease intrinsic motivation. One explanation may be that extrinsic reinforcement is more arbitrary and not directly related to behaviors produced by the student.

Intrinsic motivation occurs when students believe specific behaviors originate from their own needs. For example, a student may choose to read a book or practice the piano for personal pleasure, even if no one else knows they are engaging in those behaviors. Either extrinsic or intrinsic motivations can result in learning. However, changes in behavior are most productive and lasting when intrinsic motivation is tapped and students become, in the best sense, self-motivated.

Research on intrinsic motivation suggests students' motivation to accomplish a task may be diminished if they feel overly controlled, such as through reward and punishment incentives. Performance feedback, including grades, can be perceived by students as either controlling or as providing useful information about performance. Encouraging participative communication, providing constructive feedback, acknowledging students' points of view, clearly communicating the rationale behind assignments and evaluation schema, and allowing opportunities for students to align course objectives with personal interests can be effective means of shifting the inherently evaluative context of a university classroom from extrinsic to intrinsic motivation.

In the interest of better understanding the dynamics of classroom motivation, we have, in a series of studies,[2] invited both students and teachers to list factors that motivate students to try hard to do their best in college classes. From the students' perspective, the following factors were listed, in descending order of their importance:

The perceived relevance of and interest in the subject area

The desire to earn course credit and a good grade

The teacher's presentational ability, enthusiasm, and sense of humor

The student's own general achievement orientation or trait motivation

The opportunity to participate and receive teacher feedback

The teacher's positive attitude toward and relationship with his or her students, including the teacher's availability and approachability

The teacher's effective choice and organization of course material and textbook

The desire to please the teacher or someone else (e.g., parents)

The teacher's providing clear objectives, relevant assignments, and fair grading

The teacher's perceived knowledge and responsible behavior (e.g., timely turnaround returning assignments)

We also asked both teachers and students to list factors that decrease students' motivation in college classes. From the students' perspective, primary sources of demotivation were, in descending order:

The teacher's lack of presentational ability, lack of humor, lack of enthusiasm, tendency to digress, problems with language

Irrelevant assignments, unclear objectives, unfair grading

The student's dislike of the subject material—its being perceived as boring, difficult, redundant, or irrelevant

The poor choice and/or organization of course material and textbook

The teacher's negative attitude toward and relationship with students, including the lack of availability or approachability

The student's personal laziness

The student's lack of opportunity to participate and receive feedback

The student's perception that the teacher is not knowledgeable, is irresponsible, or is not in control of the material or class

The student's perception that there are too many demands outside of class

Negative behavior on the part of other students

Both teachers and students agreed on the importance of preconceived attitude toward the course and of grade-orientation as central to student motivation. These categories were the two sources of motivation noted most frequently by both populations, though teachers listed credit/grade motivation significantly less often than did students. Teachers also underestimated students' being motivated by a general desire to please either teachers or (most frequently) their parents, as well as the contribution of a teacher's presentational ability and enthusiasm to both motivation and demotivation. Teachers perceived a good choice of student assignments in a course, and good performance of students on those assignments and other graded work, as significantly more likely to influence motivation than did students. They also attributed student motivation to communication of their own high expectations, a category not mentioned at all by students.

Teachers were more likely than students to attribute decreased motivation to demands outside of class, and to lack of students' prerequisite knowledge or skills. Lack of satisfaction with assignments was the source of demotivation listed most frequently by teachers, who perceived irrelevant assignments and (in particular) students' failure to do well on those assignments and other graded work as more central to decreasing motivation than did students. Students, on the other hand, were significantly more critical of overall instructional process decisions related to delivery of course material—of how the instructor organized material as opposed to what they as students were asked to do.

On the whole, teachers were more likely to attribute student motivation to things they asked students to do and to how well their students did them: to the teacher's selection of course assignments and the students' success on graded work, the teacher's requirements that students act the way motivated students act (e.g., attend class, complete homework), and the teacher's communication of high expectations for and praise of that success. They were more likely to attribute student demotivation to performance-related factors: to the students' lack of success on graded work, the students' lack of prerequisite skills or knowledge that might contribute to that lack of success, and the students' heavy workload (both within and outside of their class).

Students, on the other hand, attributed more of their motivation to factors they bring with them to a course (and beyond the teacher's control): their personal credit- or grade-orientation and their desire to please others, frequently their parents. They attributed more of their demotivation to teacher behavior, in particular to poor presentational skills and lack of enthusiasm on the part of the instructor, and to the instructor's overall choice and organization of course material. In general, they saw motivation as a personally-owned state and demotivation as a teacher-owned problem.

While you as a teacher should not feel solely responsible for motivating your students, it is beneficial to understand how your demeanor, attitude, behavior, and rapport do influence your students' motivational level. Ultimately, students choose what they learn, and the extent to which they learn it. Their personal values and priorities—factors that are beyond your control—are inevitably involved. The strongest predictors of end-of-semester motivation are baseline levels of motivation. However, while students come into your classes with a clear motivational disposition, your behaviors as their teacher are instrumental in sustaining and incrementally increasing motivation. As important, your behaviors can decrease motivation. The final section of this chapter summarizes means of fostering a positive motivational environment.

What Can Teachers Do to Cultivate Motivation?

First, understand students' basic need for a safe, predictable, and orderly learning environment. Learned helplessness is a condition that occurs when students experience uncontrollable events and when that experience leads to an expectation that future events will also be uncontrollable. This situation disrupts motivation and decreases students' willingness to cope with allegedly uncontrollable situations. An individual learns through inconsistent or unpredictable reinforcement that he or she is unable to negotiate safe passage through the dangers of a given environment. The result is commonly rebellion, withdrawal, rejection, or apathy.

Because achievement motivation is linked to evaluation, teachers need to acknowledge their students' need for control over evaluative outcomes. Expectations, and their direct link to how grades will be computed, should be communicated clearly, as should the purpose of each assignment or project. When you as the teacher emphasize mastery goals—such as task involvement, improvement, learning, and an intrinsic motivational orientation—your students' attention moves toward putting forth effort, engaging challenges, learning from errors, gaining knowledge, and making progress. When rewards are largely extrinsic, students' attention moves toward outperforming others and avoiding anxiety-producing uncertainty. Students who aren't able to outperform their classmates, who feel anxiety over "what the teacher wants," or who feel no control over the grades they receive will frequently be more motivated to withdraw than to try harder. If they don't do anything, or prepare only minimally for class, they can, at least, predict the outcome.

The importance of helping students realize that they are in control of their academic progress and that they can do what is needed to succeed is essential to teachers' motivational strategies. Providing effective performance feedback is a key step in building students' intrinsic motivation and paving the way for higher achievement. To foster motivation, teachers must make every effort to establish clear and relevant goals, and to present learning in a way that is perceived as manageable as well as interesting and enjoyable.

Second, understand students' basic need for acceptance, warmth, and belonging. When a positive social-emotional climate is created, students feel supported. Their attitudes become more enthusiastic and participation increases. Once you have established a safe environment for learning, your role as a caring mentor and your engendering of respect among peers in the classroom are essential in meeting the basic motivational need for acceptance and belonging.

Teacher empathy towards students has been shown to affect students' self-concept and achievement motivation. Students who are allowed to participate in course policy-making often report higher levels of motivation at the end of the semester, and are more likely to enroll in additional courses in a subject area, to exhibit greater interest in course material, and to demonstrate more persistence with challenging coursework. Simply put, motivation to engage in on-task behavior is enhanced by a student's sense of belonging and of respect for and by his or her teacher and fellow students. Motivation to avoid an alienating environment is frequently much stronger than motivation to achieve course credit or a good grade. In contrast, a teacher's personal recognition of a student who has not found a supportive social or academic niche can have a profound impact on that student's choices, direction, and involvement throughout his or her college experience.

Third, understand students' basic need for self-esteem, self-respect, self-confidence, and feelings of strength and adequacy. From a conceptual perspective, the essence of motivation is the enhancement of self. Most of us, while accomplishing tasks, strive to do the best we can. In the classroom, a student's development of self-worth is directly related to his or her ability to achieve. When students' sense of self-worth is threatened, they act in ways to protect it. When students see school, or a particular class, as a threat to their self-worth, some are forced to choose apathy and noninvolvement as a defense.

Students enter school with differing levels of ability and motivation. They quickly discover that they must compete with others for a limited number of rewards, and that ability trumps effort. When you teach an introductory college class, you will frequently find students who are accustomed to being "easy winners" on the high school playing field just coming to difficult terms with the fact that their university peers are almost all accustomed to being at the top of their class. Even when teachers recognize, encourage, and praise a student's effort, the effectiveness of these strategies is neutralized when the expected reward of high grades doesn't follow. This is not an argument that all college students should thus earn As or Bs, or that grading scales should have no element of competitiveness. Competition need not be debilitating. It can, in concert with the grade-orientation students identify as a primary source of their motivation in college classes, serve as a strong motivating force toward higher levels of effort and achievement. Competition is only debilitating when it's forced on students of unequal abilities who do not have an equitable chance of winning.

Not only do teachers evaluate students, but students evaluate themselves on how well or poorly they have performed a given task. In psychology, this is known as *self-efficacy* and it is essential in student motivation, perhaps as important as ability. Self-efficacy does not always correspond with results. A part of your role as teacher is helping students learn to accurately and honestly evaluate the strengths and weaknesses of their own work. With proper encouragement from a teacher, it is often surprising how students *can* rise to a higher level than even they thought possible. This, of course, works to encourage future successes and overcome personal deficiencies and past failures.

Self-efficacy walks hand-in-hand with *expectancy theory*. This concept from the social sciences proposes that students determine the amount of effort expended on a task on two specific criteria, namely, their perceived probability for achieving the goal and how much they value that goal. To maximize the power of expectancy, the student needs to be assured that the results of attaining a desired goal will be equitably distributed among all participants. Teachers must reinforce all possible outcomes associated with learning the subject at hand, and convince low achievers that they can experience success by applying specific behaviors and study skills. Assignments and deadlines that produce the most satisfying work tend to be those for which the teacher monitors progress and keeps to specific schedules. Research clearly shows that vagueness, ambivalence, and disorganization undermine student confidence and motivation.

Fourth, understand the importance of presentational style. It has been well documented that *teaching style* affects student motivation and responsiveness (see Chapter 9). As a teacher, your behavior in the classroom stimulates responsive behaviors in your students; an inspired level of enthusiasm and interest in your subject is infectious and promotes a climate of interaction and participation.

Teacher immediacy is a direct motivator of your students, focusing their attention and increasing their intensity (see Chapter 6). Immediacy behaviors, both verbal and nonverbal, accomplish this task by reducing the physical and psychological distance between you and your students. An immediate teaching style is viewed by students as more positive and effective, which increases student affect towards you and your course. In terms of the previously presented model of how motivation works, this affective response is instrumental in students' choice or volition to attend to the teacher's information and direction with continued involvement throughout the course. In addition, immediacy is a direct arousal stimulus and, as such, a direct motivator. Information that has not been attended to cannot be encoded for mental storage, or learned. As discussed in Chapter 2, arousal focuses attention; it reduces the proportion of irrelevant cues attended to and increases the intensity of information processing, which results in the formation of new and stronger associative links in learning for the student.

Christophel's (1990) research supports a model of immediacy's positive influence on learning, motivating students to work to their levels of highest performance. This also serves as an effective predictor of learning. Frymier (1993) identified a student's initial motivation upon entering a course as the most accurate predictor of the student's sustained level of motivation over the course of a semester. Highly motivated students maintained their level of motivation independent of the teacher's immediacy level; however, students initially reporting low or moderate motivation increased their motivation only when exposed to highly immediate teachers. Research, therefore, informs us that teacher immediacy is particularly important to the learning capacities of students who are less motivated upon entering a course. Students who are highly *self*-aroused or *self*-motivated don't "need" teacher immediacy to lead to attention/involvement (though their affective learning will probably still be influenced by immediacy). The fact that these students appear to learn as well regardless of their teachers' immediacy does not counter the advice proposed here, since a source of both arousal and motivation are accounted for. However, when we encounter students who are *not* self-motivated upon entering our classes, teacher immediacy is the single best predictor of growth in motivation as the course unfolds.

Fifth, understand that your behavior as a teacher can decrease as well as increase motivation. We have found, across several studies, a conceptual distinction between motivating and demotivating factors in college classes. Students regard their teacher's behavior as one factor—but only one factor—contributing to their general motivation to engage and achieve in college courses. As students work with a teacher over a semester's time, the teacher's effective organization and presentation of course material, and his or her positive relationships with students, can increase students' motivation. As important, from the first day of the term and continuing throughout the course, negative teacher behaviors are clearly likely to decrease student motivation. Our research has consistently indicated that students perceive negative teacher behavior as more central to decreased motivation than positive behaviors are central to increased motivation.

We stated earlier in this chapter that you, as a teacher, should not feel solely responsible for motivating your students, that the trait motivation that they bring with them to your classes has substantial influence on the state motivation exhibited within those classes. As we have discussed, choices you make as a teacher can sustain or enhance that baseline motivation—or, quite importantly, decrease motivation. Early in the term, a teacher who is in control of the classroom and material, is an effective lecturer, has a sense of humor, is clear in her or his explanations, shows interest in students, provides opportunities for students to participate, and provides effective and timely feedback may have only a modest effect on increasing students' state motivation. However, a teacher who is *not* in control of the classroom or material, is *not* an effective lecturer, does *not* have a sense of humor, is *not* clear in her or his explanations, does *not* show an interest in students, is *not* approachable, or is *not* responsible will markedly decrease state motivation. Later in the term, positive teacher behaviors begin to have a significant influence on state motivation, as do positive assessments of course organization and procedures; however, absence of teacher behavior negatives continues to be more influential than presence of positives.

Verbal immediacy is a highly effective strategy to overcome compromised motivation. The very basics of courtesy and respect toward a student, for example, can go a long way toward countering student resistance. Encouraging students to participate, using student comments as a source of discussion, engaging in individual conversations with students, referring to students by their names, providing reactions to student assignments, asking students how they feel about projects and procedures—all of these have a strong positive effect on student motivation. While students in our studies did not directly attribute motivation to these verbal immediacy behaviors, students of verbally immediate teachers were significantly less likely to report their motivation having been diminished by something the teacher did or did not do. This finding was evident at the beginning of the course and continued throughout the term.

A teacher's nonverbal immediacy has similar effect, though the impact takes longer to establish than that of verbal immediacy. We have not found the use of nonverbal immediacy to be significantly related to either student motivation or demotivation during the early stages of a course; however, once relationships with students have been established, reports of decreased motivation are significantly associated with nonimmediate teacher behaviors.

What does this information mean for you as a teacher? First, recognize that the strongest predictor of end-of-term motivation is the baseline level (i.e., trait orientation) of your students' initial motivation, which they bring with them to your classes. Many of your students' motivational profiles will be different from yours as a student. Resist assuming that learning for the sake of learning is intrinsically motivating for everyone in your class, or that perceived relevance of the subject area is a given. Second, understand that primary needs for physical equilibrium, safety, belonging, and self-esteem must be addressed before learning for self-fulfillment is possible. Most teachers were themselves reasonably comfortable in their college courses, and generally found achievement attainable and rewarding. Their peers who did not are unlikely to have chosen, as you have, to remain in an academic environment any longer than necessary. There will be similar differences among students in your classes, some of whom will be pulled by drives that you will need to work to understand. Also, understand that the learning environment you create does influence your students' state motivation as you work together over the weeks of a quarter or semester. It is important for you, as a teacher, to develop a positive learning environment and an immediate teaching style. This includes communicating expectations to students, then providing clear, constructive feedback on their efforts and praise for their achievements. Recognize that students may rely on your organizational skills to enhance their success, and need you to prompt them to study for tests, encourage them to meet an assignment deadline, and generally keep them on track regarding your class schedule. Finally, recognize that nonimmediate behavior can significantly decrease motivation, an outcome you surely want to avoid. Effective teaching is a marriage of content and context. We trust you have command of the former, and urge you to develop sensitivity to the latter.

ENDNOTES

1. Ball, Sir Christopher (1995). Presidential Address to the North of England Education Conference, England, cited in Galloway, D., Rogers, C., Armstrong, D., & Leo, E. (1998*). Motivating the difficult to teach* (p. 3). White Plains, NY: Longman.

2. Complete results of this programmatic line of research are reported in the following studies: (a) Gorham, J., & Christophel, D. M. (1992). Students' perceptions of teacher behaviors as motivating and demotivating factors in college classes. *Communica-*

tion Quarterly, 40, 239-252. (b) Christophel, D. M., & Gorham, J. (1995). A test-retest analysis of student motivation, teacher immediacy, and perceived sources of motivation and demotivation in college classes. *Communication Education, 44,* 292–306. (c) Gorham, J., & Millette, D. M. (1997). A comparative analysis of teacher and student perceptions of sources of motivation and demotivation in college classes. *Communication Education, 46,* 245–261.

REFERENCES AND SUGGESTED READINGS

Ames, C., & Ames, R. (1985). *Research on motivation in education, volume 2: The classroom milieu.* Orlando, FL: Academic.

Ames, C., & Ames, R. (1989). *Research on motivation in education, volume 3: Goals and cognitions.* San Diego, CA: Academic.

Ames, R. (1986). Effective motivation: The contribution of the learning environment. In R. S. Feldman (Ed.), *The social psychology of education: Current research and theory* (pp. 235–256). Cambridge: Cambridge University.

Ames, R. E., & Ames, C. (1984). *Research on motivation in education, volume 1: Student motivation.* Orlando, FL: Academic.

Andersen, J. F. (1970). Teacher immediacy as a predictor of teaching effectiveness. In D. Nimmo (Ed.). *Communication yearbook, 3* (pp. 543–559). New Brunswick, NJ: Transaction.

Andersen, J. F., Norton, R. W., & Nussbaum, J. F. (1981). Three investigations exploring relationships between perceived teacher communication behaviors and student learning. *Communication Education, 30,* 377–392.

Ashton, P. (1984). Teacher efficacy: A motivational paradigm for effective teacher education. *Journal of Teacher Education, 35,* 28–32.

Bandura, A. (1982). Self-efficacy mechanism in human agency. *American Psychologist, 37,* 122–147.

Bloom, B. S. (Ed.). *A taxonomy of educational objectives. Handbook 1: The cognitive domain.* New York: McGraw-Hill.

Brophy, J. E. (1987). Synthesis of research on strategies for motivating students to learn. *Educational Leadership, 45,* 40–48.

Brown, R., & Kulik, J. (1977). Flashbulb memories. *Cognition, 5,* 73–99.

Buchanan, P. C. (1962). *The leader and individual motivation.* New York: Association.

Burda, J. M., & Brooks, C. H. (1996). College classroom seating position and changes in achievement motivation over a semester. *Psychological Reports, 78,* 331–336.

Christophel, D. M. (1990). The relationship among teacher immediacy behaviors, student motivation, and learning. *Communication Education, 39,* 323–340.

Christophel, D. M., & Gorham, J. (1995). A test-retest analysis of student motivation, teacher immediacy, and perceived sources of motivation and demotivation in college classes. *Communication Education, 44,* 292–306.

Deci, E. L. (1975). *Intrinsic motivation.* New York: Plenum.

Dreaver, J. (1924). *An introduction to the psychology of education.* London: Edward Arnold.

Dweck, C. C. (1986). Motivational processes affecting learning. *American Psychologist, 41,* 1040–1048.

Easterbrook, J. A. (1959). The effect of emotion on cue utilization and the organization of behavior. *Psychological Review, 66,* 183–201.

Eysenck, M. W. (1982). *Attention and arousal: Cognition and performance*. Berlin: Springer-Verlag.

Fayer, J. M., Gorham, J., & McCroskey, J. C. (1993). Teacher immediacy and student learning: A comparison between U.S. mainland and Puerto Rican classrooms. In J. Fayer (Ed.), *Puerto Rican communication studies* (pp. 111–126). Puerto Rico: Fudacion Arquelogica, Anthropologica, e Historica de Puerto Rico.

Frymier, A. B. (1993). The impact of teacher immediacy on students' motivation: Is it the same for all students? *Communication Quarterly, 41*, 454–464.

Frymier, A. B. (1994). A model of immediacy in the classroom. *Communication Quarterly, 42*, 133–144.

Galloway, D., Rogers, C., Armstrong, D., & Leo, E. (1998). *Motivating the difficult to teach*. White Plains, NY: Longman.

Garcia, T., & Pintrich, P. R. (1996). The effects of autonomy on motivation and performance in the college classroom. *Contemporary Educational Psychology, 21*, 477–486.

Goins, B. (1993). Student motivation. *Childhood Education, 69*, 316–317.

Gorham, J. (1988). The relationship between verbal immediacy behaviors and student learning. *Communication Education, 37*, 40–53.

Gorham, J., & Christophel, D. M. (1990). The relationship of teachers' use of humor in the classroom to immediacy and student learning. *Communication Education, 39*, 46-62.

Gorham, J., & Christophel, D. M. (1992). Students' perceptions of teacher behaviors as motivating and demotivating factors in college classes. *Communication Quarterly, 40*, 239–252.

Gorham, J., & Millette, D. M. (1997). A comparative analysis of teacher and student perceptions of sources of motivation and demotivation in college classes. *Communication Education, 46*, 245–261

Gorham, J., & Zakahi, W. R. (1990). A comparison of teacher and student perceptions of immediacy and learning. *Communication Education, 39*, 354–368.

Hall, E. T. (1966). *The hidden dimension*. New York: Doubleday.

Hancock, D. R. (1995). What teachers may do to influence student motivation: An application of expectancy theory. *The Journal of General Education, 44*, 171–179.

Hawley, R. C., & Hawley, I. L. (1979). *Building motivation in the classroom*. Amherst, MA: Education Research Association.

Johnson, L. (1998). *Two parts textbook, one part love: A recipe for successful teaching*. New York: Hyperion.

Kearney, P., Plax, T. G., & Burroughs, N. F. (1991). An attributional analysis of college students' resistance decisions. *Communication Education, 40*, 325–342.

Kearney, P., Plax, T. G., Richmond, V. P., & McCroskey, J. C. (1984). Power in the classroom IV: Alternatives to discipline. In R. Bostrom (Ed.), *Communication Yearbook 8* (pp. 724–746). Beverly Hills, CA: Sage.

Kearney, P., Plax, T. G., Richmond, V. P., & McCroskey, J. C. (1986). Power in the classroom III: Teacher communication techniques and messages. *Communication Education, 34*, 19–28.

Kearney, P., Plax, T. G., Smith, V. R., & Sorensen, G. (1988). Effects of teacher immediacy and strategy type on college student resistance to on-task demands. *Communication Education, 37*, 54–67.

Kearney, P., Plax, T. G., & Wendt-Wasco, N. J. (1985). Teacher immediacy for affective learning in divergent college classes. *Communication Quarterly, 33*, 61–74.

Kelly, D. H., & Gorham, J. (1988). Effects of immediacy on recall of information. *Communication Education, 37*, 198–207.

Kidd, J. R. (1973). *How adults learn*. New York: Association.

Kindsvatter, R., Wilen, W., & Ishler, M. (1988). *Dynamics of effective teaching*. White Plains, NY: Longman.

Klotsky, R. L. (1975). *Human memory: Structure and processes*. San Francisco, CA: W. H. Freeman.

Kolesnik, W. B. (1978). *Motivation: Understanding & influencing human behavior*. Boston, MA: Allyn & Bacon.

Livengood, J. M. (1992). Students' motivational goals and beliefs about effort and ability as they relate to college academic success. *Research in Higher Education, 33*, 247–261.

Logan, F. A. (1970). *Fundamentals of learning and motivation*. Dubuque, IA: Wm. C. Brown.

Maslow, A. H. (1954). *Motivation and personality*. New York: Harper & Row.

McDowell, E. E., McDowell, C. E., & Hyerdahl, J. (1980, November). *A multivariate study of teacher immediacy, teaching effectiveness and student attentiveness at the junior and senior high levels*. Paper presented at the annual meeting of the speech Communication Association, New York.

Mehrabian, A. (1967). Attitudes inferred from nonimmediacy of verbal communication. *Journal of Verbal Learning and Verbal Behavior, 6*, 294–295.

Mehrabian, A. (1981). *Silent messages: Implicit communication of emotions and attitudes.* Belmont, CA: Wadsworth.

Moray, N. (1959). Attention in dichotic listening: Affective cues and the influence of instructions. *Quarterly Journal of Experimental Psychology, 11*, 56–60.

Murdock, V. B., Jr. (1962). The serial position effect in free-recall. *Journal of Experimental Psychology, 64*, 482–488.

Phaf, R. H., & Wolters, G. (1986). Induced arousal and incidental learning during rehearsal. *American Journal of Psychology, 99*, 341–354.

Pintrich, P. R., Brown, D. R., & Weinstein, C. E. (1994). *Student motivation, cognition, and learning.* Hillsdale, NJ: Lawrence Erlbaum.

Pintrich, P. R., & Schunk, D. H. (1996). *Motivation in education: Theory, research, & applications.* Englewood Cliffs, NJ: Prentice Hall.

Plax, T. G., & Kearney, P. (1990). Classroom management: Structuring the classroom for work. In J. Daly, G. Friedrich, & A. Vangelisti (Eds.), *Teaching communication: Theory, research, and methods.* Hillsdale, NJ: Lawrence Erlbaum.

Plax, T. G., Kearney, P., McCroskey, J. C., & Richmond, V. P. (1986). Power in the classroom VI: Verbal control strategies, nonverbal immediacy, and affective learning. *Communication Education, 35*, 43–55.

Powell, R. G., & Harville, B. (1990). The effects of teacher immediacy and clarity on instructional outcomes. *Communication Education, 39*, 369–379.

Purkey, W. W. (1970). *Self-concept and school achievement.* Englewood Cliffs, NJ: Prentice-Hall.

Raffini, J. P. (1986). Student apathy: A motivational dilemma. *Educational Leadership, 44*, 53–55.

Raffini, J. P. (1993). *Winners without losers: Structures & strategies for increasing student motivation to learn.* Needham Heights, MA: Allyn & Bacon.

Reeve, J. (1996). *Motivating others: Nurturing inner motivational resources.* Needham Heights, MA: Allyn & Bacon.

Richmond, V. P. (1990). Communication in the classroom: Power and motivation. *Communication Education, 39*, 181–195.

Richmond, V. P., Gorham, J. S. & McCroskey, J. C. (1987). The relationship between selected immediacy behaviors and cognitive learning. In M. L. McLaughlin (Ed.), *Communication yearbook 10* (pp. 574–590). Beverly Hills, CA: Sage.

Richmond, V. P., & McCroskey, J. C. (Eds.) (1992). *Power in the classroom: Communication, control and concern.* Hillsdale, NJ: Lawrence Erlbaum.

Sanders, J. A., & Wiseman, R. L. (1990). The effects of verbal and nonverbal immediacy on perceived cognitive, affective, and behavioral learning in the multicultural classroom. *Communication Education, 39*, 341–353.

Schunk, D. H. (1985). Self-efficacy and classroom learning. *Psychology in the Schools, 22*, 208–223.

Sloane, H. N., Jr., & Jackson, D. A. (1974). *A guide to motivating learners.* Englewood Cliffs, NJ: Educational Technology.

Smith, H. A. (1979). Nonverbal communication in teaching. *Review of Educational Research, 49*, 631–672.

Stipek, D. (1998). *Motivation to learn: From theory to practice* (3rd ed.). Needham Heights, MA: Allyn & Bacon.

Vernon, M. D. (1969). *Human motivation.* Cambridge, England: Cambridge University.

Waxman, H. C. (1983). Effect of teachers' empathy on students' motivation. *Psychological Reports, 53*, 489–490.

Wlodkowski, R. J. (1978). *Motivation and teaching.* Washington, DC: National Education Association.

Yerkes, R. M., & Dodson, J. D. (1908). The reactions of strength of stimulus to rapidity of habit formation. *Journal of Comparative and Neurological Psychology, 18*, 459–482.

SECTION THREE

Special Topics in Instructional Communication

Teachers often find themselves in a variety of situations that are not "covered" by traditional discussions of teaching and learning. This section examines a number of contexts that new teachers may encounter early in their career, and offers some useful ways to approach each of these contexts.

13 Teacher Communication in the Distance Education Context

TIMOTHY P. MOTTET

SUE L. STEWART

Southwest Texas State University

Distance education is rapidly gaining popularity as a medium for teaching and learning. In fact, a 1995 national survey of two- and four-year institutions of higher education conducted by the National Center for Educational Statistics reported that 758,640 students were formally enrolled in 25,730 distance education courses delivered to remote (off-campus) locations via audio, video, and/or computer technologies during the 1994–1995 academic year (Greene & Meek, 1998). Another study by Cotton (1995) reported that over 30 percent of higher education institutions were currently engaged in some form of distance learning and another 28 percent were planning for it during the 1994–1995 academic term.

Administrators remain receptive to distance education for a number of reasons. First, distance education allows colleges and universities to reach underserved communities, a goal which remains central to the mission of many public colleges and universities. Second, serving rural and remote audiences allows institutions of higher education to increase profit margins by tapping educational markets in which minimal competition exists. Finally, distance education allows institutions to serve what Postman (1995) refers to as the technological "God." The assumption here is that all things technological remain good. Postman refers to it as "technological adoration." Although some administrators may not adore technology, they *do not* want to develop a reputation for opposing it. Therefore, developing distance education delivery systems and networks remains a way for administrators to use technology to shape their institutions. Others more opposed to instructional technologies argue that administrators are remaking the institutions to accommodate the technology.

Many teachers are not as receptive to distance education as administrators appear to be. Although they remain a bit more cautious, many teachers are warming to the idea of distance education and are becoming convinced that their futures will include teaching students at remote locations using mediated delivery systems. Some find the opportunity very challenging and rewarding where others find the opportunity problematic because it runs counter to what they consider to be good teaching. Regardless of their mixed reactions, there is a growing demand for distance educators.

Many new teachers reading this chapter may not have an immediate interest in teaching a distance education course or may believe that distance education courses are reserved for more tenured and/or seasoned faculty members. It is our belief, however, that junior faculty members may not have a choice when it comes to teaching and developing courses for the burgeoning distance education networks. In many institutions of higher education, there is a forthright determinism in terms of distance education. In the past, distance education was an option, an alternate way to reach students and for students to obtain an education. Today, distance education is no longer viewed as an option, but a necessity to accommodate contemporary lifestyles.

The purpose of this chapter is to introduce new teachers to distance education and the communication-related issues unique to this nontraditional teaching context. This will be accomplished in three sections. The first section introduces teachers to two primary distance education delivery systems including interactive television and computer or Web-based platforms. The second section addresses three questions new distance educators should understand prior to teaching their first distance education course: (1) Is your course content suitable for distance education? (2) What should you know before teaching a distance education course? And (3) What should your students know before taking a distance education course? The third and final section reviews instructional communication strategies that have been shown to be effective in the distance education context.

Definitions and Delivery Systems

Verduin and Clark (1991) define distance education as "any formal approach to learning in which a majority of instruction occurs while educator and learner are at a distance from another" (p. 8). They emphasize that "distance education occurs when more than half of the formal instruction, or teaching, is done at a distance. Teaching here means contact hours, by whatever medium, and not self-instructional work performed as an adjunct to in-class work" (p. 13).

Distance education is not a new phenomenon. Although it has been with us since the development of the postal service in the nineteenth century, the delivery systems that channel the education from teachers to students and from students to teachers have changed considerably. In many distance education contexts, the media that unite teachers and students are interactive television and/or computer-based delivery systems. Previously, these delivery systems have been examined as separate and distinct. New distance education technologies, however, remain more integrative and blended (Smith & Dillon, 1999). For example, many distance education courses delivered through interactive television also require computer-mediated communication such as e-mail and/or on-line supplemental materials. We are also beginning to see the introduction of video and audio in computer-based distance education courses.

New distance educators may find themselves using a variety of instructional technologies. Some courses are transmitted over local cable access and do not allow for teacher-student interaction. Courses transmitted via satellite, however, provide more interactive capabilities including one-way audio and two-way video, or two-way audio and video. We will refer to this as interactive television (ITV). In most remote interactive television classrooms, students attend class by watching a television monitor that displays the broadcast of the course material. When students want to participate and communicate with other locations, they activate a microphone that transmits their voice. Once they begin to speak, voice-activated cameras focus on the student and transmit the visual image. In most interactive television studio classrooms, teachers see their students at various locations on a series of smaller television monitors. Instructors teach into cameras that automatically track their movements.

Courses delivered via the computer are transmitted via the Internet and interaction is primarily text-based through the use of e-mail, bulletin boards, and/or chat rooms offering "real-time" or synchronous communication. We will refer to this as computer-mediated communication (CMC). In this context, students take courses on-line. Many distance educators design and develop Internet Web sites that allow for self-guided instruction. Depending on the course Web site, students work through a series of units that are carefully linked together. Periodically, they are instructed to interact with other students in discussion groups or to make postings to the course bulletin board. Discussion groups (called listservs on the Internet) allow for ongoing discussions via e-mail between individuals. Bulletin boards resemble listservs, but are more public allowing postings to be seen by many students at once. At many colleges and universities, these interactive capabilities are part of a larger Internet-based course management program or "platform." Course management platforms (i.e., Blackboard, WebCT, CampusCruiser, WEBSync) allow teachers to manage many functions including course documents (posting of syllabi and assignments), communication (bulletin boards, "real-time" chat rooms), assessment (quizzes and surveys), and administration (attendance, distribution of grades). For an overview of technical, network, equipment, usage, and cost considerations for distance learning, refer to Williams, Paprock, and Covington (1999).

Three Questions for New Distance Educators

This section answers three questions distance educators should understand prior to teaching their first distance education course. Oftentimes, new teachers need information in order to reduce their own uncertainty and to prepare and plan accordingly. Because of their inexperience or lack of exposure, many new teachers do not know which questions to ask. Anticipating this need, we ask and attempt to answer three questions that we consider basic to distance education.

1. *Is your course content suitable for distance education?* Before readily agreeing to teach a distance education course (assuming you have a choice), it is first necessary to ask if your course content remains suitable for a wide audience. To begin this process, you need to determine your overall learning objectives. Bloom and his associates at the University of Chicago classified learning objectives as falling into three domains: cognitive, behavioral or psychomotor, and affective (Bloom, 1956; Krathwohl, Bloom, & Masia, 1964). The cognitive domain includes those learning objectives that focus on students being able to recall, understand, apply, analyze, synthesize, and evaluate course content. An example of this would be students being able to explain balance theory and its application to persuasive communication. The behavioral or psychomotor domain includes those learning objectives that focus on students being able to perform or enact a particular behavior or skill. An example of this would be a student who can prepare and deliver a persuasive speech based on a prescribed set of behaviors. The affective domain includes those learning objectives where students cultivate a liking and/or appreciation for the content and skills they are learning. An example of this would be students who can not only explain balance theory and develop and present a persuasive speech applying balance theory, but who also enjoy and appreciate what they are doing and see themselves using and engaging in these behaviors outside of the classroom.

   Once learning objectives have been outlined, teachers need to ask what types of instructional activities may be used to bring about the objectives and if these can successfully be met in a distance learning context. This may include making use of lectures, role-plays, simulations, case studies, small group discussions, drill and practice exercises, and/or individual work. After learning goals and instructional activities have been considered, teachers then need to consider the interactive capabilities of the instructional technology used to deliver the course and choose appropriate activities. Although many distance education programs promote their technologies as being able to simulate the traditional face-to-face classroom, most instructional technologies fall short in delivering the "virtual" classroom. Over time, this problem will resolve itself as technologies become more advanced. In the interim, new distance educators need realistic expectations for what the technology can and cannot do.

   The lead author of this chapter remembers observing a graduate level course in nursing ethics in which the learning objectives, instructional activities, and the technology's ability to simulate the interactiveness of the traditional classroom were incompatible. One of the cognitive objectives of this course was to tap into students' higher order critical thinking skills. Students were expected to analyze case studies, synthesize prior content, and evaluate medical decisions. Although the instructor had experience teaching using interactive television technology, she had not used it to teach course content that remained subjective and controversial in nature. To reach her cognitive learning objectives, she had to facilitate an intensive interactive discussion among 75 students located in over ten remote locations. Unfortunately, the technology was unable to capture and transmit the type of spontaneous and synchronous interaction she needed to reach her higher order learning goals. Had she considered her learning objectives in light of the capabilities of the technology, she might have chosen other alternatives.

Introductory courses seem more appropriate and suitable for interactive television and Web-based delivery systems because the course content remains more objective or fact-based. Lower-division college content courses focus on cognitive objectives in which students are asked to recall, explain, and analyze concepts. In order for students to master introductory course learning objectives, student-to-teacher and/or student-to-student interaction remains less important. In fact, many lower division courses are delivered by faculty members and/or graduate teaching assistants who rely solely on traditional lecture rather than the interactive seminar format.

There are numerous reasons, however, why lower division courses *may not* be suitable for distance education. We will discuss two of them. The first is that less mature students are not equipped for distance learning. Distance education courses, by their nature, demand self-discipline and well-developed study habits—two traits that many new traditional college students may not possess. The second reason is that many departments use introductory courses as a way to introduce students to their discipline and department and as a way to attract majors. At Southwest Texas State University, we refer to the basic communication course as the "front porch" course. This course emphasizes affective learning goals as a way to introduce the speech communication discipline and department to prospective majors. Developing affective goals, such as getting students to like and value the course content, requires an interpersonal connection between students and teachers. To date, most delivery systems fall short in capturing and transmitting relational messages needed to cultivate affective goals. For these reasons, it may not be prudent to deliver basic courses through distance education.

2. *What should you know before teaching a distance education course?* We are going to answer this question by addressing the advantages and disadvantages of teaching a distance education course. The answer to this question will address more of the disadvantages than advantages since we believe new distance educators are more likely to be told the advantages by administrators who are anxious to get more of their courses on the distance education schedule.

Advantages to Distance Teaching

There are some clear advantages to teaching a distance education course. One advantage is that you will be helping administrators and department chairs reach their technology goals. Making friends with these key individuals remains advantageous especially for new, nontenured faculty members who are in tenure track positions. Your willingness to teach a distance education course will be recognized and noted by administrators and other faculty members who remain less willing to teach in this context.

Another advantage to being a distance educator is that you remain on the cutting edge of instructional technology. Although distance education has been around since the beginning of the U.S. postal system, the dramatic improvements in instructional technology continue to transform the systems used to mediate distance education. Your abilities and/or *willingness to learn* how to use new instructional technologies make you a pioneer and an invaluable resource as departments continue to integrate instructional technologies into their existing programs.

Disadvantages to Distance Teaching

This discussion is not intended to discourage new teachers from teaching in the distance context, but is intended to inform prospective teachers of some of the disadvantages of teaching a distance education course. One of the obvious disadvantages concerns the limitations of the instructional technology used to mediate the instruction. New distance educators must understand how they will use new technology and at the same time be used by it. It remains a love/hate relationship. Here are three ways in which the technology uses the teacher.

First, instructors do not have complete control over their classes. Distance educators are at the mercy of the technology to convey their course content and to facilitate interaction. When your link to remote locations fails, whether it is transmitted through satellite, fiberoptic cable, or telephone lines, your instruction remains interrupted and you are dependent on the technical support team, if you have one, to restore the transmission. In many interactive television classrooms this type of disruption remains problematic, especially since an instructor only has the interactive television classroom reserved for a limited amount of time and/or the institution has only purchased and reserved a limited amount of satellite time for transmission. Self-paced, computer-based delivery systems may not have these same time limitations; however, students may experience problems and frustrations stemming from difficulties in making or maintaining computer connections as well as the inability to access or download course information. Distance educators must plan for transmission disruptions and must have contingency plans for covering the remaining course content. This may include preparing prerecorded videotapes to be mailed to each remote student to recapture the part of the class that was missed, or a system to contact and distribute study guide or additional study materials to students who were unable to access the on-line course through their computer connection.

Second, distance educators are controlled by the technology in how they facilitate interaction. The distance educators we have observed complain that interactive technologies limit or retard spontaneous communication. Many comments reflect the frustration of teachers and students who have difficulty hearing, seeing, and interacting in the interactive television classroom. In an interview following her graduate course in nursing ethics, Laurie, an award winning nursing educator, discussed her experience.

> I miss the spontaneity that you get in the traditional classroom. It's very distracting; for example, tonight oftentimes the language is like watching an old film, you know, the voice components and the television monitor are not in sync. Many things happen in terms of the volume level going up and down. You can't have anything really spontaneous because it won't get picked-up. So, in other words, students within each little classroom (at the various remote sites) can have spontaneous things happening, laughter, you know, side comments. These side conversations could add or trigger another student to think of something that they might not otherwise have told us. The ability for me to facilitate a conversation between students is lost. If I interject while a student is talking, it would be so distracting in this medium because it would have meant that I would have had to cut them off, wait for the timing to come to me so that my speaker voice would be picked-up and then the comment to them. So you can't do it. You totally lose it. I have to wait until they're finished and at that point, you lose the spontaneity of the conversation. It becomes too canned. (Mottet, 1998, pp. 9–10)

Finally, current instructional technologies may fail to convey subtle nonverbal cues that are needed to both regulate the flow of communication and that have been shown to convey relational messages. Culnan and Markus (1987) refer to this as the cues-filtered-out perspective. New distance educators gain a new appreciation for nonverbal communication once they teach in an environment in which they cannot detect their students' nonverbal cues or there is a reduction and/or distortion in the nonverbal messages they receive and send to their students. Imagine not being able to see your students' facial expressions, such as their puzzlement when they are confused or their head nods that convey understanding. Imagine not being able to hear your students' vocal interrupters indicating that they would like to say something or vocal assurances that suggest their understanding of course content.

Two types of instructional communication that are highly susceptible to nonverbal cues are humor and sarcasm, both of which have been shown to cultivate affect and relational liking. These communication styles may remain less effective in the distance education context as a result of the medium's inability to convey the subtle vocal cues needed to stimulate appropriate meanings. Similarly, your enthusiasm and passion for your content and students, which are conveyed primarily through your facial expressions and animated nonverbal behaviors, may not be conveyed and transmitted because of the technology's inability to detect such relational messages.

According to Sproull and Kiesler (1986), the lack of cues makes it more difficult for the sender to communicate the mood of the message and for the receiver to choose among possible interpretations. In addition, it is more difficult to communicate a sense of individuality, resulting in the feeling of anonymity among the communicators. This may result in less emotional involvement in the communication itself, less emotional attachment to the others in the group or class, or less concern with how a student may compare with others. Overall, Sproull and Kiesler remind us that the nature of the technology allows for a feeling of detachment.

Laurie, the distance educator referenced above, indicated that the technology failed to convey or transfer her knowledge and her ability to teach. She said it was frustrating to walk away from class feeling as though the students at remote locations were not seeing her at her best. "I think they lose my personality with the television . . . and they lose my energy and passion. And I miss their energy. It's frustrating . . . I mean will they be comfortable in calling me up and asking me for advice about changing a job, or to listen to an idea that they have, or asking me to review an article they have written?" (Mottet, 1998, pp. 12–13).

Not being able to see your students' nonverbal responsive behaviors has been shown to influence the distance teaching process. Mottet (2000) found that teachers who perceived fewer student nonverbal cues in the interactive television context also perceived distance learners as being less intelligent, motivated, and interested. Additionally, interactive television instructors considered themselves less effective, satisfied, and willing to teach in the interactive television classroom as perceptions of their students' nonverbal responsive cues decreased. We suspect that the same might be true for courses delivered through the computer.

Later in this chapter, we will discuss some of the instructional communication strategies distance educators can use in both the interactive television and/or computer-based classroom to address some of the limitations referred to in this section.

3. *What should your students know before taking a distance education course?* In terms of student communication, students must *first* be introduced to the technology that mediates the instruction. In the interactive television classroom, both McHenry and Bozik (1995) and Comeaux (1995) agree that students need to be oriented to the technology. McHenry and Bozik mentioned that students need to be taught how to use the technology, especially the microphones, in both the studio and remote classrooms. In this study, students reported frustration when their peers forgot to activate their microphones when they were addressing the teacher or responding to a question. Comeaux explained how students at first were uncomfortable seeing themselves on monitors and were highly conscious of voice-activated cameras that automatically track a student's voice. According to Comeaux, students were finally comfortable with the technology by the end of the course. "For future instructors of distance learning classrooms, it might prove valuable to devote a class period to exploring and 'playing' with different camera angles and shots. The goal for such an activity would be to demystify the technology and view it as a mere tool of communication" (Comeaux, 1995, p. 361).

With on-line courses, it is important to remember that the entire inter-action with both the class and the learning institution will be through the computer. For this reason, it is important that students know how to use computer technology (both hardware and software). Some instructors begin their course with an Internet tutorial that allows them to assess their students' level of comfort and knowledge with the computer technology. This might include assessing their ability to send and receive e-mail with at-tached documents, their ability to successfully access and download infor-mation from the Internet, library database, or other research Web sites, and their ability to demonstrate sufficient working knowledge and proficiency with software such as word processing and spreadsheets (Smith & Ben-scoter, 1999). Other instructors provide a clear description in the syllabus of the skills needed in order to participate. They begin the course with an activ-ity that requires students to demonstrate their abilities by signing on to the class bulletin board for a posting, sending an e-mail message to the instruc-tor, or downloading information as part of an initial assignment.

The *second* communication-related issue that students must under-stand is how teacher–student and student–student interaction is altered. In many interactive television classrooms, audible and visual messages are not always synchronized. There may be delays in the audio transmission, caus-ing students and teachers to inadvertently interrupt each other. This can be incredibly frustrating, much like the experience of making an overseas tele-phone call in which you or your receiver constantly "step on" each other's words. Eventually, we make adjustments to allow a few extra seconds for audio transmission. In some classrooms, this interaction disruption causes students to reduce the number of questions they normally ask and may negatively influence student learning. Hackman and Walker (1990) found that factors related to the clarity of audio/video transmission and the tech-nical ease of participating and interacting in the interactive television class-room were highly related to perceived student learning. How to establish an interaction protocol will be discussed in subsequent paragraphs.

On-line courses present similar teacher–student and student–student interaction challenges. Young (2000) reported that on-line students miss professors' instant feedback. An art-history student mentioned that "[y]ou can't just raise your hand and ask a question" (p. A-42). Another student re-called the night that he and some of his colleagues gathered in the course's virtual chat room to try to figure out what the professor meant by the ques-tion he posed on the list serve, or the on-line bulletin board where teachers and students post and respond to each other's questions. "You can wait for days to get a response, and by then you've moved on to something else" (A-42).

The *third* communication-related issue examines how the filtering out of teacher nonverbal behaviors may influence student perceptions. Distance learners need clear expectations for how the course is going to look and/or sound in remote locations. Like teachers, students take for granted the nonverbal messages they receive from their instructors and have no appreciation for such messages until they are no longer apparent. In the interactive television classroom, students notice a considerable reduction in the amount of nonverbal cues they receive from their instructors (Freitas, Myers, & Avtgis, 1998). Guerrero and Miller (1998) found that students who perceived fewer instructor nonverbal cues also perceived instructors as being less likable and trustworthy and found the course content less interesting and having less value. In text-based courses delivered through the computer, these nonverbal cues may be virtually nonexistent.

Although there is ample research to suggest that there are no significant cognitive learning differences between traditional and distance learners, there is ample instructional communication research to suggest that there may be significant reductions in affective forms of learning. [We should also note that a recent study published by the Institute for Higher Education Policy (1999) criticizes much of the research examining cognitive learning on methodological grounds suggesting that there may be significant reductions in cognitive learning.] As McCroskey reviewed in Chapter 1, cognitive learning is more likely to occur if students have an affect or liking for both the teacher and the course content. Teachers cultivate liking for themselves and their content primarily through their nonverbal expression. Students need to understand how perceiving fewer, if any, nonverbal cues in the distance learning context may influence how they perceive both their instructor and course content. It could be that students may miss out on developing meaningful relationships with both teachers and course content that they will need in order to pursue their educational and/or life goals.

In conclusion, this section has asked three important questions that new distance educators need answered prior to teaching their first distance education course: Is your course suitable for distance education? What do you need to know prior to teaching a distance education course? Finally, what do your students need to know prior to taking a distance education course? Having answers to these three questions paves the way for the final section of the chapter, which examines instructional communication strategies for distance educators.

Instructional Communication Strategies for Distance Educators

There are several "how to" guidebooks that walk new distance educators through the "nuts and bolts" of teaching in the remote or distance classroom. Some of these references are cited at the end of this section. We would also like to remind readers to apply the instructional communication concepts and strategies discussed in the preceding chapters including teacher immediacy (Chapter 6), content relevance (Chapter 7), teacher clarity (Chapter 8), teacher communicator style

(Chapter 9), and teacher humor (Chapter 10). All of these concepts and strategies have utility in the remote or distance classroom.

The paragraphs that follow highlight some of the *specific* instructional communication strategies that have been shown to be effective in the distance education context including structuring interactions, developing interaction protocols, and personalizing instruction.

Structure Interactions

Much of the empirical evidence suggests that student interaction remains the critical predictor of student satisfaction in the remote classroom (Fulford & Zhang, 1993). In the distance education context, interaction doesn't just happen. It must be planned. Here are a few suggestions:

1. Require students to post weekly responses to questions and/or comments on the on-line course bulletin board. Direct students to work through e-mail to complete a group project, requiring students to complete on-line quizzes, or providing students with links to other Web sites that may have information relevant to course content.
2. Prepare breakaway activities in which small groups of distance learners are asked to respond to questions, case studies, and/or scenarios based on the assigned readings, or on content presented in the mini-lecture.
3. Assign study-guide questions for each week that pertain to the assigned readings. At the beginning of class, instructors place distance learners into small groups and ask them to respond to the questions within their group. The instructor then facilitates a guided discussion among the groups.

Develop Interaction Protocols

In many distance education contexts, students and teachers "step on" each other's words and spend an enormous amount of time pulling apart their conversation in order for it to make sense. In the interactive television classroom, students cannot monitor others' turn taking cues and many times there is a delay in the audio and video transmission that disrupts conversational patterns. Similar problems occur when using computer-mediated communication. An interaction protocol that teachers and students use to guide and facilitate responding to questions, asking questions, and/or making comments will help regulate communication.

Here are a few suggestions for teachers in the interactive television classroom:

1. Announce at the beginning of class how you would like to handle questions and/or comments from students. Some instructors remain receptive to student questions at any point throughout the televised class. Others reserve time at the beginning of class, at the end of class, or at the beginning and end of class.

2. Remind students that with some interactive delivery systems, it takes the voice-activated camera a few seconds to recognize their voice. Once the voice has been recognized, the camera will position itself to capture the student making the comment.

3. Greet students who are responding to your questions by asking for their name and location. Following their response, paraphrase what they said to ensure appropriate meaning and allow time for them to confirm or disconfirm and clarify understanding.

Here are a few suggestions for teachers using CMC:

1. Have clear instructional objectives for CMC. Post questions that specifically target your instructional objectives. This will keep students on task.

2. Give students a structure for framing their CMC. Arrange debates or roleplays. This type of structuring allows students to sequence their on-line communication. In most typical debates, opponents take turns presenting their arguments. This type of protocol prevents students from walking over each other's words.

3. Use some of the other protocols for guiding and facilitating CMC including weaving, going around the circle, arranging private conversations, and/or inviting experts to participate in chat room discussions. When teachers "weave" text-based interactions, they summarize the current state of the online discussion and identify themes or points of agreement or disagreement (Feenberg, 1989). "Going around the circle" remains effective for smaller on-line discussion groups. Here the teacher instructs each participant to respond to a question before a new question is addressed (Elsley, 1991). Two other effective and popular protocols for guiding CMC include arranging private conversations among two or more students who share similar interests and inviting experts or practitioners from the field to participate in on-line discussions with distance learners.

Personalize Instruction

Teachers who personalize their instruction or "transcend the distance" have been shown to be particularly effective as distance educators (Comeaux, 1995). Here are a few suggestions that may help personalize your distance teaching:

1. Spend the first class session allowing students to get to know the technology (how to use it) and each other by experimenting with the technology and using ice-breaker activities that help students feel comfortable interacting across the distance (Comeaux, 1995).

2. Learn students' names, faces, and especially voices when teaching in the interactive television classroom (Comeaux, 1995).

3. Have a sense of humor or personable style when dealing with technical glitches or nuances (i.e., "Dr. Smith, I think your battery is dead; we can't

hear you" or "It's the microphone that's scratchy, not my voice! Can you hear me better now?") (Comeaux, 1995).

4. Begin each class session by checking in with each remote site and allowing time for informal communication, and by visiting each remote cite for at least one class period if possible (McHenry & Bozik, 1995).

5. Distribute an e-mail list to all class members and ask students to mail a statement or paragraph introducing themselves to the group. Ask them to include in this e-mail information about their personal, professional, or educational experiences as well as their feelings and experiences about the course. This strategy has been shown to assist both teachers and students in seeing each other as individuals rather than talking heads.

6. Develop an Internet home page that lets students know who you are. Danney, a local distance educator, encourages his students to check out his Internet homepage. This location offers information about his professional and educational background, a listing of other courses that he is teaching, recommended Web sites on subjects related to course content, as well as a picture of himself and an introduction to his cats.

The preceding paragraphs have reviewed just a few of the many instructional communication strategies that have been shown to be effective in the distance education context including ways to structure and guide interactions, develop interaction protocols, and personalize instruction. New distance educators are encouraged to develop a repertoire of instructional communication strategies that can be adapted to various instructional technologies and distance education delivery systems.

Conclusion

In this chapter we have introduced new distance educators to three questions they should understand prior to teaching their first course, and several instructional communication strategies that have been shown to maximize instructional effectiveness in the distance learning context. For the past several years, rather than *using* technology as a tool to enhance teaching, many distance educators have been *used* by technology. We have been limited to a single delivery system, such as the computer or television, to channel our instructional messages. We have been limited to a single highway, which unfortunately has had numerous detours along the way. Many distance educators have accommodated the technology by taking the numerous detours and as a result, their experiences have been less than desirable. Today, the single highway has grown into an elaborate interstate highway system that networks and synthesizes numerous instructional technologies. The detours remain; however, traffic does not always come to a complete standstill. We have options. Future training of distance educators is likely to focus on selecting the appropriate technology for the instructional goals driving the course, and how to use each of the technologies to maximize instructional communication effectiveness. As new technologies are developed and used to channel distance education, so will the research examining their effectiveness. We encourage current and future distance educators to remain abreast not only of the new technologies, but also the applied research informing the practice of the new technologies. The *Journal of Distance Education, The American Journal of Distance Education,* and *Communication Education* consistently report research findings related to distance education and instructional communication related issues involving distance education. Additionally, there are several "how to" guidebooks that walk new distance educators through the logistics of distance teaching. We recommend the following resources and Web sites.

RECOMMENDED "HOW TO" WEB SITES

www.uidaho.edu/evo/distglan.html: Distance Education at a Glance, University of Idaho

www.wellspring.isinj.com: The Wellspring—An Online Community of Distance Educators

www.aber.ac.uk/media/Sections/it01.html: Computer-Mediated Communication

www.ed.psu.edu/acsde: The American Center for the Study of Distance Education

www.icde.org: International Council for Open and Distance Education

www.uark.edu/~aca/studies/cmc.html: The American Communication Association Center for Communication Studies: Computer Mediated Communication.

www.adec.edu: American Distance Education Consortium.

www.natcom.org/ctronline/index.htm: The National Communication Association's Communication Teacher Resources Online.

www.ascusc.org/jcmc/index.html: Journal of Computer Mediated Communication.

REFERENCES AND SUGGESTED READINGS

Berge, Z. L. (1995). Facilitating computer conferencing: Recommendations from the field. *Educational Technology, 35,* 22–30.

Bloom, B. S. (Ed.). (1956). *Taxonomy of educational objectives,* (Handbook I: Cognitive domain). New York: McKay.

Comeaux, P. (1995). The impact of interactive distance learning network on classroom communication. *Communication Education, 44,* 353–361.

Cotton, C. (1995). Time-and-place independent learning: The higher education market for distance learning emerges. *Syllabus, 8,* 37–39.

Culnan, M. J., & Markus, M. L. (1987). Information technologies. In F. M. Jablin, L. L. Putnam, K. H. Roberts, & L. W. Porter (Eds.), *Handbook of organizational communication: An interdisciplinary perspective* (pp. 420-443). Newbury Park, CA: Sage.

Dillon, C. L., Hengst, H. R., & Zoller, D. (1991). Instructional strategies and student involvement in distance education: A study of the Oklahoma televised instruction system. *Journal of Distance Education, 6,* 29–45.

Dillon, C. L., & Walsh, S. M. (1992). Faculty: The neglected resource in distance education. *The American Journal of Distance Education, 6,* 5–21.

Elsley, M. E. (1991). Guidelines for conducting instruction discussions on a computer conference. In A. J. Miller (Ed.). Applications of computer conferencing to teacher education and human resource development. Symposium conducted at the meeting of the International Symposium on Computer Conferencing, Columbus, OH. (ERIC document Reproduction Service No. ED 337 705)

Feenberg, A. (1989). The written world. In R. Mason & A. Kaye (Eds.). *Mindweave: Communication, computers, and distance education* (pp. 22–39). New York: Pergamon Press.

Freitas, F. A., Myers, S. A., & Avtgis, T. A. (1998).

Student perceptions of instructor immediacy in conventional and distributed learning classrooms. *Communication Education, 47,* 366–371.

Fulford, C. P., & Zhang, S. (1993). Perceptions of interaction: The critical predictor in distance education. *The American Journal of Distance Education, 7,* 8–21.

Gehlauf, D. N., Shatz, M. A., & Frye, T. W. (1991). Faculty perceptions of interactive television instructional strategies: Implications for training. *The American Journal of Distance Education, 5,* 20–28.

Greene, B., & Meek, A. (1998). *Distance education in higher education institutions: Incidence, audiences, and plans to expand.* (Report no. NCES-98- 132). Washington, DC: U.S. Government Printing Office.

Guerrero, L. K., & Miller, T. A. (1998). Associations between nonverbal behaviors and initial impressions of instructor competence and course content in videotaped distance education courses. *Communication Education, 47,* 30–42.

Hackman, M. Z., & Walker, K. B. (1990). Instructional communication in the televised classroom: The effects of system design and teacher immediacy on student learning and satisfaction. *Communication Education, 39,* 196–206.

Hiltz, S. R. (1994). *The virtual classroom: Learning without limits via computer networks.* Norwood, NJ: Ablex Publishing Corporation.

Hsu, S., Marques, O., Hamza, M., & Alhalabi, B. (1999). How to design a virtual classroom: Ten easy steps to follow. *T. H. E. Journal* (September), 96–109.

Khan, B. H. (Ed.). (1997). *Web-based instruction.* Englewood Cliffs, NJ: Educational Technology Publications.

Krathwohl, D. R., Bloom, B. S., & Masia B. B. (1964). *Taxonomy of educational objectives,* (Handbook II: Affective domain). New York: McKay.

McHenry, L., & Bozik, M. (1995). Communicating at a distance: A study of interaction in a distance education classroom. *Communication Education, 44,* 362–371.

Mottet, T. P. (1996). *Effective teaching at a distance: Three perspectives on distance education.* Unpublished manuscript, West Virginia University, Morgantown, WV.

Mottet, T. P. (1998, March). *Teaching from a distance: "Hello, is anyone out there?"* Paper presented at the University of Pennsylvania's 19th Annual Ethnography in Education Research Forum, Philadelphia, PA. [ERIC ED 417 436]

Mottet, T. P. (2000). Interactive television instructors' perceptions of students' nonverbal responsiveness and their influence on distance teaching. *Communication Education, 49,* 146–164.

Porter, L. R. (1997). *Creating the virtual classroom: Distance learning with the Internet.* New York: Wiley & Sons.

Postman, N. (1995). *The end of education: Redefining the value of school.* New York: Knopf.

Smith, P., & Dillon, C. L. (1999). Comparing distance learning and classroom learning: Conceptual considerations. *American Journal of Distance Education, 13,* 6–23.

Smith, S., & Benscoter, A. (1999). Implementing an Internet tutorial for Web-based courses. *The American Journal of Distance Education, 13,* 74–80.

Sproull, L., & Kiesler, S. (1986). Reducing social context cues: Electronic mail in organizational communication. *Management Science, 32,* 1492–1512.

The Institute for Higher Education Policy. (April, 1999). *What's the difference? A review of contemporary research on the effectiveness of distance learning in higher education.* Washington, DC.

Verduin, J. R., & Clark, T. A. (1991). *Distance education: The foundations of effective teaching.* San Francisco: Jossey-Bass Publishers.

Williams, M. L., Paprock, K., & Covington, B. (1999). *Distance learning: The essential guide.* Thousand Oaks, CA: Sage Publications.

Willis, B. (1993). *Distance teaching: A practical guide.* Englewood Cliffs, NJ: Educational Technology Publications.

Willis, B. (Ed.). (1994). *Distance education strategies and tools.* Englewood Cliffs, NJ: Educational Technology Publications.

Young, J. R. (2000, March 3). Dispatches from distance education, where class is always in session. *The Chronicle of Higher Education,* pp. A41–A42.

14 Communicating with Students from Other Cultures

CANDICE THOMAS-MADDOX
Ohio University-Lancaster

As we begin the twenty-first century, instructors at all levels are faced with the challenge of communicating with students from diverse backgrounds. The goal of many educators is to not only teach students content, but also to assist them in learning how to apply that knowledge in ways which will be beneficial to their lives. It is a challenge to accomplish this goal because we are now faced with the task of understanding the impact that student diversity has on our ability to successfully communicate with them. An essential part of being viewed as a competent teacher and a competent communicator rests in our ability to achieve shared meaning when interacting with our students. An even greater task lies in realizing the role that culture and diversity play in influencing our students' learning and behavior. These challenges are experienced by teachers at all levels of education and across a variety of instructional contexts—from the traditional classroom with students in grades K–12, to the college classroom comprised of international students and nontraditional students, to the corporate training session designed to instruct employees about new procedures for handling customer accounts. There is no doubt that we are experiencing a growing need for teachers to explore the ways in which diversity impacts communication in the classroom.

Understanding the differences specific to each and every student's individual culture is an unrealistic expectation. After all, there are many influences that could cause a student to perceive your communicative behaviors in a particular way, and vice versa. Combine this with the fact that there are often many different cultures represented in our classrooms, and you can see that it is more important to be aware of the general aspects of cultural diversity rather than focusing on the specifics of each group. The goal of this chapter is two-fold. First, you will be provided with an overview of factors which contribute to differences in perceptions that both you and your students bring to the classroom. Second, some examples of how these factors can potentially influence classroom interactions will be explored. These examples are not meant to be prescriptions or solutions to communication challenges faced in diverse classrooms, rather they are intended to inspire you to consider ways in which you can address the challenges faced when interacting with students from diverse cultures.

Diversity and Change in the Classroom

Statistics provided by the U.S. Census Bureau indicate that among students enrolled in elementary and high school in 1998, nearly 64 percent were non-Hispanic white, 16 percent were non-Hispanic African American, 4 percent were non-Hispanic Asian and Pacific Islander, and 14 percent were Hispanic. These statistics illustrate the fact that our classrooms are rapidly becoming more diverse, and projections estimate that by the year 2020 non-Hispanic whites will no longer be the majority. While these statistics reflect the ethnic and racial diversity that exists in instructional settings, individual differences span far beyond the categories of race or ethnicity. There are differences in the ability levels of students (i.e., learning disabilities, physical disabilities), the relationships or associations among students based on their common interests (i.e., joining clubs or gangs, participating in sports and activities), and their geographical location (i.e., rural or urban, those from military families who moved frequently). These factors create a unique set of cultural experiences that shapes a student's expectations for communication and learning in the classroom.

Often, teachers in K–12 classrooms are responsible for communicating with parents about their children's academic performance. However, census statistics report that approximately 20 percent of elementary and high school students have at least one foreign-born parent, while 5 percent of elementary and high school students themselves are foreign born. The new challenge for teachers goes beyond simply finding the correct words or language to communicate to parents about their child's progress. It is now a multifaceted task since the instructor must be able to not only communicate in a language that will be understood but also must have some knowledge of the cultural background of the family in order to anticipate the value that is placed on education.

Additional statistics illustrate the prevalence of diversity in college classrooms. In 1998, approximately 71 percent of college students were non-Hispanic white, nearly 13 percent were non-Hispanic African American, 7 percent were non-Hispanic Asian and Pacific Islander, and 9 percent were Hispanic. College instructors are often faced with the challenge of helping students from different cultures communicate with one another. After all, it may be the first time that many students have had the opportunity to interact with someone who is truly different from themselves. Some may have never spoken with someone of a different race or nationality, and it is likely that they have been educated primarily by teachers from cultures similar to their own. As a result, their college education experience often involves learning more than concepts and theories. It teaches students to become competent communicators when interacting with diverse others.

Defining Diversity and Culture

The term "diversity" has emerged as a "buzz word" in academic and business environments. Educational institutions and companies have created special programs designed to encourage students and employees to appreciate diversity. The goal of these programs is to foster a positive communication environment. In this chapter, diversity will be explored from a "cultural difference" perspective. While more than 800 definitions have been presented for the term *culture*, it is defined in this chapter as the social, cognitive, and/or physical factors that are shared by an identified group. This particular definition captures the aspects of culture which have the most impact for teachers who are communicating with students from diverse cultures.

Social aspects of a culture include verbal and nonverbal messages used to communicate with others. For example, many cultures have created their own language or have adopted a particular accent or dialect that makes them unique. A student's native language may be Spanish, or she may be a member of the computer club and use words such as "megabyte" and "ram" in her everyday interactions with friends. Similar differences exist when exploring the nonverbal factors that make up the social aspects of a culture. A student from India may wear her veil while studying in U.S. classrooms or a student may smile and nod in response to a teacher's question even though he does not understand what was just explained. Each of these verbal and nonverbal factors present new dimensions for teachers to understand in order to effectively communicate with students.

The *cognitive* aspects of a culture include the values, beliefs, attitudes, and needs. These components of one's cultural pattern impact the learning process, quite often in dramatic ways. An example of values impacting your classroom might include a student whose family has instilled a high value for education. The shared value for education may cause that student to be more motivated in your class. Thus, you may communicate with the student differently than with one who has little value for school. When examining the impact of needs, consider the needs that the nontraditional, adult learner brings to your classroom. These needs may be quite different from those of the traditional college undergraduate. The adult learner may be returning to the classroom after working for 10–15 years, and they have a high level of communication apprehension when asked to participate in classroom discussions. Because of this apprehension, you may need to be more supportive and encouraging in your communication with the student. Attitudes have a tremendous impact on the communication between students and teachers. An employee who has been with a company for 20 years may have a negative attitude toward changing the way things have traditionally been done, and as a result he or she may approach with a negative attitude a training seminar designed to teach employees new procedures.

In addition to these aspects of the personal orientation system, students are unique in terms of their cognitive abilities for learning. Just as teachers bring different teaching styles in the classroom, students bring unique learning styles and learning capacities to the classroom. Some students may be gifted which requires you to communicate with them in ways which engage and challenge them. Others may have various learning disabilities which require you to discover innovative ways to use communication to enable them to learn the material. Instructors who report difficulty in communicating with their students often discover that the cognitive aspects of diverse cultures are at the core of these communication barriers.

In addition to the cognitive and social aspects of culture, it is also possible that there are *physical* factors which make groups distinct from one another. While the most commonly recognized physical aspects of culture are those associated with racial and ethnic differences, there are other physical components that contribute to classroom diversity. In addition to differences in skin color or facial structure, students may differ in terms of the physical challenges that impact communication in the classroom. Programs that encourage teachers to experience the challenges faced by visually or hearing impaired students have had a tremendous impact on the approach that these instructors use.

The final component of the definition of culture emphasizes that the factors described above are *shared by an identified group*. Students can self-identify with a particular group, and/or teachers can view students as belonging to a specific group. It is important to note the *shared* perception of culture because it is a critical factor which impacts a student's view of self. This also impacts a student's sense of self. Researchers in the area of interpersonal communication have focused on the impact that a person's self-identity has on communicative behaviors. Students in the United States experience a lot of pressure to "belong" to a group. These groups may include being a member of an athletic team, part of a religious group, or an initiated member of a gang. Our feelings of belonging will likely influence our interactions with others both inside and outside the classroom.

Exploring Your Cultural Background: The First Step to Solving the Diversity Puzzle

Being an effective communicator when interacting with diverse students requires you to develop an understanding of and an appreciation for cultural differences. Consider the analogy of a puzzle. In order to solve the puzzle, you must first lay out all the pieces needed to put the picture together. An essential piece in solving the puzzle of communicating with diverse students is understanding your own cultural background. What factors influence the ways in which you communicate with your students? We often bring to the classroom communicative behaviors that were used in our own educational experiences. We may model our own teaching after instructors who we found to be effective or motivating. However, we must realize that the communicative behaviors of those who we admire have been heavily influenced by their own cultural upbringing. For example, a teacher who received primary and secondary education in a rural farm community brings a unique set of cognitive and social experiences compared to an instructor who was educated in inner-city public schools. It may be that teachers in the rural classrooms engaged in communication behaviors and adopted approaches to learning different from those required to motivate and educate students from urban areas. Similarly, an instructor or student who is educated in Thailand will probably bring a unique set of expectations to the classroom with regard to interactions in the teacher–student relationship. These expectations may be violated when communicating with instructors and students schooled in Western cultures. There are several questions to ask yourself in order to maximize both the learning and the relational aspects of a diverse classroom:

- What are my attitudes toward students of diverse backgrounds?
- How do these attitudes influence my communication with these students?
- How have my own cultural experiences shaped these attitudes?
- Does my communicative behavior denote respect for students who are different from myself?
- Does my teaching style and classroom communication allow for diverse learning and communication styles?

By answering these questions, you will begin to uncover potential barriers in becoming a competent communicator with students from diverse backgrounds. For example, in exploring the first question you may discover that you hold a particular attitude or belief about Asian students. Perhaps there is the stereotype that Asian students are more intelligent, and you assume that there is less need to solicit feedback from them when checking for comprehension at the end of a lecture. After all, the Asian students typically respond with what you perceive as being positive nonverbal responses that indicate understanding—smiling while nodding the head. When you think about the smile and head nods more closely, you may discover that your stereotype of Asian students being extremely intelligent and academically motivated are the result of interactions you had with an Asian student during your college years. Perhaps you never interacted with Asian students while in college because you thought that they would have little in common to discuss. After all, the attempts you made when trying to communicate with one another while working on a group project resulted in numerous misunderstandings because of your language differences. Because of these past experiences, you may quickly discover that you now communicate with Asian students in your own classroom in a way that does not demonstrate respect for cultural differences. You tend to avoid eye contact during lectures, and often fail to ask if they have any questions at the end of class discussions. In neglecting to explore the impact of cultural differences, you have inadvertently engaged in communication behaviors that do not encourage interaction nor do they enhance affect or motivation for learning.

In order to understand the impact of our own cultural background and the influence that our own experiences, as well as our students' cultural experiences have on communication in the classroom, four additional pieces of the puzzle should be examined: values, beliefs, attitudes, and needs. These four puzzle pieces comprise what is referred to as one's cultural pattern, and this pattern influences virtually every aspect of our communicative behaviors.

Values

Values can be described as the relatively enduring, evaluative aspect of one's cultural pattern. Our values guide us in forming perceptions or judgments about what we should or should not do. Values are a central component in the development of our personal philosophy, and the values that are part of our personal philosophies are likely to permeate our teaching philosophies as well. The values held by instructors and students may be explicitly stated, but more often than not they are implicitly communicated through nonverbal actions. We may explicitly communicate the value we have for time when telling students that we expect work to be completed and submitted by a designated deadline in order to be considered for a grade. As a result of the explicit communication of values, there is little doubt about what is expected. The problem often results from those values communicated implicitly through nonverbal channels, resulting in ambiguity and confusion. After all, it is impossible to read another person's mind! One instructor shared a story about the confusion which resulted while working with students from Bangkok and Hong Kong. A custom in these cultures is for students to present their teacher with a small gift or token of appreciation to demonstrate the value for reciprocity and respect. It is not unusual for students to offer teachers gifts in exchange for the lessons they have learned. Since many teachers in the United States would view such gift-giving as a form of bribery, much confusion developed between the teacher and her students as a result of this gesture, and subsequent interactions were quite uncomfortable. The importance of recognizing values in teacher–student interactions can be found in many other classroom examples.

Researchers have identified various dimensions of cultural values—one of these dimensions focuses on the willingness of a culture to approach or avoid change and ambiguity about the future. A student who places high value on stability and order may become frustrated with a class which uses project-based learning. In this environment, the teacher probably has high value for working and communicating in groups. If the instructor's values and goals are not clearly communicated to students, the resulting frustration may interfere with the learning process. While values are central in guiding our communication, beliefs create a different set of challenges which influence our perceptions and behaviors.

Beliefs

Teachers and students bring their own sets of beliefs to the classroom. Some students may believe that they have to earn an "A" on an exam, while others may believe that they are destined to achieve very little in life. As a result, that student may not be motivated to work for a grade higher than a "C." Beliefs are defined as personal convictions regarding the truth or existence of things. Many factors influence the formation and communication of beliefs—your religious upbringing, cultural background, or past experiences may impact your reactions to situations.

There are three types of beliefs that have tremendous implications for classroom communication—inferential, informational, and experiential beliefs.

Suppose you were to enter the classroom on the first day dressed in a navy business suit. Students may form an inferential belief that you are difficult and demanding, and they will probably avoid communicating with you. In reality, you may have simply chosen to dress that way to form a good first impression as a competent teacher who is well-organized and professional. Informational beliefs are often formed as a result of information received from outside sources such as teachers, friends, or the media. Consider the impact that the media has on the formation of beliefs held by your students—they often believe the information which they read on Web pages or hear in news broadcasts as being factual. As a result, students may form a wide range of beliefs. One student may feel that it is important to vote because she heard a celebrity on MTV say that he planned to vote. Another student may believe that education is not an important part of achieving his goal of being a professional athlete after hearing a news story about his football hero who has decided to leave college for a multi-million dollar contract as a pro quarterback. We should consider the ways in which we explicitly or implicitly communicate our own beliefs to students. In addition, our students may benefit from being encouraged to explore "why" they hold certain beliefs. For example, you could challenge a student who expresses a belief that people from the South are slow to consider why he or she believes this. You may discover that these assumptions were formed as a result of watching a television show instead of basing the information on actual interactions with people from the South.

Attitudes

Students and teachers develop learned predispositions to respond favorably or unfavorably toward specific persons, objects, or ideas. These responses are referred to as attitudes. Attitudes are perhaps the most explicitly communicated dimension of one's cultural pattern. While it is important to explore the internal factors which guide the communication of attitudes, it is also essential that you identify your own reactions to cultural differences. Instead of simply dismissing another's cultural customs or actions as being "wrong," it is important for us to understand our own attitudes and the role that our culture has played in shaping the attitude. Failure to recognize our tendencies to respond in irrational ways may produce negative results in interactions with students from diverse backgrounds.

Stereotyping is one type of attitude that results in a person's inability to discriminate and view the unique aspects of an individual. Generalizations are made about a group, and these assumptions are then linked to any individual who is a member of that group. As teachers, we may fall into the stereotyping trap as a result of our past experiences—expecting that siblings will experience similar levels of academic success and behave in similar ways, assuming that all African American students speak in Ebonics, or anticipating that a male student from a Muslim culture will have little respect for female instructors. Each of these stereotypes may result in miscommunication and a negative educational experience.

While our focus is often directed toward negative stereotypes which result in negative communication, there are instances in which stereotypes can be favorable. Viewing athletes as being organized and motivated may be an example of one such attitude. Favorable stereotypes may result in more supportive classroom communication, while negative stereotypes typically result in communication avoidance.

Another category of attitudes is prejudice. Prejudice is defined as negative communicative reactions that are the result of inflexible assumptions about a group of people. There are numerous examples of the problems caused by prejudice in the U.S. educational system, including the practice of sexism, racism, or ageism in our classrooms.

Sexism.   Many television shows and news stories have described the discrimination experienced by females in the classroom and in the workplace. The research is filled with findings on how teachers communicate sexism in the classroom. Sexism that is communicated verbally includes male students typically receiving more praise and being given more opportunities to answer questions in the classroom. Both male and female teachers have been found to discipline male students more often than female students. When examining ways in which sexism is nonverbally communicated, studies report that teachers often make more eye contact with males than with females, and instructors will typically choose to stand or sit in a location near male students, thus inviting more verbal interaction as a result of the closer distance. Conduct a personal assessment of your own communication tendencies when communicating with male and female students. Invite a colleague to observe your teaching and assess potential areas for sexist behavior. Some areas for exploration include the following: Are male students called on more frequently than females? Which students communicate more in class by asking and answering questions? Do you face male or female students more often?

Racism.   Prejudice may also be expressed through racist reactions toward those of a different race or ethnicity. Reports of hate crimes on college campuses and of violence in elementary and high school classrooms illustrate the violent nature of prejudice that is often explicitly communicated by students. In 1999, two students shot and killed a teacher and 13 classmates at Columbine High School in Littleton, Colorado. After investigating an Internet site created by one of the students, it was determined that he openly communicated his dislike for students of various racial and ethnic groups, in addition to his anger toward athletes and students of various religious affiliations. Our media has been filled with stories asking the question "why" violence occurs in schools. Many students respond that negative communication between various groups is a primary cause for the hatred that often leads to physical violence. Teachers and school administrators must consider the messages communicated to students and the community. Are you communicating and encouraging respect and tolerance? South Carolina school officials debated the decision to fly the confederate flag at schools and at athletic fields. It became clear that various groups assigned very different meanings to the symbol. Similar stories can be found regarding debates over changing school mascots, such as the Indians or Warriors, which are perceived as being offensive and degrading. Other schools have witnessed the clear communication of prejudice when students deface school property with graffiti of racist slurs or swastikas. A primary communication challenge for teachers is to discourage an "us" versus "them" mentality in the classroom. You should be cautious about using language that compartmentalizes groups. Verbal immediacy research has discovered that the use of terms such as "we" and "us" has been useful in creating a classroom atmosphere that enhances perceptions of closeness, thereby reducing the perceived distance and difference between groups. In addition to the use of verbally immediate language, you may want to encourage your school to develop policies regarding the implications of prejudicial messages. These policies should be clearly communicated to students. While the issues of sexism and racism are often familiar to people when considering prejudiced communication, we sometimes fail to recognize the differences in our communication with older, nontraditional students.

Ageism.   Ageism is a form of prejudice that is communicated primarily by college teachers and students. When exploring the challenges and needs of what has been labeled as the "nontraditional" student population, several communication issues need our attention. Some adult students who return to the classroom after working for a period of time report feeling apprehensive about many aspects of the college experience. They may be apprehensive about speaking in front of the class, especially if they find themselves to be in the minority of a class comprised primarily of students who fall in the "traditional" age category of 18–22. Nontraditional students also report high levels of apprehension and ambiguity with regard to test taking and completing projects and papers. You can have a tremendous impact on this culture of students simply by communicating supportive messages. This includes creating a learning environment that provides students with the opportunity to seek feedback or ask questions regarding assignments and exams. Traditional and nontraditional student cultures can learn a lot from one another. For example, one teacher reports that the most rewarding learning experience for her students was the result of televising a family communication class to students on a main campus and four regional campuses. While all students at the main campus were in the 20–22 age range, approximately 85 percent of the students at regional campuses were nontraditional students juggling the demands of job, family, and education. Comments on the students' evaluations of the course at the end of the academic term indicated that a unique learning experience had occurred. Traditional and nontraditional students had the opportunity to interact with students whose experiences were different from their own. Teachers may want to encourage interactions among traditional and nontraditional college students through the use of group projects or study groups to assist in reducing the potential for ageism.

Needs

Each student and teacher brings personal desires to the classroom. If these desires are not met, we experience feelings of discomfort until we have satisfied the needs. The primary means for satisfying needs is to communicate with others so that we can obtain what is desired. An international student who has difficulty understanding an assignment may need help. The request for help may be made by asking an instructor or tutor for assistance. However, the teacher may need to "read between the lines" and interpret nonverbal cues that indicate the need for additional explanation and attention. Identifying a student's needs is only one small part of the communication puzzle—if you understand how important a need is to a student you will be better able to interact and assist him or her in achieving goals. One student may have a strong need for power and status, while another has a need for friendship and inclusion. The intensity with which these needs are experienced will cause the two students to interact in very different ways with their peers and instructors. A key to understanding the value associated with various needs is to explore the value placed by one's culture on fulfilling those needs. Hispanic cultures often place high value on family, thus a student may make a decision of where to study in order to fulfill two different needs. The need to earn a college degree may be influenced by the need to be geographically close to family members. It is clear that communication is an essential piece for solving the puzzle of understanding needs and in comprehending the value placed on need fulfillment.

Exploring Diversity in Verbal and Nonverbal Communication

Verbal and nonverbal communication channels are two additional pieces in the diversity puzzle. These pieces are essential for identifying and communicating the components of one's cultural patterns. Many of the examples shared earlier in this chapter have illustrated the ways in which you can look for cues to understand student cultures. Suggestions have been offered for strategies to enhance communication in a diverse classroom. When exploring diversity in communication, it is important to consider the puzzle pieces of both verbal and nonverbal forms of communication. These pieces impact perceptions of communication competence and influence student learning.

Verbal Diversity

Language is a central element involved in learning and social interaction. Differences in language can have far-reaching implications for classroom communication. Consider the value that we place on verbal communication in the United States. Not only do we expect students to engage in verbal communication in assignments ranging from classroom participation to delivering oral reports, but they are also expected to use similar language skills in their written assignments. We are faced with the challenge of understanding the various languages that students employ, whether it be the use of slang or the use of English as a second language. Even when we think we speak the same language, there are instances that cause us to question whether we really do understand one another. Consider the following example:

> "This stuff is so bogus. Like, I don't have time to be an Einstein! Getting that 'C' was like cool beans. But it's never enough. My teacher is really phat and is up with dropping knowledge, but I'd rather hammer the trails than spend my time in this house."

In this situation, the student is expressing her frustration at the high expectations her teacher has for her. She acknowledges that she admires her teacher, but communicates that she would rather turn her attention to her interests in mountain biking than in attending classes. It becomes apparent by her statement that she is satisfied with earning a "C" on the assignment. If an instructor understands her language, he may be able to identify ways to motivate the student to place higher value on academic achievement, or he might encourage her to integrate her interest in mountain biking with her studies by writing a research paper on the topic. While this example illustrates the importance of understanding language to provide clues about a student's interest in academics, it may be more crucial for us to be aware of the language associated with a variety of potentially dangerous activities such as the language used by gangs or by students who use drugs.

Even within a culture, differences in verbal communication styles are evident. Accents and dialects provide clues as to one's home. These differences in pronunciation and forms of language shared by persons in a geographical region may produce a variety of outcomes. Stereotypes are often formed as a result of one's accent. We all have our perceptions of the stereotypical Southern accent. While some people may view the Southern form of pronunciation as sounding "dumb," others describe the accent as being pleasing to the ear and perceive it as being hospitable and friendly. Instructors should be careful about commenting on differences in pronunciation and realize that some students may have difficulty saying words in the exact way that they are being taught in class because they have heard the word pronounced differently since birth in their homes.

A different kind of misunderstanding may occur when a student speaks English as a second language. As was stated at the beginning of this chapter, nearly 20 percent of elementary and high schools students have at least one foreign-born parent, while an additional 5 percent of students are foreign-born themselves. This points to the potential challenges when communicating classroom content and when interacting with parents about their child's performance. Studies have explored the educational and personal challenges faced by students who speak English as a second language (ESL). Some schools placed ESL students in special education programs because they required additional time to interpret and complete assignments. They were falsely categorized as being learning disabled as a result of their English deficiency. As a result, the students showed a decline in their academic performance and experienced a decrease in self-esteem. Upon further investigation, it was discovered that many of the ESL students in the study achieved high grades when taught in their native languages. Language differences, and not intelligence, were at the root of their academic problems. You may assist ESL students by allowing them additional time to take exams or by arranging meetings outside of class or during office hours to discuss the student's understanding of assignments. In addition, many schools have tutors and programs devoted to assisting non-native speakers with proofreading papers and reviewing assignments. When working with ESL students in multilingual settings, you may face the task of helping parents understand how students vary in their academic development as a result of the language barrier. In addition, attention should be paid to the pacing of group activities according to the level of participation and comprehension by ESL students.

Implications of Verbal Differences

While language differences pose one set of challenges when communicating with diverse students, it is important that teachers understand other outcomes of diversity in verbal interactions. Language differences or variations in verbal patterns may produce a multitude of perceptions and learning outcomes. Even though a student from Brazil may be fluent in both Portugese and English, his cultural background has likely influenced his preference for a particular verbal communication style. It is important to explore not only the differences in language and styles, but also the perceptions and resulting implications.

Research in the area of verbal immediacy has found that students in multicultural classrooms have a variety of expectations for an instructor's verbal comments designed to enhance perceptions of closeness. A student from a collectivist culture may have a different perception when a teacher uses language such as "we" and "us" compared to the impressions formed by a student from an individualistic culture, where achievement is measured by one's own performance rather than the accomplishments of the group. Research on student perceptions of the use of behavior alteration messages across cultures may shed some light as to the relationship between a culture's value for power distance and the verbal strategies used by teachers to encourage student compliance. Students from cultures which place high value on hierarchy and distance between persons of different status levels may have diverse perceptions about the use of power in the classroom.

Mary Jane Collier examined the perceptions of students in an academic advising setting and found that while Asian American, African American, and Latino students agreed that interrupting students while speaking is perceived as being rude, they differed in their perceptions regarding other aspects of verbal interactions with Caucasian advisors. Latino and Asian American students reported that they were embarrassed when the advisor made references to their accents, while Asian American students perceived the advisor's level of openness in communication as being uncomfortable.

When exploring the impact of various verbal strategies in classrooms across cultures, different perceptions and learning outcomes have been discovered. Understanding student perceptions of question-asking in the classroom is essential to understanding the value placed on inquiry. In Japanese culture, students place high value on the knowledge shared by their instructors. To ask a question during a lecture may be perceived as challenging the instructor's knowledge on a subject. Thus, students may choose to remain silent during the class, answering questions asked by the teacher and reserving their own questions for after class or during tutoring sessions. When exploring perceptions about the use of humor by teachers in the Thai classroom, Krisda Tanchaisak discovered that Thai students' perceptions of the appropriateness of different types of humor used by U.S. teachers had a direct influence on their motivation and learning. In addition, he found that U.S. teachers reported that they alter their use of humor, often refraining from sharing many of the comical verbal examples that they would typically use when lecturing to students in their home culture. These differences point to the fact that instructors must carefully consider the different ways in which their verbal messages will be perceived by students.

One final area that should be addressed in considering the implications of verbal differences involves the communication predispositions and preferences for engaging in verbal interaction. In Chapter 3, communication apprehension was defined as the fear or anxiety associated with real or anticipated communication. Instructors should recognize that the norms for verbal communication in one culture's classrooms cannot be expected to be applied elsewhere. Studies have reported significant differences in levels of communication apprehension across cultures in Asia, Europe, Puerto Rico, the United States, and Latin America. It should come as no surprise that one's level of apprehension increases when expected to interact in a different culture. Fear of how others will judge a person's communication competence in another culture often increases anxiety. As a result, that person may demonstrate a low willingness to communicate. After all, it is often easier to remain silent than it is to risk having others form judgments of incompetence.

Nonverbal Diversity

The task of understanding the meanings behind various nonverbal behaviors in different cultures is daunting. Add to this the challenge of understanding the intentions of the nonverbal behaviors. You will soon discover that the potential for misunderstandings and confusion is even greater. While it is nearly impossible to understand the meanings for every nonverbal behavior, it is important that you attempt to gain familiarity with the nonverbal expectations and perceptions held by members of various cultures if your goal is to reduce the potential for miscommunication. An elementary teacher in the United States may touch a young child on the head in an attempt to quiet him or her during class. If the teacher were to touch the head of a Malay student, this action would be perceived as being extremely offensive since the head is considered to be the center of one's spiritual being in the Malaysian culture. The interpretations of the same behavior, touching a student's head, are quite different. Consider the differences in nonverbal rituals which impact classroom interactions. You may expect students to raise their hand in order to gain permission to talk. Other cultures may not employ such a formal process for requesting approval to speak. Even within the same school, teachers may differ in the nonverbal expectations established for their own classroom cultures.

While languages have their own sets of rules for structure and meaning, nonverbal communication is less systematized. There are no rules that govern it, and many of the behaviors which are used are culture-specific. Awareness of these differences is another piece to understanding the diversity puzzle as a result of perceptions held by students regarding nonverbal variations.

Edward T. Hall and other scholars have explored differences in nonverbal communication across cultures. There is extreme diversity when exploring the expectations for the various codes of nonverbal behavior such as body movements, gestures, eye contact, touch, use of space, and perceptions of time. Consider the value for time that is communicated by U.S. teachers. We may set deadlines for assignments and penalize students who do not adhere to these deadlines. Classes are scheduled to begin and end at specific times. Students who are late may be labeled as being lazy and unmotivated. We can communicate our values via nonverbal channels and we can form impressions of the values held by others as a result of their behaviors.

Implications of Nonverbal Differences

Research in the area of nonverbal immediacy discovered that in Australia, Finland, Puerto Rico, and the United States, students reported an increase in learning when teachers used nonverbal behaviors to enhance perceptions of closeness. While students seemed to be in agreement with the impact that nonverbal behaviors had on their learning outcomes, additional research by Collier and Powell discovered that students from diverse cultures differed in their perceptions regarding teacher effectiveness as a result of their use of nonverbal immediacy. Latino students indicated that it was more important for teachers to be immediate at the beginning of a course, while African Americans perceived the immediacy behaviors as being more important at the end of a course. Thus, there are cultural implications of immediacy behaviors that instructors should consider.

Since we are often quick to evaluate a nonverbal behavior as being positive or negative, teachers should engage in careful analysis of these behaviors when students from diverse cultures fail to react according to the instructor's expectations. One approach to achieving a level of nonverbal competence is to try and analyze behaviors on the basis of a student's cultural background. Monitor reactions to nonverbal differences. Rather than expressing disgust and perceiving a deaf student as misbehaving when she raises her hands to either side of her head and waggles her fingers, inquire as to the meaning of the gesture. You may be surprised to learn that the student is showing appreciation by this unique form of applause. It is also important for instructors to monitor students' reactions to their nonverbal behaviors. A U.S. teacher will likely experience a shocked reaction by a student from El Salvador if he or she were to point at the student to request participation in class. After all, pointing is considered to be impolite in that culture. Observe the preferred behavior when interacting with those from other cultures. Perhaps the best strategy for avoiding misunderstandings is to ask students what they mean by their behavior. The differences in the intent are often fascinating.

The Diversity Puzzle

Understanding and integrating aspects of diversity in classroom communication is analogous to putting together the pieces of a puzzle. An assortment of factors must be explored and put together in order to achieve shared understanding. Not only do we need to be aware of the various facets of cultural patterns, but we also need to recognize the ways in which these cultural patterns are communicated and the ways in which they influence our classroom interactions. This is not an easy task. After all, our cultural patterns will probably change as a result of new experiences. Interactions with teachers and peers may cause a student to form new beliefs or to express new attitudes. Just when you think that the puzzle has been solved, the pieces may change. The goal should not be defining and describing each individual difference, but to be aware of the overall potential for diverse communication in the classroom. If the instructional objective is to maximize student learning and success, careful consideration must be given to these factors which are inherent in student achievement. Following are some of the pieces to consider when solving your own diversity puzzle in communicating with diverse students:

Engage in self-analysis to increase your awareness of your own personal orientation system. Your needs, attitudes, beliefs, and values are the result of your unique experiences. Consider the ways in which your own cultural experiences have shaped these factors. How does this impact your communication with your students?

Identify your preferred teaching style. Realize that your expectations for communication and learning in the classroom may not be comfortable for students of diverse cultures.

Encourage students to appreciate cultural diversity. Provide opportunities for students of diverse backgrounds to work together on class assignments. Encourage interaction—after all, some students may choose to communicate only with those who are like themselves if not "nudged."

Consider the variety of verbal and nonverbal behaviors that are represented in your classroom. An awareness of these differences helps us to identify ways to enhance communication and understanding.

REFERENCES AND SUGGESTED READINGS

Anderson, J., & Powell, R. (1988). Cultural influences on educational processes. In L. Samovar & R. Porter (Eds.), *Intercultural communication: A reader* (pp. 207–214). Belmont, CA: Wadsworth.

Barraclough, R. A., Christophel, D. M., & McCroskey, J. C. (1988). Willingness to communicate: A cross-cultural investigation. *Communication Research Reports, 5,* 187–192.

Bennett, C. (1995). *Multicultural education: Theory and practice.* Boston, MA: Allyn and Bacon.

Bowman, B. (1989, October). Educating language-minority children: Challenges and opportunities. *Phi Delta Kappan,* 118–120.

Braithwaite, D. O. (2000). *Handbook of communication and people with disabilities: Research and application.* Mahwah, NJ: Lawrence Erlbaum Associates.

Brislin, R. (1993). *Understanding culture's influence on behavior.* Fort Worth, TX: Harcourt Brace Jovanovich.

Cazden, C. (1988). *Classroom discourse: The language of teaching and learning.* Portsmouth, NH: Heinemann.

Claxton, C. (1990). Learning styles, minority students, and effective education. *Journal of Developmental Education, 1,* 6–9.

Collier, M. J. (1988). Competent communication in intercultural unequal status advisement contexts. *Journal of Communication, 1,* 3–22.

Collier, M. J., & Powell, R. (1990). Ethnicity, instructional communication, and classroom systems. *Communication Quarterly, 38,* 334–349.

Cooper, P. J. (1995). *Communication for the classroom teacher.* Scottsdale, AZ: Gorsuch Scarisbrick Publishers.

Courts, P. L. (1997). *Multicultural literacy: Dialect, discourse, and diversity.* New York: Peter Lang Publishing.

Falvey, M. A. (1995). *Inclusive and heterogeneous schooling: Assessment, curriculum, and instruction.* Baltimore, MD: Paul H. Brookes Publishing.

Gorham, J. (1999). Diversity in classroom dynamics. In A. L. Vangelisti & J. A. Daly (Eds.), *Teaching communication: Theory, research, and methods* (pp. 257–268). Mahwah, NJ: Lawrence Erlbaum Associates.

Hall, E. T. (1966). *The hidden dimension.* Garden City, NY: Doubleday.

Hart, R., & Williams, D. (1995). Able-bodied instructors and students with disabilities: A relationship handicapped by communication. *Communication Education, 44,* 140–154.

Hollins, E. R., & Oliver, E. I. (1999). *Pathways to success in school: Culturally responsive teaching.* Mahwah, NJ: Lawrence Erlbaum Associates.

Martin, J. N., & Nakayama, T. K. (2000). *Intercultural communication in contexts.* (2nd ed.). Mountain View, CA: Mayfield.

McCroskey, J. C., Sallinen, A., Fayer, J. M., & Richmond, V. P. (1996). Nonverbal immediacy and cognitive learning: A cross-cultural investigation. *Communication Education, 45,* 200–211.

Powell, R., & Harville, B. (1990). The effects of teacher immediacy and clarity on instructional outcomes: An intercultural assessment. *Communication Education, 39,* 369–379.

Rosenfeld, L. B., & Jarrard, M. W. (1985). The effects of perceived sexism in female and male college professors on students' descriptions of classroom climate. *Communication Education, 34,* 205–213.

Sadker, M., Sadker, D., & Klein, S. (1991). The issue of gender in elementary and secondary education. In G. Grant (Ed.), *Review of research in education.* Washington, DC: American Educational Research Association.

Samovar, L. A., & Porter, R. E. (1995). *Communication between cultures.* (2nd ed.). Belmont, CA: Wadsworth

Sanders, J., & Wiseman, R. (1990). The effects of verbal and nonverbal teacher immediacy on perceived cognitive, affective, and behavioral learning in the multicultural classroom. *Communication Education, 39,* 341–354.

Sorensen, G. (1989). Teaching teachers from East to West: A look at common myths. *Communication Education, 38,* 331–332.

15 Communicating with Students of Various Ages

JON F. NUSSBAUM

DOREEN K. BARINGER

AMANDA LEE KUNDRAT
Pennsylvania State University

Learning as a Lifelong Process

As physical changes occur throughout the life span, simultaneous changes also occur in the psychological, social, and language abilities of developing adults. Although learning and formal education have traditionally been associated with the young who are attending grades K–12, many individuals of all ages are returning to formal classroom settings to improve their quality of life as they grow older (Belsky, 1988, 1990; Dychtwald, 1990; Glendenning & Stuart-Hamilton, 1995; McDonald, 1995). It should not be unexpected, therefore, that teachers are confronted with a population of age-diverse students who may create a classroom environment that is quite different from the traditional young, age-segregated classroom.

Classroom learning has received attention from researchers in diverse fields such as education, psychology, communication, and ergonomics to name just a few (McDonald, 1995). Although there appears to be a lack of consensus among theorists and researchers regarding a comprehensive definition of classroom learning (Schunk, 2000), the importance of learning within the classroom is demonstrated in the vast body of literature produced to describe, understand, and enhance the learning outcomes within the classroom (see Richmond & McCroskey, 1992; Vangelisti, Daly, & Friedrich, 1999 for good reviews).

Learning however is not confined to the classroom, but instead is an ongoing, developmental process. At a descriptive level, learning is the process of acquiring new information and encoding what is learned through practice and experience (Schaie & Willis, 1996). It is however a complex phenomena, encompassing "growth through increased awareness, knowledge, and skills" (Groombridge, 1982, p. 316) that allows one to review, relearn, and unlearn if necessary, the concepts and values of their youth (Groombridge, 1982). Learning is a necessary human requirement in our endeavors to exist and thrive in a continuously changing environment. Classroom learning and the process of aging are both lifelong developmental phenomena that directly and indirectly affect our ability to age successfully.

It comes as no surprise that teachers are experiencing a change in the student composition of their classrooms as individuals seek to make themselves more marketable to corporations and as healthy baby boomers begin to retire. As such, it may become necessary for teachers to adapt their styles of instruction in order to be able to effectively teach these students who may be in various quite diverse stages of their lives. This can be especially challenging for young college instructors who are often close in age or younger than their students, as it is reasonable to assume that more mature students have different life experiences than do younger students. Teachers must adapt to these more experienced students and often must expand their style of classroom instruction by incorporating variety and flexibility in their routines to optimize in-class learning (Shadden & Raiford, 1984).

To aid teachers in this task, we begin this chapter with a discussion of contextual age as a construct that may provide teachers a more useful focus than chronological age. We will examine age-related changes in learning styles, various age-related psychological and physical aspects of the learning process, age-related changes in motivation to learn, and the effects of life experiences of the student on in-class teaching behavior. Implications these factors will have for the teacher of students in an age-diverse classroom will then be addressed. Finally, recommendations will be offered that will provide the teacher with strategies for successful communicative adaptation with students of various ages in the classroom.

Contextual Age

Often social scientists and teachers rely heavily on student chronological age to assume certain levels of cognitive and psychological activity. Chronological age depicts the number of years that one has lived. However, communication scholars such as Rubin and Rubin (1986) have shown that individuals of any chronological age group are not homogeneous. Furthermore, research has shown that chronological age is often not the best predictor of intelligence, cognitive functioning, or the ability to learn within the classroom (Nussbaum & Prusank, 1989).

Rather, it is contextual age, the recognition that younger and older persons alike may share similar life-position characteristics in regards to physiological, psychological, social, and communicative influences that more likely explain similarities and differences among individuals. For example, two 20-year-old students may have quite different needs and motivations within the classroom. In fact, one of those 20-year-old students may be highly similar to a 40-year-old student in regards to learning style and classroom behaviors such as asking questions or time spent studying.

It is imperative for teachers to keep in mind that although similarities may exist among older students, contextual age is often a more accurate indicator of a student's in-class behavior. So at the very least, teachers must not depend on chronological age stereotyping of student abilities and should remain open that students of similar ages may have quite different classroom needs and motivations due somewhat to their contextual age.

Learning Styles

As we mentioned earlier, learning is the process of acquiring new information and encoding what is learned through practice or experiences (Schaie & Willis, 1996). We store information in our memory to retrieve at a later time. Of importance to this phenomenon is the *way* we go about learning, referred to as *learning style*. Learning style is how individuals process, concentrate, and come to understand new or difficult information. Furthermore, it is biological, developmental, affective, and behavioral in nature (Dunn & Griggs, 1988; Guild, 1994). Learning style makes us unique within the classroom. It is both our perceptual realities and our experiences that help to shape our learning styles (Guild, 1994; Kolb, 1984). The knowledge and skills we gain throughout the life span and how we go about obtaining information is not fixed and rigid, but flexible throughout our lives. Previous education, employment, and experiences may influence our learning styles, and our dominant style may change over time (Kolb, 1984).

The body of literature concerning learning styles is not only diverse but also complex (Dunn & Dunn, 1999; Kolb, 1984). Researchers differ on what they classify as learning styles. Widely used in corporate settings to assess learning styles is Kolb's (1984) questionnaire, the learning-style inventory (LSI). Through determining a person's learning style, the LSI informs managers about how workers solve problems, set goals, deal with new situations, manage others, and make career choices.

The LSI classifies people into one of four learning styles: convergers, assimilators, divergers, or accommodators based on the way in which they process and use information. Convergent and assimilator style learners focus on logic. They like ideas and concepts and tend to rely on thinking rather than on feeling. They tend to process systematically, be precise, and excel in quantitative analysis. These two styles differ however in what they do with the information they learn. Convergent style learners are concerned with what works and emphasize *doing* rather than *observing*. On the other hand, assimilators focus on understanding ideas and concepts rather than actually using them. They are good at seeing many different perspectives. Divergent and accommodative learning styles both rely on concrete experience. Divergers tend to relate information to their personal life experiences and do well in unstructured situations. They differ from accommodators who are more active than reflexive and learn best by doing.

Accommodator styles learn best through trial and error (Kolb, 1984). Divergers on the other hand simply want to answer the question of *why* ideas work as they absorb everything in the atmosphere.

Although the LSI has been used mostly in business, it is appropriately fitting to be used in the classroom as well. Students often select areas of study that are conducive to their dominant learning style. For example, very often students will change majors when (probably unbeknownst to them) a goodness of fit between learning style and specialization is not present (Kolb, 1984). Likewise, as they become more specialized in their chosen areas those same areas often strengthen their learning style. Older students who already have some formal education and learning experiences from the workplace may have strengthened their learning style or styles in some manner.

Other researchers discuss learning styles in terms of both the global and analytic processors of information (Dunn, 1998; Dunn & Dunn, 1999). Much like the LSI, this perspective focuses on how people learn and process information. But instead of a four-style classification system, individuals fall more broadly into either analytic or global learner categories. Both styles are equally capable of mastering the same information or skills. However, they benefit through differing instructional methods. Analytic processors learn best in a step-by-step process to eventually understand a concept, and most presentations are organized in this manner. Globals, on the other hand, need to understand the concept first and then concentrate on the details.

Encompassed in learning style are environmental factors such as noise levels, lighting, temperature, and seating arrangements. In addition, structure levels and conformity versus nonconformity play important roles in students' motivations and abilities. Structure levels refers to how much explicit instruction an individual needs to have concerning objectives desired, time allotted to each task, and guidelines for completing the task (Dunn & Dunn, 1999). Conformity is one's tendency to not raise questions and to respond with answers they believe authorities want to hear. Nonconformity on the other hand is one's tendency to raise questions and respond honestly. Each person has a learning style that is unique and, when necessary, this learning style can be called upon when facing new or difficult information (Guild, 1994). Being able to identify students' styles can assist in the triggering of concentration, processing, and boosting long-term memory (Dunn, 1998). Although learning style plays a primary role in learning, there are other aspects that also influence classroom learning for older adults. In the following sections, we will address psychological and physical aspects of learning, student motivation to learn, as well as implications for teachers who interact with students of various ages.

Psychological and Physical Aspects

Along with possible learning style changes that take place across the life span, changes in working memory, processing speed, name retrieval, and intelligence also change as we age (Belsky, 1990; Glendenning & Stuart-Hamilton, 1995; Nussbaum, Pecchioni, Robinson, & Thompson, 2000; Nussbaum, Hummert, Williams, & Harwood, 1996; Salthouse, 1988; Schaie & Willis, 1996). In addition, there are age-related physical changes such as a reduction in reaction time, vision, and hearing that take place as we age beyond 30. These changing psychological and physical aspects are extremely important to teachers who may have students of diverse age ranges in their classrooms. It is therefore important that educators learn to adapt to different classroom abilities, including memory and processing speed, intelligence, reaction time, vision, and hearing.

Memory and Processing Speed

As we age, declines in working memory and processing speed may hinder our ability to learn. Memory problems can occur in either long-term or short-term memory systems, or perhaps both (for more about memory, refer to Chesebro's discussion in Chapter 2). Researchers have informed us however that the meanings of words and ideas remain intact for older students. The decline they may have experienced in working memory and processing speed, however, can affect an individual's abilities to receive and produce messages (Nussbaum et al., 1996). It may take older adults more time to think of appropriate words when encoding messages. Likewise, it may also take more time to process complex sentences for older students than for younger students. When it comes to remembering, there are also general changes among younger and older adults in regards to processing types. For instance, older adults are less likely than younger individuals to use an organizational strategy when learning information, whereas younger adults are more likely to naturally remember words that may otherwise be unrelated by placing them in categories. Older adults are less likely to categorize unfamiliar words in order to remember them. However, when instructed to do so, the performance of these same older adults has been shown to improve considerably (Schaie & Willis, 1996).

According to Schaie and Willis (1996), the best way to retrieve information is to have organized that information in memory at some point. Furthermore, processing information at a deeper level, not just semantically but also at the level of the meanings of words also assists in future retrieval and the ability to prevent forgetting (to read more about processing see Chesebro's Chapter 2). Younger and older adults alike perceived that they would be more likely to recall words when they were associated with categories rather than just letters (Schaie & Willis, 1996). This may explain some of the reason older adults have more trouble remembering names than do younger adults. There are generally no synonyms for proper names, which eliminates a source of retrieval available for older adults (Cohen, 1994).

Mnemonic techniques are also useful for remembering. These devices use verbal and/or visual techniques to link pieces of information together that otherwise may not be related. Older adults can successfully be taught to create such devices (Yesavage, Lapp, & Sheikh, 1989).

Differences between recall and recognition also differ with age (Schaie & Willis, 1996). Older adults are more likely to be able to retrieve more successfully than recall specific information. Retrieving information refers to the ability to recognize information and to learn general ideas, whereas recall is the ability to remember specific words or phrases. Older adults are able to recognize words from a list such as in matching exercises and select correct answers among several choices, much more easily than writing the list from memory or filling specific words to complete actual statements. Several strategies aimed at assisting the adult learner to recall information will be discussed later when we provide suggestions.

Intelligence

Another area that changes as we age is that of intelligence (Glendenning & Stuart-Hamilton, 1995). Not to be confused with Gardner's Eight Types of Intelligence (see Chapter 2), Schaie and Willis (1996) focus on two other types of intelligence that change as we age, *crystallized* and *fluid*. Fluid intelligence can be explained as that which is related to reasoning abilities. How quickly one can take information in and out of the brain, organize, and remember, is related to fluid intelligence (Belsky, 1990; Schaie & Willis, 1996). Crystallized intelligence on the other hand pertains to the mental capacities that we develop though experience. Fluid intelligence generally declines with age, reaching a peak in early adulthood and then declining regularly. However, crystallized intelligence, follows a much different path in that cognitive ability not only can remain stable but also may increase when we learn at a rate which exceeds what we forget (Belsky, 1990). Eventually however, crystallized intelligence will begin to decline as well. Because of widely held stereotypes that older adults are not good at remembering or slower than younger learners are, the adult learner may be more anxious when confronted with a new learning experience. It is important to keep in mind that it may take older adults a little more time to get their ideas across. However, these ideas may be greatly enhanced due to crystallized intelligence level. It is also important to remember that intellectual abilities can be enhanced at any point throughout the life span (Belsky, 1990).

Just as there are psychological changes, so too there are some physical changes related to age as we progress through the life span. We highlight a few of these physical changes that may have a significant influence on adult performance in the classroom.

Reaction Time

Speed of learning involves reaction time to a perceived stimulus, the time it takes to transmit this message to the brain, and then the time that it takes to respond. Although older learners are on average slower at this process than younger adults are, pace may also be related to general personality characteristics. Older adults have generally adopted a pace that is consistent among a variety of tasks (Cross,

1981; Kidd, 1973). In sum, although the amount of time needed to learn new things increases as individuals age, once the information is learned, response times among individuals vary which accounts for the substantial individual differences that may be seen in the classroom. Speed of learning has historically been overemphasized to the detriment of learners (Cross, 1981). We need to remember that although some students in the classroom can provide the greatest number of correct answers in a short amount of time, this is not an indicator that these faster students are more intelligent or have an increased capacity to learn. As Knox (1977) concluded, "When they can control the pace, most adults in their 40s and 50s have about the same ability to learn as they had in their 20s and 30s."

Vision

Another physical change that takes place as we age is that of vision. As we age, our eyes lose some of their elasticity and transparency. Our pupils become smaller and may not react as quickly as when we were younger (Cross, 1981; Nussbaum et al., 2000). Furthermore, many older adults may suffer from cataracts, glaucoma, or other vision impairments. Seeing from a distance often becomes problematic (Nussbaum et al., 2000). Vision is at peak performance around the age of 18 and then it begins to decline until the age of 40. Between the ages of 40–55 the decline is much sharper and then returns to a slower rate of decline (Kidd, 1973). The need for illumination is much greater for individuals over the age of 50. Older students are likely to need over half more the amount of classroom light than students around the age of 20 (Cross, 1981; Kidd, 1973).

Hearing

As we age, we also experience losses in the ability to hear. Although this is a gradual decline until around the ages of 65–70, nevertheless it may impact learning in the classroom, due to increased problems with pitch, volume, and rate. This is especially true when information is provided in exceptionally high or low frequencies. Hearing loss contributes to the need of more information processing time and reaction time for older adults (Cross, 1981; Kidd, 1973).

Mobility

Motor skills also decline as we progress throughout the life span (Birren, 1996). There are overlapping explanations that contribute to this decline, such as the reduction of error (Birren, 1996). As our rate of doing a task increases there is often a decrease in accuracy. Older individuals often do things at a slower pace in an attempt to minimize potential error. They rely on more feedback than younger adults do when performing a task. Contributing to this slower pace are the declines in physical abilities such as vision and hearing (Birren, 1996). It is important for teachers to realize that they may not work or complete tasks as quickly as younger students.

Motivation to Learn

The law within a vast majority of states *requires* that children up to at least 15 years of age attend formal classroom instruction of some type. Individuals beyond the age of 15 who have fulfilled their educational obligations often *choose* to further their education. As a result of this choice, those students may be among the most highly motivated students in college classrooms (Richmond, 1999).

An intense study of adult learners by Houle (1961) nearly forty years ago resulted in a three-way motivational framework that continues to influence our thinking today (Cross, 1981). Houle (1961) states that "the desire to learn, like every other human characteristic, is not shared equally by everyone. To judge from casual observations, most people possess it only fitfully and in modest measure" (p. 3). Individuals who are returning to the classroom or are continuing their formal education may have multiple and diverse motivations for continuing the formal learning process.

Houle (1961) identifies three types of learning-oriented adults, the first of which are goal-oriented learners. Goal-oriented students pursue education in order to achieve some means, whether it be to learn how to prepare a presentation for an audience, use a new computer program, become a more effective manager, or to obtain a promotion at work. They learn through whatever method will assist them in achieving the goal whether it is through reading a book, taking a class, or joining a group (Cross, 1981; Houle, 1961).

The second type of motivated learner is the activity-oriented learner. These students are not looking for content or skill, but rather learn for something to do with their time (Cross, 1981; Houle, 1961). Although this type of learner is similarly seeking to fulfill a goal, they are different from the former in that their reasons for learning may have nothing to do with the content in which they are engaged. Similar to how religious activities may function for some adults in regards to social fulfillment so too does the classroom for other adults. In fact, loneliness influences many people to attend school, as school is considered a socially acceptable place to meet people and make friends. Other individuals may return to school as an escape from life problems or unsatisfying relationships (Cross, 1981; Houle, 1961).

The third type of learner that Houle (1961) identifies is the learning-oriented group. These students learn because they have the desire to learn for its own sake. These people have historically been avid readers all of their lives. They watch television programs, join groups, travel, and select jobs for educational experiences and growth. There is a continuity of learning among these individuals that differs from the former types of motivated learners.

It is important to realize that education seekers will have different orientations and viewpoints, and that these diverse motivations for furthering education will more than likely vary among individuals who often have multiple reasons for continuing (Cross, 1981; Tough, 1968). These motivations are also influenced by interests and lifestyles (Cox, 1991). For instance, someone who has been interested in politics all of their lives may enroll in a political science course. It would also not be surprising for someone who is a manager at work to enroll in a management course. Someone who works for the government may enroll in classes with similar or relevant content to their duties at work. The opposite might also hold that these individuals could select something to learn about which is completely different from their employment area. This may be done as an escape to think about other issues or to gain knowledge in an area that could lead them down a potentially different path than they are currently pursuing.

Motivations that are goal oriented are based upon an individual's desire to attain a certain achievement. These achievements can be the skills and knowledge that can be put to a pragmatic use for surviving and coping (Moody, 1987). Such uses relating to practical issues in life include training for the workforce, skills for coping with everyday life issues, empowerment, self-reliance and self-sufficiency, citizenship, and social welfare (to aid in community service) (Glendenning, 1995; Wirtz & Charner, 1989). As employers search for qualified personnel, adults often return for degrees and certificates in higher education in order to become more marketable in the workforce (Cox, 1991). Empowerment and skills for coping, self-reliance, and self-sufficiency result from individuals being capable and efficient with everyday tasks in life. Examples of this include how to manage money and how to manage relationships. Goals for citizenship may include helping others in their local communities. This can range from working for charities to running for local political offices. Finally, individuals return to education in order to help others on an individual or a group level. With knowledge and training, skills can be applied to social programs or even family issues in order to find solutions.

Older adults often value experiences more than they do material things (Balzas, 1995). Thus, some individuals have motivations that are activity oriented. They view education as serving a social function (Wirtz & Charner, 1989). Classroom experiences can serve as a hub for contact with other individuals. With this, older adults may view class time and study groups as a place to interact and to maintain contact with society. New knowledge and contact that education provides also allows an escape from reality (Wirtz & Charner, 1989). Difficulties and mundane routines in life can be put on hold while an individual is in class or studying.

Motivations that are based on learning serve cognitive interests and can stimulate our mind (Wirtz & Charner, 1989). These motivations for the desire to know can be thought of as learning for learning's sake (Houle, 1961). Education is viewed as a way to stimulate and engage an individual by exploring materials that are unfamiliar or unknown. The goal of learning for the sake of learning may serve as a self-satisfaction goal through enlightenment and entertainment (Cox, 1991; Havighurst, 1976).

Motivation is a hypothetical construct (Baldwin, 1967), not something that can be seen or touched, but rather inferred from what students do and say. As teachers, we tend to infer that a student who never misses class, always turns in excellent work, and fulfills every opportunity for extra credit, to be more motivated than a student who has failed to turn in the last couple of assignments, occasionally attends, and sleeps in the back of the room during lecture. There could be additional or competing motivations taking place outside of the classroom in the lives of older students that prevent the completion of assignments that are not apparent to teachers. Examples of this would be helping young children who are also of school age with homework, working overtime in their places of employment, or caring for an ill spouse or loved one.

Life Experience

Students of all ages who enter the classroom will bring with them unique life experiences. Earlier educational experiences, employment, social relationships, and media have all helped to shape the older students in the classroom. Everyday events often prove to be rich learning experiences. These include planned events such as reading the newspaper while eating breakfast, watching the discovery channel, and learning how to program a new VCR as well as spontaneous events such as engaging in an unexpected conversation, reading a brochure while waiting in the dentist's office, and being informed of an exciting event that a child witnessed at school. Family life, formal education, and social activities all provide experiences and information to individuals. These opportunities vary widely from person to person, yet we are all by necessity and habit, information seekers.

Years of experience and formal education influence the learning processes within the continuing education of older adults. Being active in the educational system gives individuals exposure to educational institutions. This includes expectations of workload, evaluations, and processes. In addition, older adults with first- or second-hand experience (siblings or children have attended college) are more likely to further their education (Cox, 1991). Individuals who have excelled academically in the past are also more likely to pursue education. "Attitudes and habits of learning" are formed in past educational experiences (Thomas, 1991, p. 27). If success is part of an individual's past academic experience, then attitudes toward learning and education are likely going to be positive. If good study habits were developed in the past, these habits will likely return as that individual continues his or her education. On the other hand, some individuals can be disenchanted when returning to school (Groombridge, 1995). With negative past experiences, subjecting themselves again to a classroom setting may worry some older adults who may fear that they are setting themselves up for failure.

With the diverse training, knowledge, and information needs of returning adults, educational programs are confronted with a significant challenge (Shadden & Raiford, 1984). As we will discuss in more detail later, this challenge transfers into the classroom where instructors are faced with the formidable task of creating lessons that suit each individual student's needs. The classroom instructor must adapt the amount and type of the course content, as well as the pace and method of instruction to effectively maximize classroom outcomes.

Communication Implications for Teachers Who Interact with Students of Various Ages

Individual student learning styles greatly affect the amount of information that each and every student consumes and utilizes. Various factors, such as background knowledge, comprehension strategies, learning strategies, and metacognitive process, produce these different learning styles (Wittrock & Baker, 1991). It is therefore pertinent that these factors be taken into consideration for the teaching and testing of students of all ages. By using a variety of classroom activities, students of different learning styles are all granted the use of their preferred style, increasing the absorption of material (Nuthall & Alton-Lee, 1995).

Providing students with a questionnaire (such as the LSI) that will assess their learning style can provide them with a more complete understanding of their strengths and weaknesses in the classroom. By having this understanding, students and teachers can both have a general idea of what they can do to assist themselves in performing more effectively in classroom situations. For instance, some students may not already know how they can most effectively study for their personal styles. Providing this information may spare them (and often instructors) unnecessary grief. Teachers can also benefit from knowing what types of learners are in their classrooms. It can aid instructors in planning lectures and activities to enhance the classroom experience and maximize each student's potential.

Careful planning as to the presentation of material must also be considered when teaching various ages. Teachers would do well for global learners by providing a general overview of concepts and providing them with "big picture" ideas before delving into step-by-step, more structured lectures appropriate for analytical learners.

Teachers also need to be sensitive to the physical and psychological aspects that influence learning in the classroom. This is especially important in introductory communication classes where students are assigned several oral presentations throughout the semester. By addressing on the first day of class, that if anyone needs special considerations to speak to you immediately as well as throughout the semester, students will likely disclose problems with hearing, seeing, and test-taking time that they have encountered in the past. Teachers can also aid the learning of older adults by preparing lesson plans that recognize additional time older adults may need to process information. Repeating information or being appropriately redundant will help students who do not quite comprehend the information the first time that it was presented. Speaking at an appropriately slower rate will also assist students in the decoding process. Soliciting audience feedback throughout classes, by asking if there are any questions, also gives students the opportunity to ask for something to be repeated or an overhead to be shown again.

Teachers must also be competent presenters of course content. Remembering to speak louder can help students who have experienced a decline in their hearing ability. Standing so that the student can read facial expressions and have a view of the mouth can assist the students who may not hear as well. Presenting content in a dramatic or animated style can enliven the classroom and make learning an interesting event.

Providing class handouts will assist students who have experienced a decline in their vision. Such handouts may be in larger font sizes as well. In addition, overheads may be more helpful than writing on the blackboard for such students. Often, chalkboard notes appear quite faded for such individuals. Furthermore, being aware of the illumination level of the classroom is important to these individuals as well. Making sure that the room is well-illuminated will enable students with vision problems to concentrate on grasping the information and what is being said rather than being distracted.

In regards to the assessment of learning, the use of recognition tests such as multiple-choice or true-false rather than recall tests such as fill-in-the-blank or short answer when possible enables the adult student to be more appropriately evaluated. They may also do well on essay questions that involve discussion of the main points or flavor of the topic (Schaie & Willis, 1996). We recommend using a variety of methods and questions when evaluating students. Projects and papers are good alternative methods to the overuse of exams. Using several question types such as true–false and multiple choice on the same exam will enable students to perform more successfully.

By providing a supportive climate in the classroom, teachers can help older students overcome fears they experience when returning to the classroom after many years. Teachers can take into account the rich life experiences of older adults by using examples in the classroom to which the older students will be able to relate. This can be done by using examples that draw upon diverse past experiences. If there is a student in the classroom with previous military experience the teacher can use a military example to assist in learning a concept. These types of examples that relate to their life experiences will also assist students in remembering the information presented. Teachers must be careful to avoid using cohort dependent examples so that students of various ages are all able to understand. For instance, if incorporating music in an example using *hip-hop*, also incorporate music that is more likely known throughout age groups, such as the oldies (e.g., Elvis, The Supremes). In addition, teaching older students to use mnemonic techniques and to organize information will enable the adult learner to recall and retrieve information more efficiently. These techniques can enhance classroom learning for older adults, enabling these students to fulfill their goals of self or instrumental satisfaction.

Self or instrumental satisfaction is related to each student's motivation. Motivations based on goals to achieve skills, activities in which to participate, and learning for learning's sake vary from individual to individual. The instructor must actively observe the things that students say and do in order to be aware of what and how students want to attain their goals (Thomas, 1991). Certain students in the classroom may be very concerned with letter grades whereas others may be more interested in the content or information the course and instructor can offer. It can be helpful to address these different goals by stressing the importance of learning the material as well as recognizing the necessity of grades.

Teachers must also be more aware of the changes individuals experience as development occurs throughout the life span. Teachers can better inform themselves about the physical, psychological, and communicative changes transpiring within their students by enrolling in continuing education classes that highlight life span development. Remembering that older students are not a homogenous group will enable instructors to have a more open and receptive attitude toward aging adults. The avoidance of stereotyping students due to chronological age can assist older students to feel more comfortable within the classroom and this comfort may lead to more positive classroom outcomes.

Conclusion

In this chapter we have discussed classroom challenges for teaching students of various ages, more specifically the older adult. We began by discussing contextual and chronological age. We then examined the complexities of learning and learning styles, age-related psychological and physical changes, age-related changes in motivation, and how life experiences influence classroom learning. It is our hope that teachers will be sensitive to the challenges and needs of older students in an endeavor enhance classroom learning outcomes for these students and teachers as well.

REFERENCES AND SUGGESTED READINGS

Baldwin, A. L. (1967). *Theories of child development.* New York: Wiley.

Balzas, (1995). Marketing to the elderly. In J. F. Nussbaum & J. Coupland (Eds.), *Handbook of communication and aging research* (pp. 263-284). Mahwah, NJ: Lawrence Erlbaum.

Belsky, J. K. (1988). *Here tomorrow: Making the most of life after fifty.* New York: Ballantyne.

Belsky, J. K. (1990). *The psychology of aging* (2nd ed.). Pacific Grove, CA: Brooks/Cole.

Birren, J. E. (Ed.). (1996). *Encyclopedia of gerontology: Age, aging, and the aged.* (Vol. 2). San Diego, CA: Academic Press.

Chibulski, O., & Bergman, S. (1981). Mutuality of learning between the old and the young: A case study in Israel. *Aging and Society, (1),* 247–262.

Cohen, G. (1994). Age-related problems in the use of proper names in communication. In M. L. Hummert, J. M. Wiemann, & J. F. Nussbaum

(Eds.), *Interpersonal communication in older adulthood: Interdisciplinary theory and research* (pp. 40–57). Thousand Oaks, CA: Sage.

Cox, C. (1991). Why older adults leave the university: A comparison of continuing and noncontinuing students. *Educational Gerontology, 17,* 1–10.

Cross, K. P. (1981). *Adults as learners: Increasing participation and facilitating learning.* San Francisco: Jossey-Bass.

Dunn, R. (1998). Teaching adults through their learning style strengths: A choice approach. In R. Dunn & K. Dunn (Eds.), *Practical approaches to individualizing staff development for adults* (pp. 3–15).

Dunn, R., & Dunn, K. (1999) *The complete guide to the learning styles inservice system.* Needham Heights, MA: Allyn & Bacon.

Glendenning, F. (1995). Education for older adults: Lifelong learning, empowerment, and social change. In J. F. Nussbaum & J. Coupland (Eds.), *Handbook of communication and aging Research* (pp. 467–490). Mahwah, NJ: Lawrence Erlbaum.

Glendenning, F., & Stuart-Hamilton, I. (1995). *Learning and cognition in later life.* Brookfield, VT: Ashgate.

Groombridge, B. (1982). Learning, education and later life. *Adult Education, 54,* 314–327.

Guild, P. (1994). Making sense of learning styles: Addressing student differences in the classroom links directly to leadership and management styles. *The School Administrator, 51,* 8–13.

Havighurst, R. (1976). Education through the adult lifespan. *Educational Gerontology, 3,* 321–330.

Houle, C. O. (1961). *The inquiring mind: A study of the adult who continues to learn.* Madison, WI: University of Wisconsin Press.

Kidd, J. R. (1973) *How adults learn.* New York: Association Press.

Knox, A. B. (1977). *Adult development and learning: A handbook on individual growth and competence in the adult years for education and the helping professions.* San Francisco: Jossey-Bass.

McDonald, L. (1995). Learning and aptitude in later life. In F. Glendenning & I. Stuart-Hamilton (Eds.), *Learning and cognition in later life* (pp. 95–113). Brookfield, VT: Ashgate.

Moody, H. R. (1987). Why worry about education for older adults? *Generations, 12(2),* 5–9.

Nussbaum, J. F., & Coupland, J. (Eds.). (1995). *Handbook of communication and aging research.* Mahwah, NJ: Lawrence Erlbaum Associates.

Nussbaum, J. F., Hummert, M. L., Williams, A., & Harwood, J. (1996). Communication and older adults. In B. R. Burleson (Ed.), *Communication Yearbook, 19,* pp. 1–47.

Nussbaum, J. F., Pecchioni, L. L., Robinson, J. D., & Thompson, T. L. (2000). *Communication and aging* (2nd ed.). Mahwah, NJ: Lawrence Erlbaum Associates.

Nussbaum J. F., & Prusank, D. T. (1989). The interface between human development and instructional communication. *Communication Education, 38,* 334–344.

Nuthall, G., & Alton-Lee, A. (1995). Assessing classroom learning: How students use their knowledge and experience to answer classroom achievement test questions in science and social studies. *American Educational Research Journal, 32,* 185–223.

Richmond, V. P. (1999). Extended Learning. In A. L. Vangelisti, J. A. Daly, & G.W. Friedrich (Eds.), *Teaching communication: Theory, research, and methods.* (pp. 497–505). Hillsdale, NJ: Lawrence Erlbaum.

Richmond, V. P., & McCroskey, J. C. (Eds.). (1992). *Power in the classroom: Communication, control, and concern.* Hillsdale, NJ: Lawrence Erlbaum.

Rubin, A. M., & Rubin, R. B. (1986). Contextual age as a life-position index. *International Journal of Aging and Human Development, 23,* 27–45.

Salthouse, T. A. (1988). Effects of aging on verbal abilities: Examination of the psychometric literature. In L. L. Light & D. Burke (Eds.), *Language, memory, and aging* (pp. 17–35). New York: Cambridge University Press.

Schaie, K. W., & Willis, S. L. (1996). *Adult development and aging* (4th ed.). New York: Harper Collins.

Schunk, D. H. (2000). *Learning theories: An educational perspective* (3rd ed.). Upper Saddle River, NJ: Prentice-Hall.

Shadden, B. B., & Raiford, C. A. (1984). The communication education of older persons: Prior training and utilization of information sources. *Educational Gerontology, 10,* 83–97.

Thomas, A. M. (1991). *Beyond education: A new perspective on society's management of learning.* San Francisco: Jossey-Bass.

Tough, A. (1968). Why adults learn: A study of the major reasons for beginning and continuing a learning project. *Monographs in Adult Education, 3,* 1–65.

Vangelisti, A. L., Daly, J. A., & Friedrich, G. W. (1999). *Teaching communication: Theory, research, and methods* (2nd ed.). Mahwah, NJ: Lawrence Erlbaum Associates.

Wittrock, M. C., & Baker, E. L. (1991). *Testing and cognition.* Englewood Cliffs, NJ: Prentice-Hall.

16 The Big Picture

"Putting It All Together" to Communicate More Effectively with Students

JOSEPH L. CHESEBRO

State University of New York at Brockport

Early in my teaching career, one of the greatest challenges I faced was seeing "the big picture" of the teaching-learning process. I had some good ideas and recommendations from a variety of sources, but all of that was difficult to synthesize and use when I entered the classroom. Similarly, if you have read through this book, you probably are left with a great number and variety of useful suggestions but may not see the ways in which those suggestions are interconnected as you attempt to use them in your classes. The purpose of this chapter is to develop some general principles of effective teaching based on what we have learned about teacher-student communication from each of the preceding chapters. As you start to recognize the connections between each of the chapters, "the big picture" should become more clear.

Four Useful Principles

Principle 1:
Think of Your Students First and Teach Accordingly

In many ways, students hold the clues and keys to good teaching. As we prepare our courses or daily class sessions, we constantly should keep our students in mind. We should consider the extent to which they are motivated to learn in general, and motivated to learn in our class in particular. We may not be able to influence their overall level of motivation, but we can play a role in their motivation in our own courses. To do so, we should keep students' needs and interests in mind and make our information as relevant to them as possible. This is likely to improve their attention and motivation, and students will be better able to remember things that are relevant to their own experiences. We should consider students' prior knowledge of the subject we are teaching and be sure that our course and class sessions are at the appropriate knowledge level and that they tie new concepts into concepts with which the students already are familiar. We also should realize that some students will communicate with us more than others and that students have different motives for communicating. This is important because it is easy for teachers to fall into a habit of assuming quiet students are unprepared or less intelligent than those who participate more often. Chances are just as good that students may be apprehensive or that they just are not motivated to communicate with their instructors. Finally, we should appreciate the influence that students have on our own teaching. We may be favoring some students simply because of certain nonverbal behaviors. By developing an awareness of our students on these various levels, we will be better able to develop our courses and class sessions in ways which are ideal for effective learning. In other words, we will be in a position to embody the other principles of effective teacher–student communication.

Principle 2:
Recognize, Develop, and Clarify Your Expectations

Once we understand our students, we can begin to take our knowledge and develop effective ways of teaching our course content. In order to have a clear vision, we should recognize our expectations for our students. Based on our students' needs, interests, experience, skills, and attitudes, we should develop clear objectives and goals for our students' cognitive, affective, and behavioral learning. Though this sounds like the kind of thing that may be beyond the control of a new teacher or teaching assistant, this approach can apply to any class session by asking yourself the following questions: "What do I want my students to know about this content?", "How do I want them to feel towards this content?", "How should this content affect students' behavior?" and, keeping in mind our long-range goals for students, "How do I want my students to feel about and use this content once they are out of the classroom or school?" Asking questions such as these helps provide focus for each course and class session, and it enables teachers to teach with a clear purpose in mind.

Another kind of expectation that teachers must consider relates to students' behavior and conduct in general. This involves expectations about things such as attendance, arriving late for class, participation, and grading standards. It is important to consider these types of expectations too, because they will influence the ways in which you teach and conduct your class sessions.

In addition to developing expectations, it is important that students clearly understand that which you expect of them. Clear teaching is more than just teaching content clearly. It also involves clear expectations. Teachers often are frustrated by their students' behavior, whether it is because students completed an assignment incorrectly, behaved inappropriately in class, complained about a grade, or failed to see why the content being taught is important. This often happens because teachers do not make their expectations clear enough. Students may not know what the teacher expects from an assignment (lack of clear objectives or good directions), what kind of behavior the teacher finds acceptable in class (they will know general norms, but may not know a teacher's individual preferences), the standards a teacher uses when grading (lack of an explanation of grading standards), or why they have to cover certain areas of content (lack of objectives which would clarify the need to cover that content). So, if a student does something "wrong," you should examine whether you have made your expectations clear. If you have not, then that may be the problem. If you have, then it will be easier for you to make your point and stick to your standards and still be fair to your students.

Principle 3:
Practice Effective Communication Behaviors

Once you understand your students and your expectations, you are ready to take advantage of what you have learned about effective teacher behaviors. You can think of ways in which you can make your content relevant to your students. You can develop ways to teach that content clearly. You can concentrate on being appropriately assertive and responsive. You can identify the potentially humorous aspects of your content. When you are in the classroom you can remember the value of immediacy in teaching. You also can be aware of misbehaviors to avoid. Finally, you can appreciate the role that each of these teacher behaviors plays in your students' motivation to learn.

Knowing the importance of these behaviors, you may be able to assess these aspects of your communication when things are not going as well in your class as you would like. Along these lines, remember the ways in which you can gather feedback on your teaching. I often hand out anonymous informal evaluations early in the semester, particularly if I do not think a class is going too well. You also can have colleagues (especially more experienced teachers) observe your teaching. This may be intimidating, but it could help you improve your teaching in important ways. You also can make a habit of reflecting on each class period. After my class sessions I often ask myself questions like: "What went well today?" or "Why did I bomb today?" I often learn important things about my teaching when I take this time to reflect. For example, I sometimes realize that I didn't really make significant eye contact with certain students or with certain areas of the classroom. Finally, remember that tests and quizzes can be good feedback on how well you are teaching certain concepts. By examining the strengths and weaknesses of your communication behavior with students, you will be better able to improve your teaching and enable your students to learn more effectively. And once again, you are likely to enjoy teaching more as you will find that students will respond to you more positively.

Principle 4: Exhibit Variety

This was discussed in Chapter 2 but the need for variety should be even more clear by now. We teach students with different intelligences, motives for communicating, levels of willingness to communicate, interests, levels of motivation to learn, amounts of background experience, ages, and cultures. If teachers stick with only one method of teaching (lecturing for example), then they may consistently fail to reach certain students. However, teachers will be more likely to reach a greater number of students if they can use lectures, discussions, questions, role-plays, case studies, and other types of learning activities. The point is not to teach each concept in five different ways, but a class session that involves a variety of approaches will hold students' attention and appeal to different types of students. Plus, knowing what we do about students' influence on teachers, positive student reaction to variety is likely to make teaching much more fun for us.

Remember also that variety applies to our nonverbal communication in the form of teacher immediacy. Students respond more positively to teachers who exhibit variety in their voice, gestures, movement around the classroom, and eye contact. Picture yourself in front of the classroom and the kind of student reactions you want to see. Chances are good that you are envisioning immediate students. As you prepare for your class sessions, keep this in mind because you probably will not see this type of reaction unless you are immediate yourself and you do your best to exhibit variety in your teaching.

Applying the Principles

So how would these principles look in action, in the course of the typical week of a teaching assistant? You could start to prepare each class session by considering your students. What do they already know about the subject? How interesting will they find this topic? How might the subject relate to their interests and needs? Based on this you could develop your expectations. What should students be able to understand, appreciate, or do with the material by the end of the class session? How should they be able to use this content once they are out of the classroom or after they graduate? At this point, you will be aware of what you want to teach and have an idea of the angles you may want to use to engage your students in the topic. You can explore these angles by thinking of ways to make the content relevant to your students (which should be easier if you already have put yourself "in their shoes"). You could begin each class session with some activity, story, or example which would demonstrate the relevance of the material to students. You also can develop ways of teaching the topic clearly so that students will understand it. As you are preparing your class, you also can consider Principle 4, variety. You can look at each area of the subject and think of different activities that may help you teach the content more clearly and in a way that applies to more students and maintains students' interest more effectively. Once you are in the classroom and interacting with students, you will be able to appreciate the value of immediacy, humor, assertiveness, responsiveness, and the effect your misbehaviors may be having on the class. If you have followed the principles so far, you are more likely to be met with positive student reactions and interests, as they will be more motivated to learn from you. However, remember that this takes time. You probably will need to examine problem areas, collect feedback, and experiement with different approaches. Quality teaching takes time to develop. You will make mistakes and experience growing pains, but if you follow these principles, you are likely to find them useful in helping you communicate more effectively with your students.

Teaching is a complex process and it would be impossible to capture it with ten principles, much less four. However, as new teachers, your goal should be to develop solid teaching skills, not be "teacher of the century!" These four principles can help you do that. Think of the best and worst teachers you have encountered and ask yourself which one was more aware of her students, had reasonable expectations which were clear to his students, taught with variety, and embodied the more positive teacher communication behaviors that have been discussed? I find these principles very important in my own teaching and suspect that by following them you will be more likely to teach effectively and help students learn more effectively. Furthermore, you probably will really enjoy teaching your students, just like your favorite teachers enjoyed teaching you!

Theory into Practice

Training Graduate Teaching Assistants to Communicate More Effectively in Their Classrooms

K. DAVID ROACH
Texas Tech University

Training TAs (teaching assistants) for the classroom is a critical factor in higher education. Many studies have addressed the topics and issues that should be included in training sessions designed to prepare graduate teaching assistants for the classroom. Much theory and research exists in the area of instructional communication and it is important that TAs are exposed to this body of knowledge. For theory and research to be practical, however, it must be applied. It is not enough for TAs to know, for instance, that instructor power/compliance-gaining communication has an important impact in the classroom. It is not enough that TAs be informed that instructor immediacy is important in the classroom. At some point, *understanding* must make way for *practice* that improves a condition or successfully deals with a problem. TA training must show TAs how to use communication principles and strategies in the classroom. TA supervisors must consider relevant instructional theory and use this in constructing effective training programs for TAs.

General Approaches to TA Training

Graduate teaching assistants constitute a large percentage of the total teaching force in U.S. colleges and universities. Though they are frequently very competent in their subject matter (e.g., biology, math, and so on), they often have had little or no training in communication or instruction. Sometimes this is true for tenure-track faculty as well. It should be noted that there are some TAs who possess previous training and/or experience in instruction when they assume their TA responsibilities. These, however, are not the norm and one can easily see the critical need for training in communication and in instruction for the majority of new TAs.

There are many approaches to TA training. Some graduate students encounter the *"no-training" approach* when they assume their TA duties. In this model, the TA does not receive any training in how to be a TA from any level of the university. He or she is merely given a book, a schedule, a classroom full of students, and told to "just do it." Such a "training model" is problematic from several perspectives. First, it has a tendency to make the TA teaching experience a torturous gauntlet for the TA. How an instructor relates interpersonally with students, how an instructor presents material, how an instructor facilitates learning activities, how an instructor organizes/apportions the course, how an instructor evaluates student performance, and how an instructor provides feedback—all are vital factors that can lead to instructional success or failure in the classroom. Second, if a TA has relatively high levels of communication apprehension and/or situational anxiety related to instruction, the experience of standing in front of a class on a weekly basis and having little or no guidance in how to communicate effectively with students will likely traumatize the TA physically, mentally, and emotionally. A third area of disadvantage lies in the area of student learning. The "sink or swim" TA training model has a high probability of fostering a serious negative learning experience for students that may well influence student attitudes toward a particular subject for the rest of their lives.

Fortunately, many TAs encounter at least some training before assuming their instructional duties. Most universities have some sort of *general institutional training* for all TAs that deals with policies of the university, job descriptions, balancing the roles of graduate student and teaching assistant, and knowing the places to go for help (e.g., personnel issues, legal council, financial aid, student services, employee benefits, and so on). Additionally, there is frequently a university concern that TAs be trained in general issues such as sexual harassment and civility in the classroom. Some universities also provide general TA training that addresses basic universal teaching strategies and issues. The advantages of this include providing some teacher training for TAs campuswide, exposing TAs to teaching ideas/strategies that work well in other disciplines, and fostering a big-picture perspective of how to conduct and maintain successful learning environments. Criticisms of this general approach often come from departments and/or graduate students who cite the need to provide applied, discipline-specific training for TAs. Notwithstanding, this type of general instructional/communication training is unquestionably beneficial.

The *departmental approach* to TA training can take many forms. One form of departmental TA training is for the TA supervisor to conduct a short session that covers only the objectives, assignments, and content of a specific course, along with a few items on classroom management and operations. Many departments, however, take a more proactive approach to TA training and use a variety of formats that are more comprehensive in nature. Some departments utilize multiple training sessions where TAs are exposed to principles of basic day-to-day classroom operations (e.g., keeping a grade book), instructional formats (conducting class discussions, and so on), and instructional style (approach, communication, and the like). These sessions, ranging in length from a few hours to a few weeks, are generally held immediately before the semester begins, and thus are beneficial in providing the new TA a solid base of preparation *before* the classroom experience. Additionally, some departments may require that TAs take a three-hour graduate level instructional communication course during their first semester as a TA. Frequently, this type of course explores theoretical and practical issues regarding classroom instruction, and is beneficial in that it addresses classroom issues and TA concerns that arise *while* the TA is teaching. A variation of this format is to require TAs to take a one-hour instructional communication course for the first two semesters they teach. This has the added benefit of providing this "as you go" TA training for a longer period of time.

Another forum of training that can be encouraged within a departmental context is that of TA mentoring by senior TAs. This can be a powerful source of TA socialization and instructional training. In some departments, closed-door orientation sessions are conducted by senior TAs for the new TAs. In these sessions, only TAs are present. The older TAs can share a variety of material with the new TAs, ranging from "here is what you do and don't do in this department" to "here is what I do as a TA that works really well in my classrooms." Such sessions are very beneficial and begin a team relationship among departmental TAs. Formally or informally, these types of meetings can foster mentor relationships among senior and beginning TAs that are very effective.

Topics of training sessions and the amount of TA training vary widely and are influenced by several perspectives. Upper-level university administration personnel have certain preferences and expectations regarding what should be included in TA training. Department chairs and basic course directors have their own views about the content to be included in TA training. TAs come with their own perspectives of what they feel should be included in their own training. Undergraduate students, parents, departmental secretaries, university regents, and so on—all may have views about what should be contained in TA training. Though it is often difficult to balance and merge these perspectives regarding TA training, each has the potential to be valuable and useful to the new TA.

Applying Communication and Instructional Theory in TA Training

Concern for effectiveness in TA training should not be limited, however, to issues of whether the training is done on a university or departmental level, whether the training is discipline-specific or not, or whether the training is a half-day session or a semester-long process. Fundamentally, TAs must be trained in how to be effective communicators—to be effective teachers in the classroom. TAs do not have to learn how to teach in a hit-or-miss fashion as they go through the semester. There is a wealth of communication and instructional theory and research. If a supervisor can construct an effective training program for TAs, this theory and research can be applied in TA classrooms.

In building such a TA training program, a supervisor must first consider what TAs should know about communicating in a classroom. Specific areas of communication research should be determined as important components of training programs. The chapters in this book provide several critical areas to be considered in a TA training program, including topics such as: effective listening, motivating students, dealing with communication apprehension in the classroom, stimulating student communication with instructors, learning how to be immediate as a teacher, learning how to be clear and humorous as a teacher, learning how to "behave" as a teacher, learning how to teach in a distance education context, learning how to be interculturally responsive, learning how to communicate effectively with students of different ages, among others. Other pertinent topics might include how to use power in the classroom effectively, the role of argumentation in a classroom, nonverbal communication in the classroom, and so on.

Once these types of decisions are made regarding topics, the supervisor next needs to determine how to teach this material and how to train TAs. There is a difference between exposing TAs to the wealth of theory and research in instructional communication and using instructional theory to show TAs how to successfully apply these principles in the classroom. TA supervisors must ask themselves, "Is this merely exposing TAs to mountains of communication and instructional literature, or is this really training them to use effective teaching behaviors found in this research?" Though teaching and training have somewhat different goals, if integrated, the TAs should *know* the research *and* be able to *put it into practice* (do it) successfully. Skinner suggests that the basic question in teaching is: "What do we want the student to do as the result of having been taught?" (Skinner, 1968, p. 707).

Training TAs to implement principles from instructional communication research requires a basic understanding and application of learning theory, and careful planning of training activities that coordinate learning theory with instructional theory. Interestingly, the way in which TA training is conducted reflects, by design or by default, the learning assumptions of those doing the training. Sometimes, TA supervisors do not use sound communication and instructional practices when they are attempting to train TAs to do this with undergraduate classes. This is a bit ironic. For optimum success in training, supervisors must use sound communication and instructional theory in constructing and implementing TA training. Two commonly known and used instructional theories are B. F. Skinner's Operant Conditioning and Albert Bandura's Social Learning Theory. The next section outlines the application and utility of these theories for TA training.

Operant Conditioning in TA Training

For TA training, operant conditioning could be used in planning a program of instruction. According to Skinner (1950), "learning is a process in the behavior of the individual" (pp. 195–196). Basically, operant conditioning involves the situational conditions in which an organism responds, the organism's response, and the consequences of the organism's response. In an educational context with students, learning can be promoted by changing the contingencies of reinforcement "progressively in the direction of the required behavior" (Skinner, 1954, p. 87). Teachers should recognize student behaviors that are already there and "selectively reinforce any part which contributes to the terminal pattern or makes it more likely that the student will behave in other ways which contribute to it" (Skinner, 1968, p. 708).

Skinnerian thought applied to TA training could be very effective indeed. A big classroom issue, especially for new TA instructors is that of classroom management. How do you get students to do what you want them to do? The influence of teacher power and compliance-gaining use in the classroom is well documented in communication literature. Overall research findings indicate that teacher use of referent (power based on the identification and positive relationship between teacher and student) and expert power (power based on the teacher's experience/knowledge in a particular area) are most effective in promoting good teacher–student relationships, gaining student cooperation, and promoting student learning and motivation. Similarly, in the area of compliance gaining, research indicates that prosocial compliance-gaining techniques/ messages (e.g., "doing this will help other members in your group and will help you learn the material much better") are much more effective in a long-term, global sense than are antisocial compliance-gaining techniques/messages (e.g., "you better do this or I will assign you a failing grade").

Implementing a unit on power communication in a TA training program would require careful consideration of and answers to the following questions:

1. *At the end of this training, what do we want the TAs to know and to be able to do? What concepts must be understood for TAs to be able to enact effective power communication in the classroom?*

    Suggested learning objectives for TA knowledge and communication patterns would certainly include a basic comprehension of French and Raven's (1959) five bases of social power: coercive power, legitimate power, reward power, referent power, and expert power. Notably, coercive power stems from the perception that the teacher can punish the student; legitimate power comes from the perception that the teacher has the right to tell students what to do; reward power comes from the perception that the teacher can provide something good/desirable in return for students complying; referent power is the degree to which the student likes and identifies with the teacher; and expert power is the perception that the teacher has knowledge of something that will prove valuable to students. In addition to understanding power bases, it is also important for TAs to have a working knowledge of research studies in the area of compliance gaining in the classroom, especially in the area of pro- and antisocial compliance-gaining techniques (e.g., Kearney, Plax, Sorensen, & Smith, 1988). *Power in the Classroom:*

Communication and Control (edited by Richmond & McCroskey, 1992) is an excellent book that provides a sequential history of research studies done in this area.

So, what should the TAs be able to do after training in effective communication and use of power and compliance-gaining? Obviously, behavioral outcomes of TA training in this area would include TA competencies in and reliance on power communication techniques that foster short- and long-term student compliance, promote positive teacher–student relationships, and motivate student learning (see Figure A.1). Specifically, TA trainers would want to be able to observe TAs effectively using referent and expert power to influence students. Also, TA supervisors would want to be able to observe an absence of antisocial compliance-gaining techniques in TA communication with students (e.g., punishment from teacher or others, guilt, appeals to authority like "I am the teacher and what I say goes," and the like). Being able to observe TA use of pro-social compliance-gaining techniques with students would be critical.

Observations of this type could be made in role-play teaching sessions in which the TA must respond to contrived situations. The true test, however, would be to observe TAs actually using these communication approaches in their classrooms.

2. *What power/compliance-gaining communication styles/skills do the TAs currently possess and how can TA supervisors discover this information? What histories of reinforcements have led to these current TA predispositions and how will these TA background factors and the current predispositions influence TA receptivity to and implementation of research-based recommendations for power communication behaviors?*

TA supervisors could take several routes to discovering current TA power communication styles/skills. First, TA supervisors could administer

---

FIGURE A.1   Examples of Prosocial Behavior Alteration Techniques

1. Immediate reward from behavior
2. Deferred reward
3. Reward from others
4. Self-esteem
5. Responsibility to class
6. Normative rules
7. Altruism
8. Peer modeling
9. Teacher modeling
10. Expert teacher

self-report paper and pencil survey instruments to the TAs to measure predispositions to power base use and compliance-gaining message use (e.g.,
Power Base Measure—Roach, 1995; Behavior Alteration Techniques/
Messages Instrument—Kearney, Plax, Richmond, & McCroskey, 1984). Because, as several studies have indicated, teachers rate themselves differently
in these areas than their students rate them, it might be advantageous to get
role-played "students" to record their impressions of a TA's communication
or get actual student perceptions of this on appropriate survey instruments.

Perceptions do not have a big place in the operant conditioning approach, so more in line with this theory, a second strategy to discover extant
TA communication patterns might be for the TA supervisor to observe TA
teaching in real or role-play situations involving a need for teacher power
use. This could be done with actual observations or videotaped sessions. Supervisors could code TA behavior and record the frequency of use.

From the operant conditioning perspective, a TA supervisor should
conduct careful consideration of current TA communication predispositions, and the history behind them. One must consider the nature of the soil
before deciding what and how to plant in a garden. A TA supervisor must
carefully consider how genetic, personality, and social environment factors
have shaped a TA's approach to power communication. Does a particular
TA have a naturally domineering, bossy communication style? How will he
or she respond when exposed to the research that says this is counterpro-
ductive in a classroom setting? What power experiences have TAs had before becoming TAs? What types of power communication have worked for
TAs in other arenas? One particularly strong area of influence to consider is
the role of the TA's cultural background and how this influences his or her
power communication predispositions. An international TA, for instance,
may come from a culture where there is a relatively high societal power distance and thus may be predisposed to use a great deal of controlling, or perhaps "ruling," communication in an instructional role. Furthermore, this TA
may have had all of his or her school experience in an educational system
where only a few people are in schools, where the teacher is expected to
wield heavy authoritative power, and where students keep quiet and take
notes. Obviously, cultural background plays a very important role in the
communication expectations, predispositions, and views of a TA. This must
be taken into account by the TA supervisor who is planning the power in
communication training.

3. *What motivations do TAs have to use power bases and compliance-gaining techniques that are proven most effective? What reinforcers, positive or negative, would
encourage TAs to use prosocial power base/compliance-gaining with their students?
What types of sequenced learning activities/contingencies can be planned to guide
TAs in enacting positive power communication in the classroom? How can new
power communication behaviors be reinforced after the training session is over?*

The concept of reinforcement is vital in Skinner's approach to learning.
The TA supervisor must determine reinforcers that are salient for TA

instructors. What reinforcers, positive or negative, would foster effective TA communication? On a general level, a TA's job will depend on the ability to communicate effectively with students. Bad teaching evaluations from the TA supervisor, poor student ratings of instruction, and so on, could cost a TA a teaching position. This is an especially critical factor for international TAs in U.S. universities. Learning or honing one's communication skills to keep one's job is a strong reinforcement. A second area of reinforcement could come from the TA's intrinsic motivation to be a good teacher and to promote a positive teacher–student relationship. From this perspective, a TA so motivated would naturally find that positive student learning and relationship results from effective instructor power communication. The flip side of this would be that TAs are likely to want to avoid the conflict, anger, frustration, public confrontations, bad teacher-student relations, potential grade appeals, and the like that often come from poor TA power communication.

More specific or direct reinforcement for TA power communication would be given in actual training sessions, using various training strategies. As a prelude to each strategy, basic power communication principles and models could be shared with the TAs. Building on this, *strategy one* might involve providing TAs with written scenarios of common student situations that require TA power communication. TAs would be required to write what they would do and say to deal with these situations. Each TA response would be shared with and discussed by the group. The TA supervisor could praise, affirm, hand out candy rewards, give grade rankings, or the like when TAs use the most effective power communication strategies. *Strategy two* might involve role-playing in which a TA would be required to actually respond to a contrived "classroom" event with TA peers and/or the TA supervisor serving as the "students." The "students" could be coached before the simulation to allow the conflict to resolve if the TA instructor uses positive power communication and to emulate negative student response (and to keep the conflict going) if negative TA power communication is used. Each TA could be given a chance to experience one of several scenarios several times, allowing him or her to try out several power communication strategies and "experience" the results thereof. It should be noted that one of the key difficulties in this training strategy is controlling the "student" responses. For this reason, Skinner was a big advocate of teaching machines, through which degrees and directions of reinforcements could be carefully controlled. Though Skinner was limited in his day in terms of teaching machine capabilities, current advances in computer technology allow for very sophisticated construction of computer simulations that could be used to simulate TA power communication situations in the classroom.

Notably, the TA supervisor is a major source for reinforcement during the training sessions, but ultimately, actual student responses to TA power communication in the classroom will serve as strong reinforcements. Optimally, actual students' responses will be similar to those experienced in the

TA training sessions. One must realize too, that sometimes students can respond negatively even if an instructor uses prosocial power communication. TAs must be prepared for this and consider these behaviors in view of the average/typical student responses. To supplement the reinforcement effects from average/typical student responses, TA supervisors could observe TA teaching and provide continuous feedback on the effectiveness of TA power communication.

With the many advantages of operant conditioning as a framing theory and as a perspective leading to many advantageous instructional activities, one must note that this is only one approach to teaching and learning. If indeed triangulation is beneficial for research, it is beneficial for teaching as well. The best teachers are the ones who can use many different approaches and learning theories, separately or in conjunction with each other, to promote learning in students. A second instructional theory that can be used to promote effective TA training is the Social Learning Theory.

Social Learning Theory in TA Training

Albert Bandura's Social Learning Theory is a notable instructional theory that takes an interactionist perspective. Bandura posits that "most human behavior is learned observationally through modeling" (Bandura, 1977, p. 23). "The ability of individuals to abstract information from the behaviors of others, make decisions about which behaviors to adopt, and later, to enact the selected behaviors" is a major part of this theory (Bell-Gredler, 1986, p. 234). Essentially, the theory suggests that individuals observe and consider the behavior of others, and then choose to behave (imitating or otherwise) in ways that are perceived as desirable or beneficial. Hergenhahn and Olson (1993) frame these post observation/consideration response behaviors as "advantageous behaviors."

Though this may sound very similar to the assumptions of operant conditioning, it differs in some very fundamental ways. Bandura (1978) suggests that "it is true that behavior is influenced by the environment, but the environment is partly of a person's own making. By their actions, people play a role in creating the social milieu and other circumstances that arise in their daily transactions. Thus, from the social learning perspective, psychological functioning involves a continuous reciprocal interaction between behavioral, cognitive and environmental influences" (p. 345). These factors are more than just linked; they affect and effect one another. This dynamic relationship is referred to as "reciprocal determinism" (Bandura, 1978). The idea is that each of these three factors shapes and determines the other factors. An individual observes behavior, processes it cognitively, and then chooses a path of behavior. Perhaps the most important distinction from operant conditioning is that Social Learning Theory advocates the important role of personal factors in determining behavior and/or learning. Personal factors consist of several things including cognitive processing, personality, attitudes, assessments of self and of observed behaviors, and so on. Operant conditioning excludes such "black box" phenomena.

In communication literature, the concept of teacher immediacy has been found to have a strong influence in the classroom. "Immediacy" refers to the level of psychological and physical distance between two individuals (Mehrabian, 1971; Andersen, 1979). A wealth of literature exists on the influence of instructor immediacy, linking it specifically to student cognitive and affective learning (e.g., Richmond, Gorham, & McCroskey, 1987; Frymier, 1994), motivation to learn (e.g., Richmond, 1990), student ratings of instruction (e.g., McCroskey, Richmond, Sallinen, Fayer, & Barraclough, 1996), and perceptions of interpersonal attractiveness (e.g., Rocca & McCroskey, 1999). Given the powerful influence of this communication variable, TAs and their students would be well served if immediacy were included in TA training programs.

A supervisor would do well to consider and use the Social Learning Theory in teaching/training TAs in effective instructor immediacy. Implementing Bandura's three-part model of behavioral, cognitive, and environmental influences in this type of training would require a careful examination and use of each of the component parts. The *environment component* contains the modeling aspect of the theory that is so critical for fostering/explaining learning. Bandura (1977) recognizes three types of behavior models: verbal, symbolic, and live. *Verbal modeling* is being used when the instructor describes or instructs students orally in a particular body of academic content or behavior. Lecturing on the concept of instructor immediacy could be a good first step in behavioral modeling. In training sessions, TAs can be shown lists and descriptions of immediate and nonimmediate behaviors. TAs can be exposed to research findings that explore the effects of instructor immediacy in the classroom and on students.

To avoid the sins of the past in TA training and to ensure maximum effectiveness in enhancing TA immediacy, however, the modeling cannot be limited to verbal alone. *Symbolic modeling,* especially in the area of nonverbal immediacy, could be very effective in TA training sessions. Symbolic modeling is used when the instructor shows students drawings, pictures, or videos of content specific behaviors. TA supervisors could display pictures of an instructor looking and smiling at the class, and then pictures of the same (or another) instructor frowning and/or "teaching to the chalkboard." Pictures of instructors with relaxed and tense body positions could be projected and discussed. Video clips of instructors using gestures and instructors not using gestures could be very powerful examples for TAs regarding effective and noneffective nonverbal immediacy behaviors. Video or audiotapes of actual teaching sessions could be played and judged according to the variety of vocal expression used by the instructor. All of these methods could foster lively discussion and reflection from TAs on their own personal reactions to instructor immediacy behaviors they have encountered.

The third type of modeling TA supervisors could use in immediacy training for TAs is *live modeling.* Live modeling is used when students get to see real incidents and examples of content/behaviors in action. First and foremost, TA supervisors must be able to be immediate with TAs in their own training sessions. This is critical. Supervisors who attempt to elicit immediate behaviors from TAs but who cannot demonstrate them in their own training style are not apt to meet with much success. In training sessions, other live modeling techniques could be used as well. TAs might be challenged by the supervisor to role-play the immediacy behaviors of a favorite and least-favorite teacher they had encountered in their undergraduate experience. Playing both roles would clearly highlight the contrast between immediate and nonimmediate behaviors. TAs could be required to visit the classroom of another TA or a faculty instructor who has very pronounced and positive immediacy behaviors, and to record or code the observed instructor immediacy behaviors during an entire class period. A follow-up discussion with other observers and the TA supervisor could serve as an important forum for this live model experience.

Verbal, symbolic, and live modeling are all critical parts of the environmental component of the Social Learning Theory. Additionally, all three of these types of modeling are essential in training TAs to be more immediate in their classrooms. Supervisors should make sure to construct training sessions that use each of these.

The second major component of Bandura's three-part model is the *personal/ internal cognitive processing factor*. Social Learning Theory advocates that there are four basic internal processes that influence observational learning: attention, retention, motor reproduction, and motivational processes. Though TA supervisors cannot directly influence personal cognitive/internal events of TAs, they should at least consider these factors and shape training environments accordingly. Specifically, attention should be given to the four-component process that influences observational learning.

The *attention process* must be carefully considered in planning immediacy training. Bandura (1977) notes that "attentional processes determine what is selectively observed in the profusion of modeling influences to which one is exposed and what is extracted from such exposures" (p. 24). An individual simply cannot process all of the constant stimuli received. Notably, this is especially true in TA training sessions as new TAs experience information overload. Filters are constructed and stimuli that are not perceived as important are screened out. Because of this, individuals will notice or "attend to" certain stimuli and not even be aware of other stimuli. Chapter 2 of this book specifically addresses the concept of attention in detail. How can the TA supervisor elicit TA focused attention on instructor immediacy behaviors?

As one might expect, "need to know" is a powerful determinant of attention. Generally, attention is given to observed behaviors of others that are perceived as potentially important or relevant to the observer. Chapter 7 of this book goes into great detail regarding the concept of relevance in an instructional setting. There are a few things inherent to being a new TA that may promote "need" for and/or visibility of instructor immediacy for TAs. Most TAs have some level of an intrinsic personal drive to perform well in their role as a TA. At the very least, if not for personal reasons, TAs want to be successful to keep their jobs as TAs. TA supervisors, recognizing this, can frame the concept of instructor immediacy for TAs as an important, research-documented factor that leads to success in the classroom. Presenting data and results from the many immediacy studies, and showing how immediacy is fundamentally relevant to even how TAs respond to their own graduate instructors should make the concept of immediacy salient for new TAs. Also, most TAs are inherently interested in how they look and how they come across to other people. Seeing themselves on videotape and rating their own immediacy behaviors would be interesting to most TAs. It might be useful to video a group of TAs before or during a training session, and play back the video later for discussion and assessment of individual immediacy.

There are other determining factors that influence an individual's attention to a given modeling stimuli. The distinctiveness of the observed behavior is important. Does the behavior stand out from other behaviors? The affective valence of the observer toward the observed behavior also influences observer attention. The prevalence and the functional value of the observed behavior also influence attention. A second major category of variables affecting attention have to do with the characteristics of the observer. Sensory capacities, the arousal level, the perceptual set, and the collection of past reinforcements of TAs will all have an impact on attention.

The second internal process that influences observational learning is *retention*. Observed behaviors that are attended to and deemed important are then *"retained"* or remembered by the learner. "People cannot be much influenced by observation of modeled behavior if they do not remember it" (Bandura, 1977, p. 25). Retention involves coding observed behaviors into verbal or visual codes and then storing them mentally (Bell-Gredler, 1986). Visual codes provide a mental image of the observed behavior and outcomes, and can be stored and retrieved at a later time. Frequently individuals translate visual images into easily stored verbal codes. These verbal codes account "for the notable speed of observational learning and retention in humans" (Bandura, 1977, p. 26).

Retention processes would be a key element in enhancing TA immediacy behaviors. Even the best of students retain only small portions of what they hear a trainer say. The effects of time on this make retention from verbal modeling even more problematic. Individuals have a tendency to remember visuals and experiences more deeply and longer. Symbolic and live immediacy modeling would create strong visual memories for TAs and thus would allow them to remember vivid examples of immediate and nonimmediate behaviors they observed in TA training sessions. Another factor affecting retention is learner perception of the consequences or outcomes of modeled behavior. "Typically, learners will tend to retain and use behavioral models that promote desired results" (Roach & Jensen, 1997–98, p. 83). Observed behaviors that result in negative consequences for the student will generally not be retained or will be retained as verbal/visual memories of "how not to behave." TA supervisors need to set up training or real-world exercises that allow TAs to experience and remember examples of "student" responses to immediate and nonimmediate behaviors. Positive and negative experiences in this regard serve as reinforcers and enhance retention.

Perhaps the biggest omission in immediacy training is the lack of time and attention devoted to allowing trainees to *do* immediacy in a controlled environment. *Motor reproduction* is the third major process that influences observational learning. It is the process whereby the student tries to physically imitate or enact the retained observed behavior. Bandura suggests that "A capability is only as good as its execution" (1982, p. 122). Hergenhahn and Olson (1993) state that behavioral production processes determine the extent to which that which has been learned is translated into performance" (p. 328). TAs can know about immediacy and its effects but this really does not help them unless they can enact successful immediacy behaviors in their classrooms. The value of role-play in training sessions is critical in this regard. TA supervisors need to construct situations in which TAs can practice and rehearse immediacy behaviors. Some TAs will have already acquired these skills but others may find immediacy behaviors very new and uncomfortable. It may be, indeed, that some TAs are too immediate and will likely encounter negative consequences in the classroom. In addition to feedback from the TA supervisor, feedback from other TAs can be extremely helpful in this regard.

One should realize, however, that motor reproduction of observed behavior may be awkward, incomplete, or flawed initially. A naturally nonimmediate TA may feel and act awkward at first when trying, for instance, to maintain good eye contact with students. It may take a while for individuals to comprehensively and accurately enact observed behavior. Bandura (1977) recognizes that "people usually achieve a close approximation of the new behavior by modeling, and they refine it through self-corrective adjustments on the basis of informative feedback from performance and from focused demonstrations of segments that have been only partially learned" (p. 28).

The fourth basic internal process under the category of personal/internal cognitive processing is *motivation.* Bandura (1977) notes that "social learning theory distinguishes between acquisition and performance because people do not enact everything they learn" (p. 28). Individuals must be motivated to enact an observed behavior. Motivation to enact a particular behavior will be high for an individual if it is perceived that this behavior will produce a reward. Conversely, if the behavior brings punishment or negative consequences, motivation will be low to enact the behavior. Rewards that prompt motivation can come from several sources. A learner can receive direct reinforcement from a behavior he or she enacts. Interestingly, a learner can also receive vicarious reinforcement from observing how other people are rewarded for a given behavior. Thirdly, a learner can receive self-reinforcement for a behavior. Reinforcements of this type are internal and are focused on accomplishing personal goals. Notably, this type of internal reward may be very strong. Bandura states that learners "are more likely to adopt modeled behavior if it results in outcomes they value than if it has unrewarding or punishing effects" (p. 28).

Motivation for TAs to enact immediacy behaviors will depend largely on the reinforcements TAs receive. A TA supervisor should carefully consider potential external, vicarious, and self-reinforcements in planning immediacy training for TAs. Experiencing the consequences, positive or negative, of immediacy behaviors from role-play participants, from TA supervisors, from TA peers, and ultimately from "real" students will be powerful external reinforcements for TAs. It is very important for TA supervisors to foster immediacy experiences that are positive and nonthreatening for TAs in training sessions. It is very important that a TA supervisor consider the cultural background of TAs and how this will frame external reinforcements that TAs will garner from immediacy behaviors. It is very important that TA supervisors let TAs know that sometimes immediacy behaviors can be too much in certain situations and/or that sometimes students will respond negatively no matter what. External reinforcements must be viewed in terms of the normal, most probable responses to immediacy.

If TA supervisors create training situations in which TAs can watch other TAs enact immediacy behaviors (in role-play or live situations), TAs will be afforded the opportunity for vicarious reinforcement. This type of reinforcement comes from watching other TAs enact modeled immediacy behaviors and being able to observe the effects of these behaviors for the other TAs. This is effective reinforcement for "what to do" and "what not to do" as well. TA self-reinforcement will be an important factor in training sessions and in the live classroom as well. Bandura (1977) notes that "the evaluative reactions that people generate toward their own behavior also regulate which observationally learned responses will be performed" (pp. 28–29). Again, opportunities to view themselves enacting immediacy behaviors on video will be extremely useful in allowing TAs to evaluate and adjust their own immediacy behaviors.

After considering the various types of modeling under the environmental component and the internal process found in the personal/internal processing component, one can turn attention to the third major component of the Social Learning Theory—that of *behavior*. In many learning models behavior is seen as the linear end of the instructional process. From the perspective of the Social Learning Theory, behavior is indeed influenced by environment and internal personal factors (e.g., cognitive processing). Behavior also, however, has a dynamic influence on the environment and on an individual's cognitive processing. In a classroom situation, the lack of immediate behaviors from a TA instructor has great potential to foster nonimmediate behaviors in students as well. Conversely, immediate behaviors from a TA often foster immediate behaviors in students (the environment), which in turn has a further influence on the immediacy behavior of the TA. Certain learning activity behaviors that are repeated over and over can actually have a positive influence on a student's internal processes (e.g., attitudes toward content, motivations to participate and learn, and so on). Examples of this can be seen running drills for basketball practice, rehearsing a piano piece over and over, and even giving multiple speeches in class. "Doing" affects thinking. "Doing" affects the environment. A TA supervisor who can set up multiple opportunities for TAs to engage in immediate instructor behaviors will find that the actual behavior itself will impact the TA.

It is one thing to tell new TAs about the value of being immediate with their students, showing them the relevant research in this area, and it is quite another thing to use theoretically based training to enhance TA immediacy in the classroom. Obviously, the goal of TA immediacy training is to enhance and promote TA immediacy *behaviors* in the classroom. Within the framework of Bandura's Social Learning Theory, TA behavior will influence and be influenced by *environment*, *personal cognitive/internal events*, and *behavior*. From the Social Learning Theory perspective, the task for the TA supervisor then is to shape TA training such that it addresses a concept from each of the three domains.

Conclusion

To be a good teacher, one must remember that learning has knowledge and skills components. What real value does knowledge have if it does not change you and if you cannot do something better or different as a result of having it? What real value does skill ability have if you do not know why a behavioral skill is effective or how to make it better or how if fits into the grand scheme of things? The goal of teaching TAs a lesson on listening is not that they remember your lecture notes. The goal of a lesson on listening is that a TA be better able to understand and perform listening behaviors. This book has explored theories and research in areas of listening, affective learning and motivation to learn, student motives for communicating with instructors, teacher immediacy and nonverbal communication, making content relevant for students, teacher clarity, verbally effective teachers, instructional humor use, teacher misbehaviors, teacher motivating and demotivating behaviors, communication in distance education contexts, intercultural communication, interage communication, and issues in instructional communication research. Research and theory in all of these areas are positioned to have a major positive impact on instructional communication in the classroom *if* it is understood and *if* it is put into practice.

TAs frequently come to the classroom with limited experience, knowledge, and skills. The purpose of TA training is not only to expose them to the wealth of research and theory in instructional communication, but also to show them how to make practical use of this wealth in ways that will make instruction effective in their classrooms. Exposure is not enough. TA supervisors must plan and implement training sessions in a way that exemplifies the very principles that are being taught. TA supervisors must understand basic instructional theory and use it in framing and presenting training content. TA supervisors must show TAs how to enact and use recommended instructional communication practices. Though only two basic learning theories were explored and applied to TA training in this unit, there are many more learning and communication theories that can be applied effectively in this context. "Since no single teaching strategy [or theory] can accomplish every purpose, the wise teacher will master a sufficient repertoire of strategies to deal with the specific kinds of learning problems he or she faces"

(Joyce & Weil, 1980, p. 19). The task for the TA supervisor is to strategically choose and implement theories and principles of learning and communication to meet the basic needs of TAs as they approach the marvelous and magical environment of classroom instruction.

REFERENCES AND SUGGESTED READINGS

Andersen, J. F. (1979). Teacher immediacy as a predictor of teaching effectiveness. In D. Nimmo (Ed.), *Communication yearbook 3* (pp. 543–559). New Brunswick, NJ: Transaction Books.

Bandura, A. (1977). *Social learning theory.* Englewood Cliffs, NJ: Prentice Hall.

Bandura, A. (1978). The self-system in reciprocal determinism. *American Psychologist, 33,* 344–358.

Bandura, A. (1982). Self-efficacy mechanism in human agency. *American Psychologist, 37,* 122–147.

Bell-Gredler, M. E. (1986). *Learning and instruction: Theory into practice.* New York: Macmillan.

French, J. R. P., Jr., & Raven, B. (1959). The bases for social power. In D. Cartwright (Ed.), *Studies in social power* (pp. 150–167). Ann Arbor, MI: Institute for Social Research.

Frymier, A. B. (1994). A model of immediacy in the classroom. *Communication Quarterly, 42,* 133–144.

Hergenhahn, B. R., & Olson, M. H. (1993). *An introduction to theories of learning* (4th ed.). Englewood Cliffs, NJ: Prentice-Hall.

Joyce, B., & Weil, M. (1980). *Models of teaching* (2nd ed.). Englewood Cliffs, NJ: Prentice-Hall.

Kearney, P., Plax, T. G., Richmond, V. P., & McCroskey, J. C. (1984). Power in the classroom IV: Alternatives to discipline. In R. Bostrom (Ed.), *Communication yearbook 8* (pp. 724–746). Beverly Hills, CA: Sage.

Kearney, P., Plax, T. G., Sorensen, G., & Smith, V. R. (1988). Experienced and prospective teachers' selections of compliance-gaining messages for "common" student misbehaviors. *Communication Education, 37,* 150–164.

Littlejohn, S. W. (1992). *Theories of human communication* (4th ed.). Belmont, California: Wadsworth.

McCroskey, J. C., Richmond, V. P., Sallinen, A., Fayer, J. M., & Barraclough, R. A. (1996). Nonverbal immediacy and cognitive learning: A cross-cultural investigation. *Communication Education, 45,* 200–211.

Mehrabian, A. (1971). *Silent messages.* Belmont, CA: Wadsworth.

Richmond, V. P. (1990). Communication in the classroom: Power and motivation. *Communication Education, 39,* 181–195.

Richmond, V. P., Gorham, J., & McCroskey, J. C. (1987). The relationship between selected immediacy behaviors and cognitive learning. In M. McLaughlin (Ed.), *Communication yearbook 10* (pp. 574–590). Beverly Hills, CA: Sage.

Richmond, V. P., & McCroskey, J. C. (1989). *Communication: Apprehension, avoidance, and effectiveness* (2nd ed.). Gorsuch Scarisbrick.

Richmond, V. P., & McCroskey, J. C. (Eds.). (1992). *Power in the classroom: Communication, control, and concern.* Hillsdale, New Jersey: Lawrence Erlbaum.

Roach, K. D. (1995). Teaching assistant argumentativeness and perceptions of power use in the classroom. *Communication Research Reports, 12,* 94–103.

Roach, K. D., & Jensen, K. K. (1997–98). TA training: Social learning theory into practice. *The Journal of Graduate Teaching Assistant Development, 5,* 81–87.

Rocca, K. A., & McCroskey, J. C. (1999). The interrelationship of student ratings of instructors' immediacy, verbal aggressiveness, homophily, and interpersonal attraction. *Communication Education, 48,* 308–316.

Skinner, B. F. (1950). Are theories of learning necessary? *The Psychological Review, 57,* 193–216.

Skinner, B. F. (1954). The science of learning and the art of teaching. *Harvard Educational Review, 24,* 86–97.

Skinner, B. F. (1963). Operant behavior. *American Psychologist, 18,* 503–515.

Skinner, B. F. (1968). Teaching science in high school—What is wrong? *Science, 159,* 704–710.

APPENDIX B

About the Editors and Contributors

Terre H. Allen (Ph.D., Louisiana State University, 1990) is an Associate Professor of Communication Studies, Administrative Co-Director of the Hauth Center for Communication Skills, and Director of Graduate Studies at California State University, Long Beach. In addition, she coordinates and teaches the largest general education oral communication course offered at CSULB. She conducts research on how individuals use knowledge structures when engaging in interpersonal, small group, and classroom contexts. She has contributed to journals such as *Human Communication Research*, *Communication Education*, *Communication Research*, and *Communication Research Reports*. She has served on the editorial boards of *Speech Communication Teacher*, *Women's Studies in Communication*, and NCA's Committee on Assessment.

Doreen K. Baringer (M.A., West Virginia University, 1998) is a Doctoral Student and Research Assistant within the department of Speech Communication at the Pennsylvania State University. Her interests are in health and instructional communication. Her work has been published in *Communication Theory* and *Communication Education.*

Joseph L. Chesebro (Ed.D., Educational Psychology and Instructional Communication, West Virginia University, 1999, M.A., Speech Communication, Ball State University, 1995) is an Assistant Professor of Communication at the State University of New York at Brockport, where he enjoys teaching courses in interpersonal communication, communication in business and the professions, communication theory, and communication training and development. His articles on clear teaching and listening behavior appear in *Communication Education*, *Communication Quarterly*, and *Communication Research Reports*. He also serves on the advisory board of Brockport's Center for Excellence in Learning and Teaching.

Ann Bainbridge Frymier (Ed.D., Curriculum and Instruction, West Virginia University, 1992) is an Associate Professor at Miami University, in Oxford, Ohio. She teaches classes in interpersonal communication, instructional communication, intercultural communication, organizational communication, nonverbal communication, and persuasion. Her primary area of research is instructional communication. In particular, she has focused on teacher immediacy, affinity-seeking, content relevance, empowerment, and humor and their impact on student learning and motivation. Her research appears in *Communication Research Reports, Communication Education, Communication Quarterly,* and *Journal of Applied Communication Research.* Frymier has presented numerous competitive papers at regional and national conventions. She also is Director of Graduate Studies for the Speech Communication Area of the Department of Communication at Miami University.

Joan Gorham completed her undergraduate work at the University of Wisconsin-Madison and received master's and doctoral degrees from Northern Illinois University. She currently is associate dean for academic affairs in the Eberly College of Arts and Sciences and a professor of communication studies at West Virginia University. Dr. Gorham serves as editor of the Dushkin/McGraw-Hill series *Annual Editions: Mass Media.* Her research over the past fifteen years has focused primarily on how teacher behavior affects student learning, attitudes, and motivation.

Patricia Kearney (Ed.D., West Virginia University, 1979) is a Professor of Communication Studies and Co-Director of the Hauth Center for Communication Skills at California State University, Long Beach. Her research focuses on communication in the instructional process. A current member of seven journal editorial boards, she has written 4 books and more than 50 research articles, chapters, and commissioned research reports. Her research utilizes quasi-experimental and survey research designs typical of the social sciences.

Amanda Lee Kundrat is a Master's student of Speech Communication at the Pennsylvania State University. She studies medical and organizational communication, currently is focusing on the interplay between illness, identity, and communication. Amanda teaches communication classes and is involved as a research assistant for a project focusing on patient-physician communication with the elderly population. Her background also includes studies in business and French.

Matthew M. Martin (Ph.D., Kent State University) is an Associate Professor of Communication Studies at West Virginia University. His primary research interests include communication traits and communication competence. The courses he teaches include interpersonal communication, nonverbal communication, and communication theory.

James C. McCroskey (Ed.D., Pennsylvania State University, 1966) is a Professor of Communication Studies at West Virginia University. He has published a number of articles relating to the role of communication in instruction. His publications in this area have focused primarily on credibility, communication apprehension, immediacy, power, and clarity. He has authored, co-authored, or co-edited three books on communication in instruction, the most recent being *An Introduction to Communication in the Classroom,* 2nd edition, Acton, MA: Tapestry Press, 1998.

Linda McCroskey received her master's in instructional/organizational communication from West Virginia Uuniversity and another master's in interpersonal/intercultural communication from Arizona State University. Her Ph.D. in intercultural/instructional communication was earned in 1998 from the University of Oklahoma (home of the national football champion Sooners!). Currently she is an assistant professor at Cal State University, Long Beach in Information Systems and is teaching two seminars in intercultural business in the MBA program, as well as an upper-division business communication course.

Diane Millette completed her bachelor and master's degrees at California State University, Sacramento, and received her doctoral degree in instructional communication from West Virginia University. Currently an associate professor in the School of Communication at the University of Miami, she serves as program director for Communication Studies and director of the university's Instructional Advancement Center. Dr. Millette has served on several editorial boards of scholarly communication journals. Her research focuses on classroom motivation, apprehension, and intercultural communication.

Timothy P. Mottet (Ed.D., West Virginia University, 1998) is assistant professor at Southwest Texas State University in San Marcos. He directs and teaches the basic course and also teaches courses in instructional communication and communication assessment. Mottet's research examines the effects of student communication on teachers and their teaching in traditional and distance education instructional contexts. His work also examines the role of emotion in the teaching and learning process. Mottet has presented papers at regional and national conferences and his research appears in *Communication Education*, *Communication Quarterly*, *Communication Research Reports*, *Journal of Psychology*, and *Psychological Reports*. He currently serves on a university-wide task force funded by the Kellogg foundation to improve teaching effectiveness. He is co-authoring a textbook on communication training and development with David Roach and Steven Beebe. Mottet also has worked as director of in-flight service training and development for Northwest Airlines.

Scott A. Myers (Ph.D., Kent State University, 1995) is an Assistant Professor of Communication Studies at West Virginia University. His research has been published in journals such as *Communication Education*, *Communication Research Reports*, and *Western Journal of Communication*. His research interests include the training and socialization of graduate teaching assistants, the effects of instructor argumentativeness and verbal aggressiveness on student outcomes, and student use of information-seeking strategies.

Jon F. Nussbaum (Ph.D., Purdue University, 1981) is a Professor of Communication Theory within the Department of Speech Communication at Pennsylvania State University. He has published numerous journal articles and book chapters concerning teacher effectiveness and teacher communicator style. In addition, he has authored or edited eight books and numerous articles dealing with communication across the life span.

Timothy G. Plax is Professor of Communication Studies at California State University, Long Beach. He received his B.A. and M.A. degrees from California State University, Long Beach and his Ph.D. from the University of Southern California. He joined CSULB in 1987. Dr. Plax has been on the faculty at the University of New Mexico and West Virginia University and spent several years as a member of the Executive Staff at Corporate Headquarters and the Satellite and Space Divisions of the Rockwell International Corporation. His programs of research focus on persuasion and communication in instruction and training. He teaches in the areas of instructional and organizational communication and persuasion. He has received a variety of awards for his writing, research, teaching, and consulting activities.

Virginia P. Richmond (Ph.D., University of Nebraska, 1977) is a Professor of Communication Studies at West Virginia University. She has published a number of articles relating to the role of communication in instruction. Her publications in this area have focused primarily on communication apprehension, nonverbal communication, power, and immediacy. She has authored, co-authored, or co-edited three books on communication in instruction, the most recent being *Nonverbal Communication in the Classroom,* 2nd edition, Acton, MA: Tapestry Press, 1998.

K. David Roach received his Ed.D. in Education Administration and Communication from Texas Tech University in 1989. He is an Associate Professor and Chair of the Department of Communication Studies at Texas Tech University. His primary teaching and research interests are in instructional communication. He has published numerous research articles in this area and maintains an active membership in the Instructional Development Division of the National Communication Association.

Sue L. Stewart (M.A., Southwest Texas State University, 2000) is an adjunct professor in the Communication Department at St. Edward's University in Austin, Texas. She also is a doctoral student in Education at the University of Texas at Austin, with an area of focus on instructional communication . She teaches courses in presentational speaking, professional communication, and computer-mediated communication (an on-line course). She has presented papers at several regional conferences and in May 2000 she was named Outstanding Graduate Student and was recognized for outstanding teaching by a graduate student in the Department of Speech Communication at Southwest Texas State University.

Candice Thomas-Maddox (Ed.D., Communication in Instruction, West Virginia University, 1994) currently is an assistant professor at Ohio University-Lancaster, where she teaches both graduate and undergraduate courses in instructional communication, including Communication with Diverse Students. She has co-authored two textbooks, two instructor's manuals, and four book chapters. She has earned awards for her teaching and research from the National Communication Association, the International Communication Association, and the Eastern Communication Association, and is a member of Phi Beta Delta, an honorary organization recognizing international scholarship. In addition to serving on the editorial boards of *Communication Monographs* and *Communication Research Reports*, Thomas-Maddox serves as the Executive Secretary for the Eastern Communication Association and as the Executive Director for the Speech Communication Association of Ohio.

Melissa Bekelja Wanzer received her Ed.D. in Communication in Instruction from West Virginia University in 1995. She taught one year at Kutztown University before joining the Communication Studies Department at Canisius College. She has taught instructional communication courses such as Nonverbal Communication in the Classroom and Interpersonal Communication in the Classroom and has developed instructor's manuals for courses in Nonverbal Communication and Interpersonal Communication. In addition to teaching courses in Instructional Communication, Wanzer has both presented and published instructional articles in areas such as student affinity-seeking, teacher misbehaviors and student learning, and the impact of teacher humor on student learning. In addition to studying humor in the classroom context, Wanzer has explored individual differences in humor production and nurses' use of humor in healthcare. Wanzer has received teaching awards from Syracuse University and The International Communication Association.

INDEX